T0139939

Advances in Information Security

Volume 79

Series editor
Sushil Jajodia, George Mason University, Fairfax, VA, USA

The purpose of the *Advances in Information Security* book series is to establish the state of the art and set the course for future research in information security. The scope of this series includes not only all aspects of computer, network security, and cryptography, but related areas, such as fault tolerance and software assurance. The series serves as a central source of reference for information security research and developments. The series aims to publish thorough and cohesive overviews on specific topics in Information Security, as well as works that are larger in scope than survey articles and that will contain more detailed background information. The series also provides a single point of coverage of advanced and timely topics and a forum for topics that may not have reached a level of maturity to warrant a comprehensive textbook.

More information about this series at http://www.springer.com/series/5576

Kim-Kwang Raymond Choo • Ali Dehghantanha
Reza M. Parizi

Editors

Blockchain Cybersecurity, Trust and Privacy

 Springer

Editors
Kim-Kwang Raymond Choo 🆔
Department of Information Systems
and Cyber Security
University of Texas at San Antonio
San Antonio, TX, USA

Ali Dehghantanha
Cyber Science Lab
School of Computer Science
University of Guelph
Guelph, ON, Canada

Reza M. Parizi 🆔
College of Computing and Software
Engineering
Kennesaw State University
Marietta, GA, USA

ISSN 1568-2633   ISSN 2512-2193   (electronic)
Advances in Information Security
ISBN 978-3-030-38183-7   ISBN 978-3-030-38181-3   (eBook)
https://doi.org/10.1007/978-3-030-38181-3

© Springer Nature Switzerland AG 2020
This work is subject to copyright. All rights are reserved by the Publisher, whether the whole or part of the material is concerned, specifically the rights of translation, reprinting, reuse of illustrations, recitation, broadcasting, reproduction on microfilms or in any other physical way, and transmission or information storage and retrieval, electronic adaptation, computer software, or by similar or dissimilar methodology now known or hereafter developed.
The use of general descriptive names, registered names, trademarks, service marks, etc. in this publication does not imply, even in the absence of a specific statement, that such names are exempt from the relevant protective laws and regulations and therefore free for general use.
The publisher, the authors, and the editors are safe to assume that the advice and information in this book are believed to be true and accurate at the date of publication. Neither the publisher nor the authors or the editors give a warranty, expressed or implied, with respect to the material contained herein or for any errors or omissions that may have been made. The publisher remains neutral with regard to jurisdictional claims in published maps and institutional affiliations.

This Springer imprint is published by the registered company Springer Nature Switzerland AG.
The registered company address is: Gewerbestrasse 11, 6330 Cham, Switzerland

Contents

Blockchain in Cybersecurity Realm: An Overview

Reza M. Parizi (iD), **Ali Dehghantanha, Amin Azmoodeh,**
and Kim-Kwang Raymond Choo (iD)

Abstract Cybersecurity is a pressing need for governments, businesses, and individuals, which is compounded by the fast-pace technological changes and changing cyberthreat landscape. A large number of solutions have been proposed to address the changing security requirements, and one of such solutions is based on blockchain. Blockchain is a promising infrastructural technology, with potential to be leveraged in different aspects of cybersecurity. For example, blockchain characteristics such as decentralization, verifiability and immutability can facilitate one to achieve authenticity, reliability and integrity of data. Yet, little is known about factors related to the adoption decisions and how it can systemically be put into use to remedy current security's issues in the digital world. In order to advance the body of practical and theoretical knowledge, this book seeks to provide a sample of cutting-edge research from both academia and industry to perceive blockchain cybersecurity and its current solutions in a clearer context and pave the way for the future.

R. M. Parizi (✉)
College of Computing and Software Engineering, Kennesaw State University, Marietta, GA, USA
e-mail: rparizi1@kennesaw.edu

A. Dehghantanha
Cyber Science Lab, School of Computer Science, University of Guelph, Guelph, ON, Canada
e-mail: adehghan@uoguelph.ca

A. Azmoodeh
School of Computer Science, University of Guelph, Guelph, ON, Canada
e-mail: aazmoode@uoguelph.ca

K.-K. R. Choo
Department of Information Systems and Cyber Security, University of Texas at San Antonio, San Antonio, TX, USA
e-mail: raymond.choo@fulbrightmail.org

© Springer Nature Switzerland AG 2020
K.-K. R. Choo et al. (eds.), *Blockchain Cybersecurity, Trust and Privacy*, Advances in Information Security 79, https://doi.org/10.1007/978-3-030-38181-3_1

1   Introduction

As a cryptographic-based distributed ledger, blockchain technology enables trusted transactions among untrusted participants in the network. Most notably, there is an emerging trend beyond cryptocurrency payments, transforming the blockchain into a new paradigm of decentralized systems development for Internet security [1]. Since the introduction of the first Bitcoin blockchain in 2008, blockchain technology has been the subject of increased scientific research and development, and has raised significant interest among researchers, developers, and industry practitioners [2–5].

The potential of utilizing blockchains into decentralized computing platforms has been explored in various contexts ranging from identity management to health data records, Internet of Things (IoT), automobile, risk management, public and social services, far beyond the underlying mechanism of cryptocurrencies and payments. The immutable nature of the blockchain can facilitate security and transparency, since it is computationally challenging for ledgers to be altered in a way not instantly clear to every single user involved. Therefore, granting that the features of blockchain technology guarantee more reliable and expedient services, it is important to consider the security and privacy issues and challenges behind the innovative technology [6–9].

To let blockchain's values to be more practically and scientifically realized in the field of data privacy and security, it is critical to have a clear understanding of current achievements and its challenges moving forward. This is the focus of this book.

2   Book Outline

This book presents the state-of-the-art advancements and achievements from both academia and industry in the blockchain space for security and privacy of software and systems. The remainder of the book is structured as follows.

In order to face with heterogeneous IoT networks challenge, the second chapter [10] introduces a decentralized framework for authentication, authorization and accounting based on ERC721 standard to secure IoT networks and devices. Besides, the chapter reports experiments of applying the framework on Ethereum blockchain as a testbed. Nazmul Islam and Kundu in the third chapter [11] pursue the security, trust and privacy in IoT sharing economy (e.g. a surveillance camera in an Airbnb room) and propose a method to mitigate security, trust, and privacy issues related to leasing IoT-enabled contractual home using blockchain-based smart contract. Worley et al. [12] in Chap. 4 propose a lightweight mining and secure algorithm for cryptocurrencies based on Scrybe architecture.

In the fifth chapter, Moh et al. [13] propose a cloud-based public key model that employs blockchain to improve access to certificate data and certificate revocation lists. Furthermore, they present a run-time sharding of Tendermint that uses the blockchain to provide Byzantine-fault tolerance.

To utilize blockchain technology for facing with real-world challenges, Tiba et al. [14] in Chap. 6 leverage blockchain to propose a secure solution for traffic congestion by detecting, identifying and counting vehicles using reinforcement learning to predict traffic congestion as the first step of traffic management. The subsequent Chap. 7 [15] highlights the importance of power systems and provides a bibliographic analysis of the blockchain application in power systems related researches. Ekramifard et al. [16] in Chap. 8 present a systematic literature review that investigates intersection researches of artificial intelligence and blockchain.

Healthcare has always been an important and appealing target for conducting innovative researches. In Chap. 9 [17], Srivastava et al. give an overview of IoT health technologies that use blockchain and investigate positive and negative aspects of this integration. Similarly, Chap. 10 [18] proposes a healthcare framework that uses public key cryptography to secure data. Singh et al. [19] in Chap. 11 comprehensively review the state-of-the-art of sharding and segregated witness in public and permissionless blockchain models and argue about possible improvements.

In Chap. 12 [20], Click et al. investigate structure of blockchain and security challenges associated with its networking and explore the effectiveness of their approach for preserving digital identity by presenting experimental implementation. Bello and Perez [21] in Chap. 13 study the blockchain within the financial applications and adapt the Payment Application Data Security Standards (PA-DSS) to blockchain platforms and revise the standard to satisfy both financial and blockchain requirements. Finally and in Chap. 14 [22], Liu et al. utilize blockchain for educational and employment purposes to decrease prolonged and inaccurate background screening. They propose a novel $E^2C\text{-}Chain$ that create new blocks upon request of organization to verify education and employment information. Then, they use a Vickrey-Clarke-Groves mechanism to discover the Nash Equilibrium and ensure social cost minimization and encourage the participants of the framework to take part in verifying proposed skills of requesters.

References

1. P.J. Taylor, T. Dargahi, A. Dehghantanha, R.M. Parizi, K.-K.R. Choo, A systematic literature review of blockchain cyber security. Digit. Commun. Netw. https://doi.org/10.1016/j.dcan.2019.01.005
2. A. Yazdinejad, R.M. Parizi, A. Dehghantanha, K.-K.R. Choo, Blockchain-enabled authentication handover with efficient privacy protection in SDN-based 5G networks. CoRR abs/1905.03193. arXiv:1905.03193. http://arxiv.org/abs/1905.03193
3. S. Homayoun, A. Dehghantanha, R.M. Parizi, K.-K.R. Choo, A blockchain-based framework for detecting malicious mobile applications in app stores, in *Proceedings of the 32nd IEEE Canadian Conference of Electrical and Computer Engineering, IEEE CCECE'19*, 2019
4. R.M. Parizi, A. Dehghantanha, On the understanding of gamification in blockchain systems, in *2018 6th International Conference on Future Internet of Things and Cloud Workshops (FiCloudW)* (2018), pp. 214–219

5. E. Nyaletey, R.M. Parizi, Q. Zhang, K.-K.R.C. Choo, BlockIPFS - blockchain-enabled interplanetary file system for forensic and trusted data traceability, in *Proceedings of 2nd IEEE International Conference on Blockchain, IEEE Blockchain-2019*, 2019

6. Q. Zhang, R.M. Parizi, K.-K.R. Choo, A pentagon of considerations towards more secure blockchains, in *IEEE Blockchain Technical Briefs*, 2018

7. R.M. Parizi, A. Dehghantanha, K.-K.R. Choo, A. Singh, Empirical vulnerability analysis of automated smart contracts security testing on blockchains, in *Proceedings of the 28th Annual International Conference on Computer Science and Software Engineering, CASCON '18* (IBM Corp., Riverton, NJ, 2018), pp. 103–113

8. R.M. Parizi, S. Homayoun, A. Yazdinejad, A. Dehghantanha, K.-K.R. Choo, Integrating privacy enhancing techniques into blockchains using sidechains, in *Proceedings of the 32nd IEEE Canadian Conference of Electrical and Computer Engineering, IEEE CCECE'19*, 2019

9. R.M. Parizi, A. Singh, A. Dehghantanha, Smart contract programming languages on blockchains: an empirical evaluation of usability and security, in *International Conference on Blockchain – ICBC 2018*, ed. by S. Chen, H. Wang, L.-J. Zhang (Springer International Publishing, Cham, 2018), pp. 75–91

10. A.S. Omar, O. Basir, Capability-based non-fungible tokens approach for a decentralized AAA framework in IoT, in *Blockchain Cybersecurity, Trust, and Privacy*, ed. by R.M. Parizi, A. Dehghantanha, K.-K.R. Choo (Springer International Publishing, Cham, this volume)

11. M.N. Islam, S. Kundu, IoT security, privacy and trust in home-sharing economy via blockchain, in *Blockchain Cybersecurity, Trust, and Privacy*, ed. by R.M. Parizi, A. Dehghantanha, K.-K.R. Choo (Springer International Publishing, Cham, this volume)

12. C. Worley, L. Yu, R. Brooks, J. Oakley, A. Skjellum, A. Altarawneh, S. Medury, U. Mukhopad-hyay, Scrybe: a 2nd-generation blockchain technology with lightweight mining for secure provenance and related applications, in *Blockchain Cybersecurity, Trust, and Privacy*, ed. by R.M. Parizi, A. Dehghantanha, K.-K.R. Choo (Springer International Publishing, Cham, this volume)

13. M. Moh, D. Nguyen, T.-S. Moh, B. Khieu, Blockchain for efficient public key infrastructure and fault-tolerant distributed consensus, in *Blockchain Cybersecurity, Trust, and Privacy*, ed. by R.M. Parizi, A. Dehghantanha, K.-K.R. Choo (Springer International Publishing, Cham, this volume)

14. K. Tiba, R.M. Parizi, Q. Zhang, A. Dehghantanha, H. Karimipour, K.-K.R. Choo, Secure blockchain-based traffic load balancing using edge computing and reinforcement learning, in *Blockchain Cybersecurity, Trust, and Privacy*, ed. by R.M. Parizi, A. Dehghantanha, K.-K.R. Choo (Springer International Publishing, Cham, this volume)

15. H.M. Rouzbahani, H. Karimipour, A. Dehghantanha, R.M. Parizi, Blockchain applications in power systems: a bibliometric analysis, in *Blockchain Cybersecurity, Trust, and Privacy*, ed. by R.M. Parizi, A. Dehghantanha, K.-K.R. Choo (Springer International Publishing, Cham, this volume)

16. A. Ekramifard, H. Amintoosi, A.H. Seno, A. Dehghantanha, R.M. Parizi, A systematic litera-ture review of integration of blockchain and artificial intelligence, in *Blockchain Cybersecurity, Trust, and Privacy*, ed. by R.M. Parizi, A. Dehghantanha, K.-K.R. Choo (Springer International Publishing, Cham, this volume)

17. G. Srivastava, R.M. Parizi, A. Dehghantanha, The future of blockchain technology in healthcare internet of things security, in *Blockchain Cybersecurity, Trust, and Privacy*, ed. by R.M. Parizi, A. Dehghantanha, K.-K.R. Choo (Springer International Publishing, Cham, this volume)

18. R. Kumar, R. Tripathi, Secure healthcare framework using blockchain and public key cryptog-raphy, in *Blockchain Cybersecurity, Trust, and Privacy*, ed. by R.M. Parizi, A. Dehghantanha, K.-K.R. Choo (Springer International Publishing, Cham, this volume)

19. A. Singh, R.M. Parizi, M. Han, A. Dehghantanha, H. Karimipour, K.-K.R. Choo, Public blockchains scalability: An examination of sharding and segregated witness, in *Blockchain Cybersecurity, Trust, and Privacy*, ed. by R.M. Parizi, A. Dehghantanha, K.-K.R. Choo (Springer International Publishing, Cham, this volume)

20. K. Click, A. Singh, R.M. Parizi, G. Srivastava, A. Dehghantanha, Immutable and secure IP address protection using blockchain, in *Blockchain Cybersecurity, Trust, and Privacy*, ed. by R.M. Parizi, A. Dehghantanha, K.-K.R. Choo (Springer International Publishing, Cham, this volume)
21. G. Bello, A.J. Perez, On the application of financial security standards in blockchain platform, in *On the Application of Financial Security Standards in Blockchain Platforms*, ed. by R.M. Parizi, A. Dehghantanha, K.-K.R. Choo (Springer International Publishing, Cham, this volume)
22. L. Liu, M. Han, Y. Zhou, R.M. Parizi, M. Korayem, Blockchain-based certification for education, employment, and skill with incentive mechanism, in *Blockchain Cybersecurity, Trust, and Privacy*, ed. by R.M. Parizi, A. Dehghantanha, K.-K.R. Choo (Springer International Publishing, Cham, this volume)

Capability-Based Non-fungible Tokens Approach for a Decentralized AAA Framework in IoT

A. Sghaier Omar and O. Basir

Abstract The proliferation of IoT devices across various application domains led to a high level of heterogeneity which introduced new device management challenges. These challenges include, bringing the capability of the service delivery and the underlying accounting, authentication and authorization mechanisms. Moreover, IoT devices tend to no longer require a centralized authority to authenticate and authorize access to the services offered. In this work, we address this by introducing a decentralized Authentication, Authorization and Accounting (AAA) framework using Capability-based Tokens based on the ERC721 standard to provide secure authentication and authorization for IoT devices. The approach is tested on a private Ethereum Blockchain node to analyze performance factors related to access time, timeout ratio and overhead.

1 Introduction

The IoT device proliferation is on a continuous rise, where according to Gartner report on "Value and Impact of IoT on Business" in Gartner Symposium/ITxpo in November 2015 [1] and other industry insights a number of 20 50 billion connections is expected to exist by 2020 with a volume of around $2 trillion in revenue. On the operations side, many challenges exist and among them is secure service delivery and the underlying authentication and authorization mechanism.

Furthermore, the dynamic IoT connections and the trend of peer-to-peer applications in IoT impose other challenges on how devices' authentication and authorization is handled. The need for automated mutual authentication on device-to-device basis is an important scenario where less user intervention is needed thus devices need to perform the mechanism of authentication and authorization autonomously. On the other hand, the constrained environment of IoT devices limits the capability

A. Sghaier Omar (✉) · O. Basir
Electrical and Computer Engineering, University of Waterloo, Waterloo, ON, Canada
e-mail: a2sghaie@uwaterloo.ca; obasir@uwaterloo.ca

© Springer Nature Switzerland AG 2020
K.-K. R. Choo et al. (eds.), *Blockchain Cybersecurity, Trust and Privacy*, Advances in Information Security 79, https://doi.org/10.1007/978-3-030-38181-3_2

of IoT devices to perform the authentication and authorization step using currently adopted frameworks.

Certain approaches opt for offloading those functionalities to the gateways [2, 3], yet this does not fulfill the requirement of ensuring a more secure framework. Gateways vulnerability are addressed in many studies as a result of the shared usage of gateway representing a single point for attack.

OAuth 2.0 and OpenID Connect 1.0 definitely highlights two standardized frameworks for authentication and authorization [4, 5]. However, the main challenge is that OAuth and OpenID Connect have mainly been bound to HTTP which introduces a limitation in case of IoT devices that usually due to the constraints in power don't run on HTTP. New authentication and authorization schemes in IoT are needed for enabling devices to interact with each other in applications where devices exchange services in an autonomous and decentralized way.

Our proposed decentralized approach is based on a decentralized device identity and builds on that to enable a decentralized mechanism for devices authentication and authorization which will enable decentralized service exchange among IoT devices that we finally augment with a token to make it transactional and suggest it for accounting and billing purposes.

This chapter is structured as follows. Section 2 describes the concepts of AAA framework and highlights the suggested and used approaches. Section 3 introduce the concept of Blockchain, its main features, and how smart contracts can be used to implement tokens of both fungible and non-fungible operations, while Sect. 4 explains access control models. The proposed system architecture is described in Sect. 5 and highlighting core functionalities. The details of smart contract implementation and sequence of processes are detailed in Sect. 6. To evaluate the performance and demonstrate the proposed approach feasibility Sect. 7 shows the used testbed and provides insights on the analysis carried out. Finally, Sect. 8 concludes the work.

2   Authentication, Authorization and Accounting

Authentication, authorization, and accounting (AAA) is a framework of controlling access to devices resources, enforcing policies, auditing usage, and providing the information necessary to bill for services [6].

Authentication is the process by which a user or device identifies itself to another user/device. For example, a device can authenticate to a service or a device can authenticate to another device. The process of authentication is based on each user/device having a unique set of attributes (credentials) grouped as a unique identity. The authorization is the process pertaining to the means by which a device determines what privileges other devices/users have on the device and what actions they can perform. Thus, it defines the process of policies enforcement by determining the types of activities, resources, or services a device/user is permitted to perform or access.

The third A is for accounting, and it considers the process of measuring the resources usage during access time. This includes the amount of time or the amount of data a device has used during a session. The accounting function mostly performed by logging of session statistics and usage information to be used for control, billing and analysis.

In existing IT and Telecom networks major frameworks coexist, including the RADIUS, DIAMETER and KERBEROS frameworks, to provide the AAA functionalities [6]. In IoT networks, and due to the need to support heterogeneous networks with intermittent connectivity and dynamic authentication/authorization relationships an automated and autonomous authentication/authentication with less centralization and support for scalability framework need to be devised.

Moreover, most of the existing frameworks are based on a central authority that controls the storage of all identities, perform the matching of authentication requests and then providing access upon authorization requests. Those centralized systems represent a major single-point-of-failure condition, where an adversary that compromises the central AAA servers can disturb the authorization and policy management of the entire network. This becomes even more challenging when we consider peer-to-peer transactions that is characterized as a main stream application domain in IoT networks.

The devices and the data ownership and the fact that many regulatory frameworks such as General Data Protection Regulation (GDPR) [7] require granting users the ownership of the data their devices generate, and thus the devices themselves, show clearly that a decentralized approach would be a necessity to satisfy technical, business and regulatory requirements.

Furthermore, analysing further how current telecom operators and service providers run the AAA systems show that the centralized approach is limiting the granularity level of the AAA functionality required to enable per device or per owner policy design and enforcement [8]. As per the current situation an operator of a AAA service enables authorizing access to services or devices based on coarse-grained attributes such as IP address, port or QoS level, and this does not offer fine-grained access control on resources and services deployed on IoT devices.

In our suggested approach, the central AAA authority is replaced with a set of smart contracts deployed on Ethereum Blockchain, [9], and the AAA operations are handled according to the logic engraved in the smart contracts code. This offers a decentralized, immutable and trackable ledger of transactions. We suggest using a Blockchain for various tasks in IoT, see [10], where we introduced a device identity management framework in IoT using Blockchain and smart contracts. The work of decentralized identity management is a cornerstone in building a decentralized AAA framework. Thus, we build on that to enable the authentication and authorization processes based on the IoT device identity stored on the Blockchain.

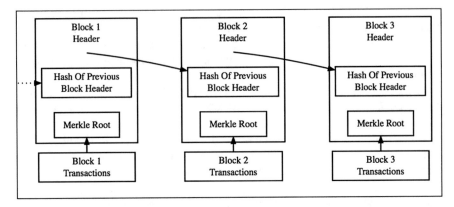

Fig. 1 Visualization of Blockchain concept

3 Blockchain Concepts

Blockchain is defined as a distributed shared digital ledger for transactions. It employs public key cryptography in forming the identity and pseudo-anonymity of all participants and decentralized consensus algorithms to maintain the ledger intact and to verify any transaction. The distributed ledger is constructed by combining a number of transactions in a block, and hash their content with the hash value of the previous block to construct the hash value of the new block, Fig. 1. This happens for each newly generated block except for the genesis block [11].

3.1 Ethereum Blockchain and Smart Contracts

Among the widely adopted Blockchain platforms is Ethereum, and it is a Blockchain architecture with an associated state database, capable of storing programs and their state, known as Smart Contracts. A smart contract can be deployed by any Ethereum user and it has a function-based interface or Application Binary Interface (ABI).

Once deployed the smart contract can be referenced by its address, which is a cryptographic identifier. To Access a smart contract function, a user calls the smart contract function by sending a transaction to its address as the destination, and with the data payload of the transaction containing the function signature and input parameters [9].

3.2 Tokenization in Blockchain

Smart contracts in Ethereum are implemented in one of the supported languages (Serpent and Solidity) with defined user interface through libraries [12]. The cryptocurrencies and tokens used in Blockchain applications represent a viable solution for establishing accounting and billing transactions.

This has been largely attributed to the standardized and well-defined ERC20 token standard authored by Fabian Vogelsteller and Vitalik Buterin in 2015 [13].

In addition to ERC20 tokens, which is considered a fungible (interchangeable) token, non-fungible tokens (NFTs) also started to become a main asset exchanged on Blockchain platforms based on the ERC721 token standard [14]. That includes examples of game cards and other tradable collectible assets such as CryptoKitties, Decentraland and DotLicense [15].

The main difference between these two types of tokens is summarized by the fact that ERC20 tokens are the class of identical interchangeable tokens more of a fiat currency example, while ERC721 NFT is the class of unique non-interchangeable token. The main feature of NFTs is that they represent ownership over digital or physical assets, that include a diverse list of assets such as real-estate, unique artwork, virtual collectables—unique pictures of kittens and collectable cards. This makes NFTs distinguishable and their ownership is trackable on individual basis.

The authors demonstrate through the combination of these two token standards a foundation to enable decentralized AAA framework. While the fungible tokens provide a simple, fast and frictionless transactional mean, NFTs offer the verifiable immutability and authenticity required in addition to other features such as delegation, transfer of ownership, and revocation.

4 Access Control Models

An access control system is described as the set of rules that define the control functions of the who, what and when. Entities such as users or devices are normally called subjects, which based on a rule can define what actions can be performed based on the rights granted on which resources; resources usually called objects. Therefore, an access control system can be modelled by a relationship model that describes the set or rules U that connects objects O subjects S, rights r and context C, Eq. 1.

$$U = \{u_0, u_1, u_2, \ldots u_n\}, where \ u_i = (o_i, s_i, r_i, c_i) \tag{1}$$

Most access control (AC) frameworks implement the policies to control access to network resources with different access control models that can be mapped to one of the following main categories: Access Control Lists (ACLs), Role-based Access

Control (RBAC), Attribute-based Access Control (ABAC), and Capability-based Access Control (CapBAC).

The most common form of access control is based on access control lists (ACLs). ACL is a centralized approach to support administrative activities, which assigns access rights to specific subjects. However, as the number of subjects and resources increase, confused duty problems are identified in ACL and access rules become much more complex to manage [16].

To overcome the challenges of simple ACLs systems, the Role Based Access Control (RBAC) approach [17–19] was designed: it assigns access rights to roles and subjects to roles. RBAC supports access control principles such as least privilege authorization and partition of administrative functions. RBAC suffers from the roles explosion problem as the number of resources grow, which makes it unsuitable to implement security policies that require interpreting complex and indistinct IoT scenarios.

Recently, capability-based access control CapBAC was proposed in few studies [16, 20–22], CapBAC is based on issuing a communicable and unforgeable token that the owner can assign to other subjects. The core principle is that those capability tokens are issued by the object owner and granted to the subject with minimal interaction of a central authority which makes it more aligned for decentralized architectures.

The main factors to define a CapBAC is that a capability token once issued to a subject, the subject should not be able to tamper with. Also, the token should have a specified data structure that has at least major fields such as the capability identifier, the delegation rights, the access rights, the issuer and subject identifiers and timing-related fields. In a CapBAC model, major functions are also defined which includes token creation, token revocation and delegation function. Additionally, to accommodate the constrained environment of IoT networks the representation should be light and compact.

4.1 Access Models Suitability

Assessing the suitability of those different approaches to the IoT scenarios and specifically to the decentralized architecture proposed in this work is based on number of factors. The works of [23, 24] provide solid analysis of the different approaches and highlights the major advantages and disadvantages which is compiled here in a radar chart to depict the coverage each approach is providing considering those multivariate factors, Fig. 2.

The CapBAC shows wider coverage in most aspects except the interoperability factor which defines the portability of any access control rule between different systems. This, however, is not a relevant feature for a decentralized approach as object owners have more granular control over the resources in a heterogeneous and ad-hoc established connections. The context-awareness aspect also ranks low which

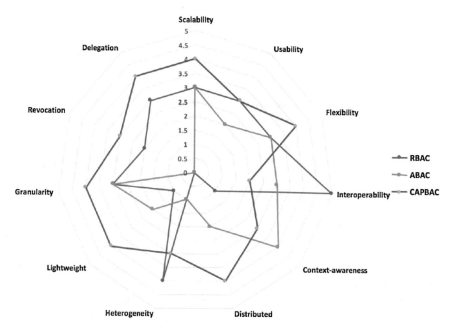

Fig. 2 Radar view of AC models fitness to AAA requirements in IoT networks

can be improved by augmenting more contextual information in the capability token issued in compromise of lightweight representation.

4.2 Centralized vs. Decentralized Access Control

The AAA architecture is made of certain components that focuses on how to authenticate the user/device and authorize access and that is performed by querying, making a decision, and enforcing the decision against defined access policy. Those functionalities are defined in AAA frameworks by the terminology of Policy Administration Point (PAP) responsible on policies creation and modification, Policy Enforcement Point (PEP) responsible for triggering entitlement policy decisions, Policy Decision Point (PDP) provides the actual entitlement decisions on behalf of the PEP, and Policy Information/Retrieval Point (PIP/PRP) that supplies the PDP with the information required for a decision [25]. Figure 3 depicts the flow of actions among those different points.

The difference between a centralized and a decentralized AC model depends on placement of those functionality and which entity owns and controls that point and the decisions made.

In a decentralized approach, which is proposed in this work, the approach goes far beyond a distributed approach which distributes the policy points among

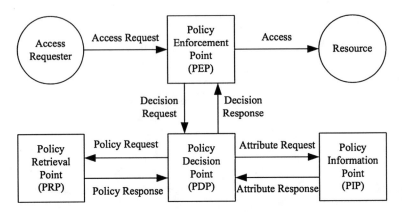

Fig. 3 Policy management functions interactions in AAA architecture

different actors in the network yet under a global supervision by the centralized authority. A decentralized approach will put, most importantly, the policy definition and decision making under the control of the device/owner. In such case, the envisaged architecture of a decentralized access control model grants the PAP and PDP functions to the object owner as they pertain to the points for policies creation and decision making. The object owner will define the policies make them available for retrieval to a PEP, which can be implemented inside the device or pushed to a gateway to accommodate for device resource limitations.

5 Proposed Architecture and Protocol Stack

As mentioned in the introduction, industry trends aim for a fully decentralized architecture in IoT, which is considered very important in the service layer. Therefore, the underlying functionalities represented by authentication and authorization should build the foundation for that. In this paper, we suggest a decentralized architecture that can enable devices to authenticate each other in peer-to-peer fashion and authorize access and service requests.

The proposed decentralized framework is based on the Blockchain and smart contracts technology. The framework highlights four main principles: AAA operations in IoT tend more for a decentralized setting to enable decentralized applications; decentralization of services require that device(s)' owners have full control over device operation; portability of devices and specifically data is a must for decentralized IoT applications and thus users should be to do that under no control of service providers; and finally that services provisioning and de-provisioning should be automated also in a decentralized way. Figure 4 shows the proposed protocol stack.

Fig. 4 Proposed architecture
and protocol stack

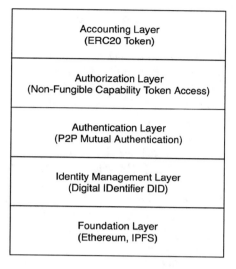

5.1 Foundation Layer

This foundation layer provides implicitly the infrastructure required for cryptography, virtual machine and storage. The Ethereum Blockchain will enable the tracking of all transactions and ensure the existence of an immutable record, which is required for auditing and analysis purposes. The distributed file storage system represented here by the Interplanetary File System IPFS [26], provides the distributed storage infrastructure necessary to ensure that IoT devices and the generated data has the required portability and is offered in a provider-agnostic approach.

The two platforms Ethereum and IPFS are used to complement each other, so to avoid storing large data volumes inside the Blockchain, all data, including policies metdat, are stored into the IPFS and the hash value of the stored data is linked to the transaction stored in the Blockchain.

5.2 Identity Management Layer

The second layer is the identity management, which we briefly highlight its functions in this text and we refer the reader to the authors previous work [10] for further details. This layer enables the devices to issue an identity stored on the Blockchain that can be tracked to the time of device origin. The Blockchain-hosted identity establishes a unique and global digital identity that can be maintained throughout the device life cycle. In addition, this provides the means for supporting the device ownership management and identity update.

5.3   *Authentication Layer*

The authentication layer in this architecture provides a peer-to-peer authentication mechanism based on the Blockchain-hosted device identity. The fundamental component of this layer is defined by the mutual challenge handshaking authentication mechanism [27]. Upon establishing a connection between two devices the flow of messages as in Fig. 5.

First party (party A) will create a challenge (based on the set of attributes used to generate the device identity and a nonce) and send a message containing the challenge (CHa) and the party DID-Blockchain identity (DIDa) with digital signature using it private key SIGa(DIDa,CHa). Upon receiving the message, party B issues a query to the identity management smart contract to query the owner of the identity DIDa, which will return its Ethereum address and thus public key. Party B verifies the SIGa(DIDa,CHa) and if verified then Party A identity is authentic. In the next exchange of messages Party B sends a message containing DIDa,CHa,DIDb,CHb with a digital signature SIGb. Party A as well queries the identity management smart contract to confirm the ownership of DIDb by party B and uses the public key PUBb to verify the digital signature. If successful then the mutual authentication has been completed.

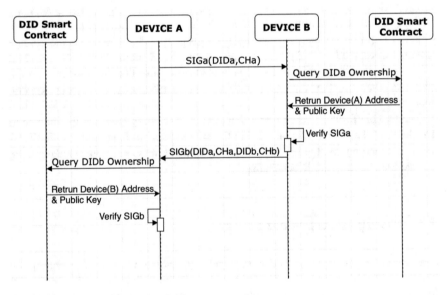

Fig. 5 Peer-to-peer mutual authentication sequence diagram

5.4   Authorization Layer

To permit a decentralized service requests authorization, devices are required to deploy smart contracts that provide the function of access control. In traditional networks, access control is performed using either role-based access control RBAC or attribute-based access control ABAC, and each serves certain applications and offer certain advantages. As it was described in Sect. 5, the CapBAC provides more features that aligns with the requirement of implementing a decentralized authorization mechanism.

The proposed framework consists of several access control smart contracts that each device submits on the Blockchain. Each access control smart contract provides a number of functions to enable defining the access control rules for resources and services provided by the device. The architecture also includes a registrar contract that is used to list the different access control contracts information with a metadata and utilized for resources and service discovery.

The CapBAC model is implemented using the principle of NFT tokens by extending the ERC721 smart contract standard to provide functionalities of Cap-BAC tokens generation with features of delegation, revocation and contextual information.

The access control smart contract is implemented on a device basis, where a device will define multiple access control roles for the resources/services available and issue the required amount of CapBAC tokens. As a result, one access control smart contract will exist for each device with a supply of access tokens as per the rules defined for each resource. In the proposed architecture, to enable dynamic management, the main template for the access control smart contract includes a set of management functions (ABIs) that includes:

- *issueTokens()*: is used to generate new tokens by the device owner when a new resource is available or new policy is required.
- *revokeTokens()*: enables access tokens deletion as an existing policy becomes obsolete or the resource is not available.
- *obtainToken()*: provides the interface for any requesting device to be granted access by obtaining CapBAC token issued by the device owner.
- *destroyContract()*: it provides a tool to remove the access control smart contract from the Blockchain and enables generating a new contract.

Upon a successful device-to-device mutual authentication, a subject device issues an access request for an advertised resource to the access control smart contract. That is handled by having the subject device issuing a call to obtainToken function. The function upon success issues a new NFT access token and transfer the token ownership to the subject device.

Having obtained the token, the device then can access the resource according to the access control rule defined within the token. The PEP functionality deployed either within the device or a gateway can query the access control smart contract upon receiving access requests. The smart contract in this case is providing the PDP functionality as set by the rules defined in each specific token.

In case of failure, the requesting device negotiate with the offering device to amend the authorization rules and generate a token with the desired access rights. The object device through the management ABIs generates new tokens or deletes obsolete ones and to ensure only the authorized device/owner can access the management ABIs, each of those functions are restricted in access based on a set of modifiers.

5.5 Accounting Layer

Blockchain technology main application is cryptocurrency, and Ethereum Blockchain is one of few platforms that offers the capability to create a cryptocurrency for entities to use as a transactional mean. The Ethereum ERC20 token standard is a feasible tool to introduce a mean of transaction between IoT devices once authorization is granted. The logging and immutability features of Blockchain provide a tool to enable the accounting functionality in a decentralized AAA framework.

Thus, in this framework we introduce a special token that will be utilized by the IoT devices to charge for resources usage. The concept of a token has been used for many decentralized applications including IoT, and here we follow a similar approach but with a focus on AAA functionality to support the accounting capability.

The token contract is based on the ERC20 token standard with an addition of top-up function that will allow a device balance to be topped up to be able to perform transactions with other devices. This function is usually called by the device owner through an external interface. The ERC20 contract provides an interface for the ERC721 to charge subjects for granting access tokens based on the defined cost. The accounting model used in this framework is a pre-paid model, where based on the defined set of access rights requested for the access token (either per resource or time) the object device upon access token generation will set the price.

6 Details of Smart Contract Implementation

In defining the details of smart contracts implementation, the work required to address the IoT context and list the main requirements to fulfill a decentralized AAA functionality, and those can be described as:

- Full control of devices and owners on policy rules creation/revocation.
- The need to offload AAA management functions out of the constrained IoT devices with the least minimal external authority control.
- The capability to revoke any access rights in a dynamic arrangement and the to easily delegate rights with full auditing on resource access.

- The capability to support usage of time-based access tokens that can support spontaneous as well as long-lived connections.

The implementation is based on three smart contracts handling the mechanisms of discovery, access control and accounting. The first smart contract is used as a registrar to enable devices and owners of publishing their newly deployed access control smart contracts. The registrar contract represents a repository for the information of available resources and to obtain information on access control smart contract addresses.

The second set is the core of the decentralized AAA architecture where it includes the authorization logic. Specifically, the access control smart contract includes the PAP, PDP and PIP functionalities, while the PEP functionality is left to be implemented as an application that can reside either in the IoT device or on a gateway that controls few devices. The PEP application has interfaces with the access control smart contract as per the standardized interfaces including PEP-PDP and PEP-PIP. The third set is the ERC20 token smart contract that provides the mechanism of accounting which includes the functions to transfer a defined amount of the billing token in return of obtaining an access control token.

6.1 Registrar Smart Contract

The main function of this part is to allow subjects to discover available resources, specifically the access control smart contract and the information of available resources. It is designed with the assumption that an operating entity handles the smart contract management; in terms of adding a registrant or authorizing features.

The registrar contract contains a data structure that holds records of registrants and the information about available resources, policies and addresses of access control contracts deployed. The data structure includes three main identifiers: the registrant is identified by the global identifier based on the Blockchain identity; policies are identified by a unique policy identifier; and the access control smart contract by the Blockchain address.

6.2 Access Control Smart Contract

This smart contract is designed as set of templates that a device based on the scenario can deploy a specific template that serves certain access control scenario. The access control smart contract utilizes the principle of NFT tokens where capability-based access tokens are defined as an NFT token that is unequivocal and manageable. The skeleton of the access control smart contracts inherits the functions defined by the ERC721 standard including tokenGeneration, tokenRevocation, tokenOwnership and tokensBalance.

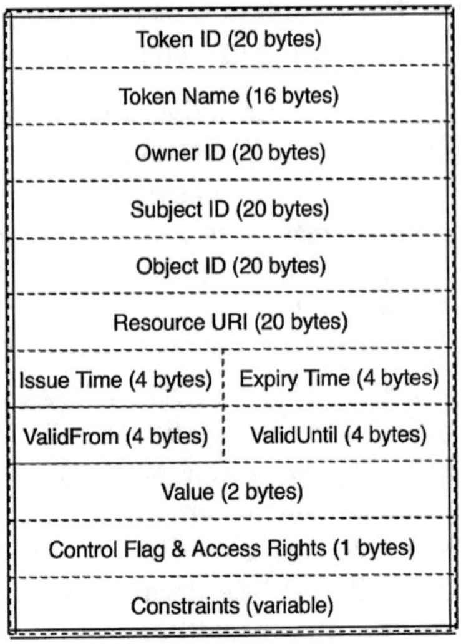

Fig. 6 Non-fungible
capability-based token
structure

Token ID (20 bytes)
Token Name (16 bytes)
Owner ID (20 bytes)
Subject ID (20 bytes)
Object ID (20 bytes)
Resource URI (20 bytes)

Issue Time (4 bytes)	Expiry Time (4 bytes)
ValidFrom (4 bytes)	ValidUntil (4 bytes)

Value (2 bytes)
Control Flag & Access Rights (1 bytes)
Constraints (variable)

6.3   Non-fungible Capability Token Structure

The access control smart contract utilizes the NFT token concept to build the CapBAC token. The token structure, as in Fig. 6, is defined in JSON format to provide a compact representation and allow easy integration with the underlying communication protocol. The structure of the CapBAC token is defined by a number of fields described hereafter:

- *Token ID*: this is a unique identifier of the token which is composed from hashing three other identifiers, subject ID, object ID and resource URI.
- *Token Name*: this field is a descriptive filed to be human readable.
- *Subject ID*: this is represented by either the device or user ID, which represents the token holder.
- *Object ID*: this is the ID of the object to be accessed.
- *Owner ID*: this field manages token ownership and also used in delegation confirmation. Different values of Owner ID and Subject ID show that access token rights have been delegated.
- *Resource URI*: a string representing the resource to be accessed as per the communication protocol.
- *Issue Time*: a timestamp for when the token was issued to the subject.
- *Expiry Time*: a timestamp for a token and access right granted expire.
- *ValidFrom*: a timestamp for when a token is valid, this is always set to be greater than Issue Time.

- *ValidUntil*: a timestamp for when this token is valid, this is always set to be less than Expiry Time. Both fields are used by the token holder to delegate access rights for a limited time.
- *Value*: this represents the value defined by the resource owner to offer the defined access rights.
- *Control Flags*: a number of flags used to handle token management and represent validation on whether a token can be delegated, transferred or if it has been revoked.
- *Access Rights*: a field describing the actions according to the CoAP protocol GET, FETCH, PUT, UPDATE, PATHC and DELETE.
- *Constraints*: this field is made of zero or more entries to define granular access rights and it currently supports merging contextual information either by ANDing or ORing. The entries should have those subfields:
  - Type: the contextual condition type such as location, battery level.
  - Condition: control condition on access right (e.g. >, <, =)
  - Value: to define the desired value for condition verification.

- *Token Digest*: a hashed value of the token JSON document that is used to protect against usage of forged tokens.

6.4 Authorization Process

The authorization sequence diagram, Fig. 7, shows the steps in a device to device authorization process. The requesting device sends an access request to the device where the resource/object exists, with no access token the object device redirects the requester to the address of the deployed access control smart contract. The requester issues a transaction to the smart contract address to obtain a token, which triggers the smart contract to generate a token with the specified arguments define the value associated and charge the requester by calling the ERC20 accounting contract.

Upon a successful transaction, the issued token is forwarded to the requesting device. Henceforth, and based on the expiry period of the access token, the requester starts issuing access commands (GET, PUT, ... etc) that passes through the PEP point, which in this diagram is represented by the gateway.

The policy enforcement is performed by the gateway as most decision factors are already embedded in the access token. The only calls need to be made to the access control smart contract is to retrieve the token hash value and check the ownership and delegated authority on the token.

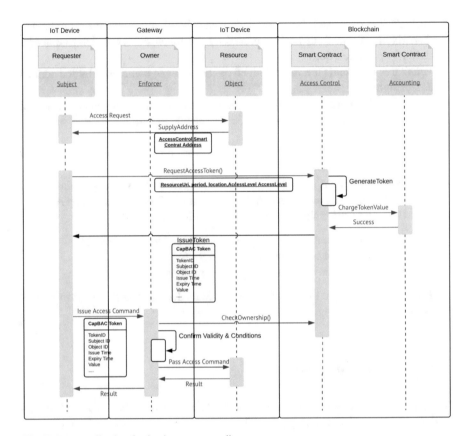

Fig. 7 Decentralized authorization sequence diagram

6.5 *Delegation Process*

The delegation process, as per Fig. 8, describes how the CapBAC token design provides the mean for a token holder to delegate access rights to other devices. The token field is Delegable defined by the token issuer dictates if the holder can delegate rights or not.

Once a delegaee submits a delegation request the token holder (delegator) confirms delegation capability and then issues a transaction to the access control smart contract to update the fields of subject ID to match the delegaee ID, define the delegation period by setting the validFrom and ValidUntil fields and then if required update the access rights and define other constraints on the delegation. The constrains refinement can be only made to further fine the detail the permitted zone and not to exceeded. For example, if the holder is granted UPDATE right the delegaee cannot obtain PUT right yet it can still be restricted only to GET operations.

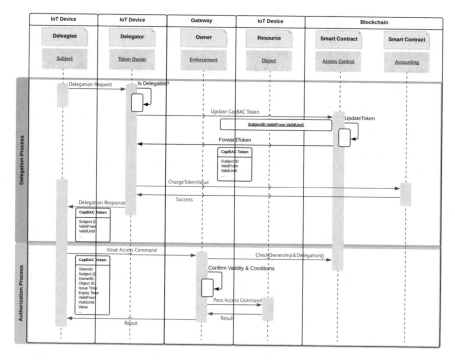

Fig. 8 Delegation process sequence diagram

The revocation of delegation is not shown in the figure above; however, it is performed by the holder issuing a transaction to the access control smart contract to reset the Subject ID to match the Owner ID and the validity fields to match the issue and expiry time.

6.6 Placement of Policy Management Functions

In the authorization steps, the different policy management functions handle the flow to grant or deny access to a certain resource. The access control smart control hosts the functions of PAP, PDP and PRP, where it describes the flow of actions and map them to the different components. This approach provides a high level of dynamicity where CapBAC tokens can be generated on-demand according to a negotiated set of attributes.

PAP functionality is provided through the tokenIssuance function which creates the CapBAC token with the set of attributes defined by the issuer. The PRP function is offered by the capability to query the available CapBAC tokens in a smart contract and retrieve all details.

The PDP function is embedded in the CapBAC token itself since all parameter required to make a decision are already compiled and once a device presents the token and proves its ownership access should be granted. This design allows for resource constrained devices to handle decentralized authorization with less burden on computing, storage and battery requirements as the smart contracts are hosted and executed on the Blockchain.

The only functionality that is left to be either implemented at the device or a gateway is the PEP functionality since any request should pass through it before access is granted. The PEP function also has access to the smart contract to perform actions that confirm the validity and ownership of the presented CapBAC token in any access request.

6.7   PEP Process Steps

The application residing on the device or the gateway handles the enforcement process by applying a checklist to confirm the token validity and match access rules. These steps are carried out once receiving the CoAP access command with the issued CapBAC token. The process design opted for embedding the CapBAC token so the PEP function is more self-contained.

The PEP process as depicted in the process chart, Fig. 9, is a series of checklist with a final outcome of the PEP process to be either deny access or grant access response, those check points are:

- *Check against Revocation*: firstly, the PEP application checks the is Revoked flag to handle the case of revoked tokens, and if revoked then it replies with denied access.
- *Check for Forgery*: the PEP queries the token hash value from the smart contract and compares it with the hash value of the presented token. On an unmatched event the PEP replies with denied access.
- *Confirm Token Ownership*: to ensure that the request has been issued by the legitimate token holder, the receiving party check both the subject ID and Owner ID. If both fields are equal then it is only required to check token ownership by querying the specified interface on the smart contract. If fields have different values that shows the case of a delegated access, thus again the receiving party will confirm the ownership and delegation rights through the smart contract.
- *Check Token Validity*: once more, if the token rights have been delegated then the gateway will check the validity of token delegation by ensuring that current timestamp lays between ValidFrom and ValidUntil timestamps. If the token is still held by the original owner then the validity is checked against both Issue and Expiry timestamps.
- *Check Access Rights*: by comparing the access method used in the CoAP request received and the access right defined in the token metadata against the specified object URI, the PEP application will either deny or grant access to the specified resource.

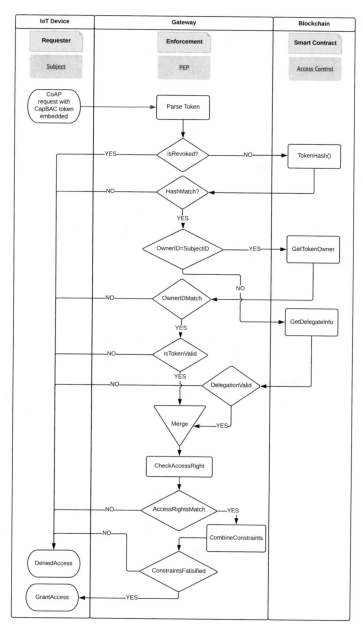

Fig. 9 Policy enforcement process flow chart

- *Check Constraints*: Upon successful check of access rights, the PEP application validates the condition set in the constraints array. The application pulls the different conditions and values defined and fuse them according to the defined operator (OR/AND).

6.8   Accounting Smart Contract

The functionality of accounting is performed using a simplified pre-paid usage model implemented using an ERC20 token. The token is used to represent the value of transactions involving obtaining a CapBAC token or to charge for a delegation right. Such an approach provides the entities participating in the authorization step the autonomy needed to price the services offered and flexibility in offering services to the different actors interested.

The implemented accounting tokens is a straightforward translation of the ERC20 standard with uncapped total supply and one additional function which is the top-up function to allow any device/owner to top-up its account balance that is tied to the total supply. The accounting smart contract design defines an assumption that minting new accounting token is linked to an external crypto or fiat currency.

The ERC20 main functions are mapped to certain usages in the accounting mechanism as per the following:

- *balanceOf()*: used when obtain a new Token to check sufficient balance.
- *transferFrom()*: the main function used whenever a CapBAC token issued to transfer the corresponding value of the token from the requester to the issuer.
- *Transfer()*: used also for crediting against CapBAC tokens issuance as well in funding device accounts by the owner.
- *Approve()*: offers the device owner the ability to grant a device a certain balance to be used for transacting, yet the accounting token is still under the authority of the owner and this balance can be updated at any time.
- *Allownace()*: provides the same functionality of balanceOf() but for tokens available and approved by the owner to the device.

The accounting smart contract implements the events to record the transactions involving a token transfer and approve as well as the minting transactions, thus all accounting information are registered.

7   Test Bed and Performance Evaluation

To evaluate the performance of the suggested approach and highlight main issues a test bed was built hosting an implementation of a use case of few IoT nodes providing sensor data consumed in a p2p approach, Fig. 10.

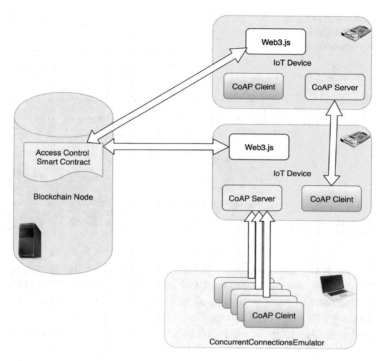

Fig. 10 Testbed configuration

The test bed architecture was based on 2 IoT nodes hosted on raspberry pi boards and a sense-hat shield. The test bed emulates a group of environmental nodes providing measurements of temperature, humidity and barometric pressure. Each node work as an end node and as a gateway and hosts a client and server interface of the CoAP protocol based on the node-coap library [28], and interfaces to the Blockchain using the Web3.js library [29].

A laptop was used to emulate number of concurrent connections, the application resides on the laptop uses the node-coap library to create multiple instances of the client and issue access requests. The smart contracts for the identity management, access control and accounting were deployed on a private Ethereum node with the following specifications. The overall architecture of the testbed is defined by the following figure, and here we explain the main performance factors considered in the analysis.

7.1 Timeout Ratio

Transactions on Blockchain require confirmation and in case of Ethereum public network confirmation time is estimated at 5–20 s. Thus, it is expected that

Fig. 11 Results of timed-out requests ratio vs. number of concurrent connections

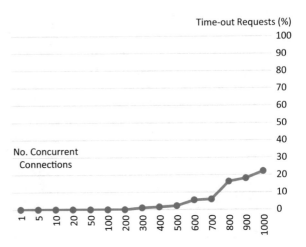

offloading the AAA functionalities to the smart contract will introduce latency. The CoAP confirmable message exchange specifies default transmission parameters for message timeout and number of retries, which we use in this analysis as per the transmission parameters section in the CoAP Protocol Standard [30].

The timeout ratio factor is measured in a scenario of one IoT device serving a resource with a number of concurrent connections initiated within 30 s, equivalent to half the value of the default MAX_TRANSMIT_SPAN value in CoAP [32]. The number of concurrent connections were increased from 1 to 1000 concurrent connections in steps {1, 5, 10, 20, 50, 100, 200, 300, 400, 500, 600, 700, 800, 900, 1000}.

The results, Fig. 11, show that for as low as 200 concurrent connections no timeouts were recorded and the number of timed-out requests rose slightly above 5% of total requests sent at 600 concurrent connections with a spike appearing at 800 concurrent connections represented by a timeout ratio of 16.25%, and at 1000 connections the timeout ratio is measured at 22.1%. Once more, we attribute this sudden increase to the fact that the CapBAC token generation step introduces significant processing delay waiting for block confirmation and the congestion in block production is the main attributing factor.

7.2 End-to-End Access Time

This parameter is the time measured from the time a device issues an access request for a resource till it receives the response for the resource requested, encompassing all steps in the authorization sequence diagram. Measuring the average time over 1000 runs between two devices in a scenario of newly established connections, that require new CapBAC token generation, shows an average value of 729 ms and measuring a maximum value of 1411 ms. While in the case of established connections and already issued CapBAC tokens, the average time is at 246 ms and a maximum value of 316 ms.

The analysis of the authorization sequence show that the bottleneck is present the first time the CapBAC token is generated as it requires changing the state of the smart contract. The subsequent access requests, when the token is still valid, are only querying the smart contract for ownership and delegation information. This shows the benefit of utilizing the NFT capability token approach to issue a self-contained policy decision point.

7.3   Overhead

The proposed approach defined a capability token that the requester embeds in any request such that it offloads the policy management functions into the smart contract and make the capability token self-contained for policy decisions. However, that results an overhead in the data to be sent in each CoAP packet. According to the proposed token data structure, the maximum length is 120 bytes which in case of having IPv6 as the underlying protocol (1152 packet size), [31], that represents 10.4% overhead in the data link budget.

8   Conclusion

Building distributed and decentralized applications on heterogeneous IoT networks require that lower level layers to support these operations. The IoT device management layer is among the layers responsible on enabling decentralized service consumption model. The core is the AAA functionality which in this work we presented a working solution thorough the utilization of the standardized Ethereum ERC20 and ERC721 tokens.

The work defined a framework that has a foundation of a decentralized identity management and built on top of it a mutual authentication scheme with forward perfect secrecy. Moreover, by mapping the CapBAC access model to the ERC721 the authors demonstrated how access tokens can be defined as collectibles which can be extended to an economy of tradable and collectible access tokens.

The testbed results show the feasibility of the approach with further investigation required to compare the performance when the same approach is implemented on top of PoS and DPoS consensus algorithms. The data overhead issue observed in the testbed results also require an assessment of a trade-off between embedding the token as a whole or just the token ID and leave the token retrieval at the PEP end which can also suffer from communication overhead as the token need to be retrieved on each request.

References

1. Gartners, Inc. The value and impact of IoT on business, 2015. http://www.gartner.com/newsroom/id/3114217
2. E. Bertino, N. Islam, Botnets and internet of things security. Computer **50**(2), 76–79 (2017)
3. B. Ali, A.I. Awad, Cyber and physical security vulnerability assessment for IoT-based smart homes. Sensors (Basel, Switzerland) **18**(3), 817 (2018)
4. OAuth 2.0. https://oauth.net/2
5. D. Recordon, D. Reed, OpenID 2.0: a platform for user centric identity management, in *DIM '06: Proceedings of the 2nd ACM Workshop on Digital Identity Management*, 2006, pp. 11–16
6. M. Nakhjiri, M. Nakhjiri, AAA and network security for mobile access: radius, diameter, EAP, PKI and IP mobility. (Wiley, New York, 2005), pp. 1–24
7. General Data Protection Regulation, 2018. https://gdpr-info.eu
8. O. Liberg, M. Sundberg, E. Wang, J. Bergman, J. Sachs, *Cellular Internet of Things: Technologies, Standards, and Performance* (Academic Press, London, 2018)
9. V. Buterin, Ethereum: a next-generation smart contract and decentralized application platform. Ethereum Foundation. 2014. https://github.com/ethereum/wiki/wiki/White-Paper
10. A. Sghaier Omar, O. Basir, Identity management in IoT networks using Blockchain and smart contracts, in *Proceedings of the 2018 IEEE International Conference on Blockchain*, Halifax, NS, Canada, 2018
11. G. Wood, Ethereum: a secure decentralised generalised transaction ledger, 2014. http://gavwood.com/paper.pdf
12. Solidity Documentation. https://solidity.readthedocs.io/en/v0.4.25/
13. F. Vogelsteller, V. Buterin, ERC 20 Token Standard, 2015. https://github.com/ethereum/EIPs/blob/master/EIPS/eip-20.md
14. W. Entriken, D. Shirley, J. Evans, N. Sachs. ERC-721 Non-fungible token standard, 2018. https://github.com/ethereum/EIPs/blob/master/EIPS/eip-721.md
15. Non-fungible token Market. https://nonfungible.com
16. R. Xu, Y. Chen, E. Blasch, G. Chen, Blendcac: a Blockchain-enabled decentralized capability-based access control for iots, in *IEEE International Conference on Blockchain, Selected Areas in IoT and Blockchain*, 2018
17. D. Ferraiolo, R. Kuhn, Role-based access controls, in *Proceedings of the 15th National Computer Security Conference*, 1992, pp. 554–563
18. S. Gavrila, J. Barkley, Formal specification for role based access control user/role and role/role relationship management, in *Proceedings of the 3rd ACM Workshop on Role-Based Access Control (RBAC'98)*, 1998, pp. 81–90
19. G. Zhang, J. Tian, An extended role based access control model for the internet of things, in *Proceedings of the International Conference on Information, Networking and Automation, Proceedings*, 2010, pp. 319–323
20. J.L. Hernandez-Ramos, A.J. Jara, L. Marin, A.F. Skarmeta, Distributed capability-based access control for the internet of things. J. Internet Serv. Inform. Secur. **3**(3/4), 1–16 (2013)
21. A. Ouaddah, A. Abou Elkalam, A. Ait Ouahman, Fairaccess: a new Blockchain-based access control framework for the internet of things. Secur. Comm. Network. **9**(18), 5943–5964 (2016)
22. R. Xu, Y. Chen, E. Blasch, G. Chen, A federated capability-based access control mechanism for internet of things (iots), in *SPIE Defense & Commercial Sensing. Conference on Sensors and Systems for Space Applications*, 2018
23. S. Gusmeroli, S. Piccione, D. Rotondi, A capability-based security approach to manage access control in the internet of things. Math. Comput. Model., 1189–1205 (2013)
24. A. Ouaddah, H. Mousannif, A.A. Elkalam, A.A. Ouahman, Access control in the internet of things: big challenges and new opportunities. Comput. Netw. **112**, 237–262 (2017)
25. Study of Authorization Architecture for Supporting Heterogeneous Access Control Policies (2016) OneM2M Technical Report, TR-0016-V-2.0
26. IPFS Documentation, Protocol Labs, https://docs.ipfs.io

27. L. Chen, G. Guang, *Communication System Security* (Chapman & Hall/CRC, London/Boca Raton, 2012)
28. M. Collina, COAP Node.js Library, https://github.com/mcollina/node-coap
29. Web3.js Ethereum Javascript API. https://github.com/ethereum/wiki/wiki/JavaScript-API
30. Z. Shelby, K. Hartke, C. Bormann, The Constrained Application Protocol (CoAP), IETF RFC 7252, 2014. http://tools.ietf.org/html/rfc7252
31. S. Deering, R. Hinden, Internet Protocol, Version 6 (IPv6) Specification, Internet Engineering Task Force (IETF) RFC 8200, 2017. https://tools.ietf.org/html/rfc8200

IoT Security, Privacy and Trust in Home-Sharing Economy via Blockchain

Md Nazmul Islam and Sandip Kundu

Abstract The phenomenal growth of Internet-services has created a vibrant new domain for sharing economy. Millions of users around the world share personal services and possessions with others—often complete strangers. Such sharing schemes have been defined by a strong centralization of power and processes, which results in disadvantageous prices and deals for consumers alongside distrust. They also increase the risk of violation of one's informational and physical privacy and security. Strangers often have to trust each other with their privacy (e.g. a surveillance camera in an Airbnb room). However, very little research has been devoted to investigate security, trust and privacy in sharing economy. In this paper, we explore the security, trust, and privacy concerns associated with contractual renting or leasing of IoT (Internet-of-Things) devices-enabled home. We propose a methodology to eliminate security, trust, and privacy threats from IoT-enabled telematics devices in a smart home via blockchain-based smart contract. For the purpose of illustration, we focus on how we can circumvent the threats from indoor surveillance IP cameras in a smart home sharing economy.

1 Introduction

Sharing economy platforms such as Airbnb have recently flourished in the tourism industry. However, relying on a centralized third party sharing platform inevitably leads to single point of weakness, higher fees, lack of trust and governance issues for both users and service providers [1], creates an inherent bias, fraud in the system. Such intermediaries charge a large service fee (up to 15% for guests and up to 5% commission off the homeowner), can arbitrarily change the terms and conditions [1]. Hence, it is imperative to find a technological solution to eliminate distrust in sharing economy scheme.

M. N. Islam (✉) · S. Kundu
University of Massachusetts Amherst, Amherst, MA, USA
e-mail: mislam@umass.edu; kundu@umass.edu

© Springer Nature Switzerland AG 2020
K.-K. R. Choo et al. (eds.), *Blockchain Cybersecurity, Trust and Privacy*, Advances in Information Security 79, https://doi.org/10.1007/978-3-030-38181-3_3

33

Moreover, sharing any IoT-devices enabled smart house poses a serious threat to user's privacy and security. Airbnb hosts prefer to know what's going on in their rentals. Because of this, hosts may opt to have surveillance cameras in key places. This allows Airbnb hosts to spy on guests which is a serious infringement upon the guests' expectation of privacy. Similarly, by accessing the smart door lock, an intrusive homeowner can compromise the security system. By accessing the stored credentials on connected devices, hosts can take control of the IoT devices' sensors and can even disable an apartment's control of HVAC systems [21]. Hence, it is essential to find a technological solution to preserve IoT privacy in sharing economy.

Additionally, an IoT device can be compromised by a malicious attacker by counterfeiting, infecting with Trojan, tampering, etc. [16]. A compromised IoT device can leak secret information to a malicious party, thus violating user's security. To ensure security, each IoT device must be authenticated before using it for any data transaction and transmission.

In this chapter, we propose blockchain technology-based smart contract as a potential solution to manage the security, trust, and privacy concerns in sharing economy. Often introduced as the technology behind Bitcoin, blockchain has the potential to revolutionize numerous industries beyond financial services, such as, energy distribution, health care, Internet of Things (IoT), forecasting, insurance and so on [3, 14, 19, 25, 27]. With the advent of the Blockchain, we have a new tool to establish this trust by using an algorithm. No longer do customers and sellers need to rely on central authorities anymore.

Blockchain is a decentralized, immutable ledger that keeps records of digital transactions [29]. This immutable blockchain record can establish trust and eliminate the need for middlemen and data silos across thousands of platforms selling users' personal details. Everything from finding and booking a property to payments, reviews and post departure sequences can be handled through smart contracts on blockchain. With no source of power or control, there cannot be a single authority controlling the system.

The major contributions of this chapter are:

1. Proposing a blockchain-based solution to eliminate distrust in third-party control by decentralizing home-sharing economy.
2. Proposing a smart contract solution to ensure security, and privacy of IoT-enabled telematics devices in a sharing house.
3. Designing a hardware collateral to implement the proposed smart contract.
4. Demonstrating the proposed solution in Ethereum blockchain. The code has been made publicly accessible in Github [22].

The paper is organized as follows: Sect. 2 presents the threat model in a conventional home sharing economy and then describes our motivation for the proposed solution. Section 3 briefly presents backgrounds related to our proposed methodology for establishing security, trust and privacy in sharing economy. Section 4 introduces the system requirements and implemented smart contracts for our proposed protocol. In Sect. 5, we present our proposed methodology to establish security, privacy and trust using blockchain and embedded PUF. Section 6 presents the hardware collateral designed for implementing our proposed protocol. Section 7 outlines a demonstration of the protocol and discusses future directions. Finally, Sect. 8 concludes the paper.

2 Threat Model and Motivation

In this section, we present the security, trust, and privacy threats in a conventional home sharing economy and then describe our motivation for the proposed solution.

2.1 Threat Model

Home-sharing economy platform, such as, Airbnb currently sits in between a homeowner and a guest. They provide an extremely well designed interface, which allows millions of guests to find and book homeowners homes. Additionally, Homeowners and managers are at the mercy of continually changing terms and structure. They raise the prices because their services are expensive to maintain, and thus need to take a large share of the profits. They have the power to arbitrarily make decisions, the consequences of which can be disastrous to individuals and small businesses. Finally, they can develop a bureaucracy that makes dealing with them slow and onerous.

Figure 1 presents the security, trust, and privacy threats in a conventional home-sharing economy. Here, firstly, relying on a centralized third party sharing platform inevitably leads to threat to trust. Secondly, an IoT device can be compromised by a malicious attacker by counterfeiting, infecting with Trojan, tampering, etc. [15]. A compromised IoT device can leak secret information to a malicious party,

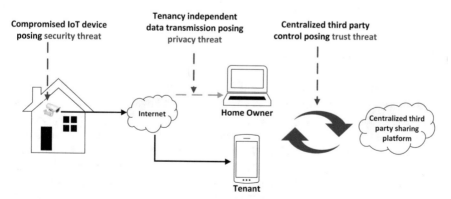

Fig. 1 Threats associated with accessing indoor IP camera by home-owner from remote location in a home-sharing economy scenario

thus violating user's expected level of security. Thirdly, an intrusive homeowner can compromise the privacy of the tenant by accessing the stored credentials on connected devices.

2.2   Motivation

In this section, we present our motivation behind protecting the trust, privacy, and security.

2.2.1   Protection of Trust

Sharing is a special case among business models. In a sharing economy, companies do not sell their own products or services to other businesses (B2B) or consumers (B2C). Rather, they sell goods that they receive from other consumers—essentially C2C, consumer to consumer. Companies in B2B and B2C often produce real value. For example, it is hard to imagine how one could make a steel factory or a bakery redundant by establishing a Blockchain around their business models. However, this is different in the sharing economy, in C2C: Here, companies are really only middlemen who can be cut out of the process by establishing an alternative source of trust between consumers. Thus, the sharing economy is uniquely suited to decentralization via the Blockchain.

For IoT in home-sharing economy, blockchain can provide an infrastructure for direct, safe and secure transfers between devices, without the need for a centralized authority. Smart contract can translate the existing contractual clauses into embedded hardware and software in such a way that it can self-verify that conditions have been met to execute the contract [6]. Smart contracts contain code functions and can interact with other contracts, make decisions, store data, and send tokens/money to others.

2.2.2   Protection of Privacy

Smart contracts can also facilitate efficient IoT devices by automating their operations and decision making. This can be achieved by allowing IoT devices to interact with smart contracts and make decisions defined by the fixed contract logic. For example, in order to safeguard surveillance data, modern IP cameras are equipped with an on-board security chip, Trusted Platform Module (TPM) [5]. Using a symmetric cryptographic key, the TPM encrypts the data stream (Fig. 2). In this paper, we leverage the TPM to change its encryption key whenever there is a tenancy change recorded in smart contract. This key can only be computed using the device and the tenant's private key so that no one else can access the surveillance data other than the current tenant.

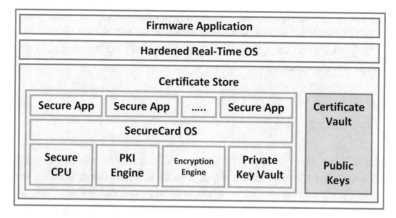

Fig. 2 Block diagram of a Trusted Platform Module (green block) embedded into the camera's software architecture [5]

2.2.3 Protection of IoT Device Security

To protect the home sharing economy from IoT device security threats, the device ownership information and the device authentication information must be securely recorded and verified. Blockchain can enable the device ownership information to be verified, recorded and prevent any malicious party from altering or challenging the legitimacy of the information recorded. This verifiable and immutable ledger can enable identification and authentication of a device throughout the supply chain and its deployment lifetime. To corroborate a record in the blockchain against a physical device, the device must be authenticated securely and uniquely.

For this purpose, we utilize physical unclonable functions (PUFs) as the hardware root-of-trust. PUFs are innovative, lightweight circuit primitives which harness the intrinsic disorder in an IC (Integrated Circuit) introduced during the fabrication process. Various PUFs have been proposed and developed in recent years and are generally classified as either Strong or Weak PUFs. Strong PUFs [7, 28] can enable secure, low-cost authentication using Challenge-Response Pairs (CRP) [24]. The start-up behavior of a Weak PUF [13] can also be used for unique identification and authentication [2, 11]. In this paper, we propose a method of securely and uniquely identifying a device using Weak PUFs to corroborate the blockchain information. An authenticated device can eliminate the security threat from leaking secret information to a malicious adversary.

3 Background

In this section, we introduce some relevant concepts related to our proposed blockchain-based protocol. First, we discuss about blockchains and smart contract required for automated execution of enrollment, authentication, ownership trace-ability, and ownership transfer, tenancy transfer of an IoT device. Next, we discuss about PUFs which are used for securely and uniquely authenticating a device to corroborate the blockchain information.

3.1 Blockchain

Blockchain is an encrypted, shared ledger where a single transaction addition is updated across all the people having access to it. Blockchain stores transaction information permanently across a network of personal computers. This not only decentralizes the information but also distributes it too. All the people who runs the blockchain system, use their own computers to hold bundles of transaction records submitted by others. The records are known as blocks. Each block has a timestamp and a link to previous block, forming a chronological chain.

3.1.1 Smart Contract

Smart contracts are blockchain-powered autonomous computer programs that, once started, execute automatically the conditions defined beforehand, such as the verification, facilitation, or enforcement of the negotiation or performance of a contract [26]. Smart contracts give us distributed trustworthy computations on blockchain platform. They translate the existing contractual clauses into embedded hardware and software in such a way that it can self-verify that conditions have been met to execute the contract [6]. Smart contracts contain code functions and can interact with other contracts, make decisions, store data, and send tokens/money to others.

The main advantage of deploying smart contracts in a blockchain is the assurance provided by the blockchain that the contract terms cannot be modified. The blockchain makes it impossible to modify or tamper the contract terms. It generates the confidence and security necessary to automate the declarative phrases without resorting to a third party.

3.2 PUFs

Physical unclonable functions (PUFs) harness the intrinsic disorder in an IC introduced during the fabrication process and provide a set of *unique* input to output mappings, called challenge-response pairs (CRPs)[9, 24]. Based on the implementation, a PUF that provides a limited set of CRPs is classified as a *Weak* PUF, while a design that can produce an exponential number of CRPs is called a *Strong* PUF.

3.2.1   Weak PUFs

Weak PUFs can be leveraged for secure cryptographic key generation to combat semiconductor device counterfeiting, theft of service and tampering. Weak PUFs rely on intrinsic process variations to produce repeatable and unique fingerprint. This fingerprint is further processed to generate a unique cryptographic key. For generating a reliable key, the fingerprint needs to be reproducible over time, even under changing environmental conditions. However, noise in the system can affect the fingerprint and introduce errors. To alleviate noise and generate stable keys, a number of solutions have been proposed, such as, fuzzy extraction and error correcting codes [8], accelerated device aging [17, 18], built-in self-test [4], etc.

4   System Requirements and Smart Contract Implementation

In this section, we present the key system requirements and implemented smart contracts for our proposed protocol. First, we describe the approach and operational requirements of our protocol. Next, we outline the implementation of smart contracts.

4.1   *Approach*

The blockchain will contain the record of PUF data, used for authentication, and relevant tenancy transfer information, used for establishing trust between transacting parties. The smart contract will preserve the privacy of IoT devices by automating their operations and decision making. This enables IoT device security, trust and privacy without an explicit need for trusted intermediary. Before detailing the protocol, we enumerate the key requirements for creating the blockchain and explain their necessity for our protocol.

1. Legitimate IoT device vendors can claim the initial ownership and write the relevant PUF data in the blockchain. This facilitates authentication and enables security of the IoT device.
2. The owner of a house sends a transaction to the smart contract to transfer the tenancy. The smart contract defines all the necessary conditions related to tenancy transfer, which facilitates trust between two parties.
3. With the tenancy transfer, the smart contract autonomously changes the encryption keys of all IoT devices in a home. This facilitates privacy of IoT devices. In the next section, we detail the smart contract implemented in our proposed protocol.

Algorithm 1: Pseudo-code of `registerDevice()` for registering a device claimed by a manufacturer

---

Inputs: Manufacturer's address (*addrManufacturer*), and device information (*deviceInfo*)

if *Message sender is in manufacturer's list* **then**
  | Specify owner of the device as *addrManufacturer*
  | Register *deviceInfo* on the blockchain
else
  | Do nothing
end

Algorithm 2: Pseudo-code of `checkOwnership()` for verifying the ownership information of a device

---

Inputs : Seller's public key (*seller PubKey*), and device identifier (*deviceIdentifier*)
Output: A boolean `True` or `False`
if *(hash(seller PubKey) == blockchain[identifier Device].owner)* **then**
  | return `True`
else
  | return `False`
end

4.2   Implementation of Smart Contract

In our proposed protocol, a smart contract is created by the manufacturer to maintain uniform applicability and usability for all users. After creating the smart contract, it is sent to the blockchain network as a transaction that assigns an address to the contract. After this initial transaction, the contract becomes forever a part of the blockchain and its address never changes. Smart contract provides the services for device registration, checking the ownership information, device authentication and ownership transfer, tenancy transfer and change of the encryption key. Next, we explain these services and how these are implemented by our proposed smart contract.

4.2.1   Device Registration

A manufacturer must register a device first to introduce it into the supply chain. This is implemented by the smart contract function `registerDevice()`. Algorithm 1 presents the pseudo-code of function `registerDevice()`. The *deviceInfo* in the function includes data for *identification* and *authentication*. The identification data can be a serial number fo the device (e.g. Electronic Product code, or EPC). It is used to look up the targeted device being queried among a collection of devices. Here, the device identifier is being used for the purpose to *identify*, and not as the primary means to *authenticate*. For *authentication* purpose, manufacturer includes PUF data as input to the function `registerDevice()`.

Algorithm 3: `authenticateDevice()` for authenticating a device

Inputs : Identifier of the device to be transferred $(deviceIdentifier)$
Output: A boolean `True` or `False`
set $deviceChallenge$ = blockchain$[deviceIdentifier].Challenge$
get $deviceResponse$ from the device after applying $deviceChallenge$
if $(deviceResponse == blockchain[deviceIdentifier].Response)$ **then**
| return `True`
else
| return `False`
end

Algorithm 4: `transferOwnership()` for transferring the ownership of a device from seller to buyer

---

Inputs: Buyer's address $(addrBuyer)$, and device identifier $(deviceIdentifier)$
if $(addrMessageSender == blockchain[identifierDevice].owner)$ **then**
| set blockchain$[identifierDevice]$.owner = $addrBuyer$
else
| Do nothing
end

4.2.2 Ownership Verification

Before buying a device, a potential buyer needs to verify the ownership to confirm that the owner is a genuine one. It is necessary when the ownership is transferred from the manufacturer to the first buyer, and also any subsequent transfer of the ownership from the first owner to other owners. This is implemented by the smart contract function `checkOwnership()`. Algorithm 2 presents the pseudo-code of function `checkOwnership()`. This function verifies the ownership of the device against the seller's address. If the device with the provided identifier is owned by the seller, it returns `True`. The function is invoked when any potential buyer wants to verify the ownership of the device. Additionally, the function can return the ownership history till the provenance.

4.2.3 Device Authentication

An owner may sell a house including all the IoT devices in it. A potential buyer must be able to authenticate a device before buying to confirm that the device is authentic; not a counterfeit one. This is implemented by smart contract function `authenticateDevice()` Algorithm 3 presents the pseudo-code of `authenticateDevice()`. This function starts device authentication process for a given device identifier. The process includes getting the challenge-response data for particular $deviceIdentifier$, applying the challenge to the device via verifier's wallet, calculates the response and matching the challenge-response pairs.

Algorithm 5: transferTenancy() for renting the possession to a new tenant

---

Inputs: Tenant's address (*addrTenant*), Tenant's public key (*pubKeyTenant*), rent period
       (*rentPeriod*), rent cost, device identifier (*deviceIdentifier*)
if *(addrMessageSender == blockchain[identifier Device].owner)* **then**
  | set blockchain[*identifier Device*].owner = *addr Buyer* for *rentPeriod*
else
  | Do nothing
end

Algorithm 6: pollTenancy() for polling the current tenant's public key

---

Inputs: device identifier (*deviceIdentifier*)
if authenticateDevice() == *True* **then**
  | send Tenant's public key (*pubKeyTenant*) to device
else
  | Do nothing
end

4.2.4 Ownership Transfer

An owner may sell a house including all the IoT devices in it. For transferring the ownership of a device, the smart contract implements the function transferOwnership(). Algorithm 4 presents the pseudo-code of transferOwnership(). This function transfers the device (*deviceIdentifier*) from the seller (*addr Seller*) to buyer (*addr Buyer*). First, the function checks whether the message sender is the owner of the device with *deviceIdentifier*. If that is true, then the function assigns the *addr Buyer* as the new owner of the device.

4.2.5 Tenancy Transfer

This function defines all the necessary information related to tenancy transfer, such as, new tenant information, tenancy period, cost etc. Algorithm 5 presents the pseudo-code of transferTenancy(). The transaction includes tenant's public key which will be used by the IoT device for computing the data encryption key. If the sender of the transaction is the current owner of the device, the smart contract updates its new tenant and the new tenant public key.

4.2.6 Poll Tenancy

An IoT device intermittently (e.g. once in a day) checks whether the tenancy has been changed. If so, the device autonomously calculates the new encryption key using the new tenant's public key. The proposed smart contract has a function `pollTenancy()` which provides the public key of the current tenant when the function is called by an IoT device. Algorithm 6 presents the pseudo-code of `pollTenancy()`. The IoT device calls the `pollTenancy()` function of the smart contract. The smart contract authenticates the device by calling `authenticateDevice()`. If the device is authenticated, then the smart contract function provides the public key of the current tenant.

5 Proposed Methodology

In this section, we present the details of the algorithmic procedures between all parties necessary for the realization of the proposed protocol. The procedure for enrolling a device by the manufacturer is first outlined. This is followed by the procedure for transferring the tenancy which is the key part of our overall traceability protocol. The protocol consists of the following steps.

5.1 Enrollment of IoT Device by the Manufacturer

In the first step of our proposed protocol, the manufacturer of an IoT device (an IP camera, for example, in our case) creates a smart contract (*possessionContract* in Fig. 3). This contract offers functions for managing the possession transfer and polling the possession of the device. The manufacturer sends a transaction to the smart contract function `registerDevice()` to enroll the IoT device. It then deploys the contract in blockchain and embeds the address of the contract in the device. The blockchain can be a public blockchain (e.g Ethereum), maintained by its community, including its developers, users, service providers (exchanges), miners and others. Finally, the manufacturer transfers the ownership to the first owner of the device.

The contract consists of *code* (its functions) and *data* (its state). The functions are *transferTenancy*, *pollTenancy* and the state variables are owner, tenant, tenant public key, device public key etc. Once the smart contract is appended to the blockchain, an IoT device executes whatever the contract makes it to execute. As the contract is immutable once it's uploaded onto the blockchain, no one can tamper with the code.

5.2 Transferring the Ownership

Before buying a device, a potential buyer needs to verify the ownership to confirm that the owner is a genuine one. It is necessary when the ownership is transferred from the manufacturer to the first buyer, and also any subsequent transfer of the ownership from the first owner to other owners. For this purpose, any potential new

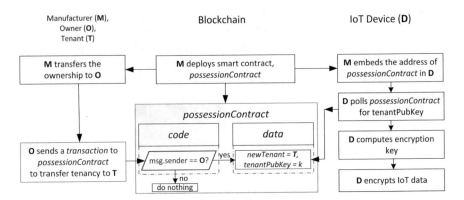

Fig. 3 Detailed diagram of showing the role of all entities in the proposed privacy protection protocol

buyer verifies the ownership by calling `checkOwnership()` and authenticates the device by calling `authenticateDevice()`. The detailed procedure for device authentication using stored Weak PUFs credentials is described as following.

Several Weak PUF based public key cryptography for authentication have been proposed in the literature [2, 11]. Figure 4 presents a hardware authentication module to generate cryptographic key from SRAM-based Weak PUF [12]. The manufacturers first records Weak PUF data in the blockchain by issuing a transaction `registerDevice()`. At any stage of the supply chain, any buyer can authenticate the device by invoking `authenticateDevice()`. The components of the authentication module and their functions are described as follows.

5.2.1 Key Generation Module

During enrollment phase, the key generator in the authentication module generates a private-public key pair. Using the private key, a device can create signature of a message protecting the message's integrity and proving its authenticity. At a receiving end of message, the digital signature can be verified for authenticity using the public key corresponding to the private key. The private-public key pair may be keys for RSA, DSA, Schnorr, El Gamal, Elliptic Curve based public key cryptosystems etc. For the purpose of illustration, we describe RSA public key cryptography here. First, the key generator finds two prime numbers from a seed which is derived from PUF output, e.g., the contents of an SRAM. Finding prime numbers can be done on an appropriately programmed device or Hardware Security Module (HSM). Once two prime numbers of appropriate sizes are found, an RSA private-public key pair is constructed. The RSA key pair generation is computationally intensive process and done only during enrollment phase.

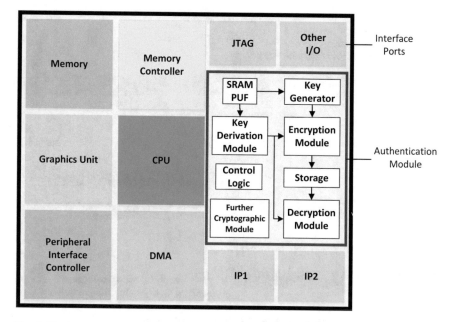

Fig. 4 Hardware authentication module for generating cryptographic key from PUF embedded in an SoC [12]

5.2.2 Encryption Module

The private key is encrypted with a second key (encrypting key) generated from the same PUF and stored in a non-volatile memory. This encryption is done using symmetric encryption algorithm, like AES and the encrypting key is obtained from any random 128-bit string from the PUF. The manufacturer records the public key in the blockchain by issuing a transaction registerDevice() for the device (Fig. 5a).

5.2.3 Decryption Module

During authentication phase, the encrypting key can be generated instantly from the PUF output. Using the encrypting key, the decryption module generates the private key of the device.

When a potential buyer wants to authenticate the device, he invokes the function authenticateDevice() with the device identifier. The smart contract sends the device's public key to buyer's wallet. The buyer's wallet then sends a challenge message generated with a pseudo-random number generator to the device. The device's further cryptographic module creates the device signature using the private key. Using the public key, the buyer's wallet can verify the digital signature for the authenticity of the device as shown in Fig. 5b.

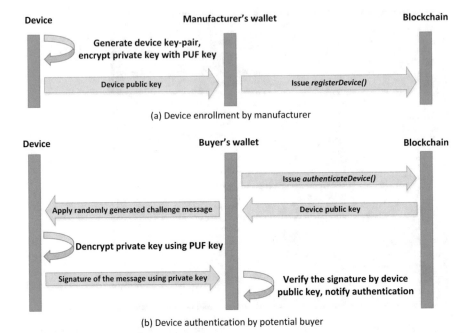

(a) Device enrollment by manufacturer

(b) Device authentication by potential buyer

Fig. 5 (**a**) Device enrollment and (**b**) authentication process via weak PUFs

5.3 Transferring Tenancy to a Tenant

To transfer the tenancy to a tenant, the owner sends a transaction to *possession-Contract*. This transaction defines all the necessary information related to tenancy transfer, such as, new tenant information, tenancy period, cost etc. The transaction includes tenant's public key which will be used by the IoT device for computing the data encryption key. If the sender of the transaction is the current owner of the device, the smart contract updates its new tenant and the new tenant public key.

5.4 Establishing a Shared Encryption Key

Figure 3 presents our proposed protocol for decentralizing home sharing economy and preserving IoT security, privacy and trust. The IoT device polls the address of the embedded smart contract intermittently (e.g. once in everyday). After the tenant includes public key in the smart contract, the IP camera can encrypt the video data with tenant's public key and the tenant can decrypt the data with private key using any standard Public Key Cryptography (PKC) algorithm. But for large amount of data like video stream, encryption/decryption with asymmetric PKC (e.g.

RSA, ECC) is very slow. Instead we choose symmetric key cryptography (AES) for encryption/decryption which is several orders of magnitude faster [10].

For video stream encryption purpose, a symmetric key is established using the Diffie-Hellman protocol. On one hand, the device calculates the symmetric key using its private key stored secretly inside the device and the tenant public key from the smart contract. On the other hand, the tenant calculates the symmetric key using his own private key and the device public key. The computation happens based on some pre-established large prime number, p and generator, g which is a primitive root modulo p.

If the tenant's private key is t, and the device private key is d, the corresponding public keys are calculated according to the ECDSA protocol as follows:

Tenant's public key, $T = g^t \bmod p$

Device public key, $D = g^d \bmod p$

Next, the public keys are exchanged via smart contract. The tenant and the device computes a shared symmetric key (s) according to Diffie-Hellman protocol using their private keys.

Tenant computes $s = D^t \bmod p = g^{dt} \bmod p$

Device computes $s = T^d \bmod p = g^{dt} \bmod p$

5.5 Encrypting IoT Data with the Shared Encryption Key

The encryption engine of the TPM changes the encryption key to newly computed symmetric key. Then it encrypts all the video data stream or other payload with encryption key (Fig. 6). The tenant can also decrypt the video data with the shared key. On the other hand, the owner can no longer decrypt the surveillance data as the key has been changed.

5.6 Change of Encryption Key After Tenancy Period

The *transferTenancy()* function in *possessionContract* defines that after the tenancy period, the tenant will be the original owner. So, the encryption key will be changed autonomously according to original owner's public key.

6 Hardware Collateral for Smart Contract

For implementing the proposed smart contract, the IoT device's system-on-chip (SoC) needs to be equipped with an authentication module, an encryption engine, such as AES, DES, 3DES etc (Fig. 4). Most of the modern IoT devices (e.g. IP cameras) are equipped with such security engines for safeguarding the data [5]. Similar security and privacy protection methodology can be applied to any other

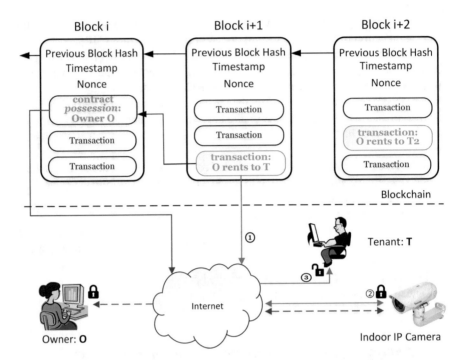

Fig. 6 Detailed diagram of the privacy protection protocol: (1) the smart contract notifies the IP camera about the tenancy change, (2) IP camera computes the symmetric key from tenant's public key and encrypts video data, (3) tenant calculates the symmetric key and can decrypt the video data. The dotted lines indicate inaccessible data

IoT devices present in a home. Alternatively, a Smart Home Hub [23] can perform the security and privacy protection for all the IoT devices connected to it.

7 Protocol Demonstration and Discussion

We implemented the proposed protocol in Solidity scripting language and evaluated in terms of its operational cost. The code is publicly accessible in Github repository [22]. In particular, we calculated the total cost by measuring the total gas amount (execution fee for each operation made in Ethereum) for all of the functions involved in the process, that is, (1) registering device (registerDevice()), (2) transferring ownership (transferOwnership()), and (3) transferring tenancy (transferTenancy()) and then converting it into a real currency. As the amount of gas is fixed for each operation in Ethereum, e.g. an SHA3 calculation costs 20 gas, the total gas amount for executing a function is also fixed. We experimented using Ethereum's test environment tool, *testrpc* [20], to measure the gas amount since this tool has the ability of automatically counting the gas

Table 1 Operation cost for a chip in supply chain

Operation	Gas limit	Gas price	Cost (in ETH)	Cost (in USD)
registerDevice()	121,478	10.89×10^{-9}	0.0013229	0.11
transferOwnership()	30,365	10.89×10^{-9}	0.00033067	0.03
transferTenancy()	23,365	10.89×10^{-9}	0.00023067	0.02

amount. With current value of 1 ETH = 83.15USD and 1 Gas = 10.89×10^{-9} ETH (10.89 Gwei), the operation cost for a chip in supply chain is calculated in Table 1. Finally, the total cost of maintaining the identity of a chip in a supply chain with N entities is:

$$\text{total cost} = \text{cost of enrollment} + (N - 1) \times \text{cost of ownership transfer}$$

For practical implementation, the protocol can be implemented in an application and all the steps, like creating transaction, verifying ownership, authenticating the device, transferring the tenancy can be done by using the application. Participants can mange their keys and addresses using a digital wallet.

8 Conclusion

In this paper, we present a novel methodology to fully disintermediate home-sharing economy and protect users' IoT device privacy in home-sharing economy. In this protocol, the smart contract facilitates the decentralization of home-sharing economy. Our proposed protocol enables users controlling their own information and transactions. By implementing unique device authentication, the data transaction and transmission security is ensured. At the same time, by facilitating the change of encryption key via smart contract, it can preserve the IoT privacy.

References

1. Abraham, Decentralizing airbnb (2017). https://www.smarthosts.org/posts/Zr4w8SEK5BH42CPZF/airbnb-blockchain-loyalty-travel
2. A.B. Alvarez et al., Static physically unclonable functions for secure chip identification with 1.9–5.8% native bit instability at 0.6–1 V and 15 fJ/bit in 65 nm. IEEE J. Solid-State Circ. **51**(3), 763–775 (2016)
3. A. Back et al., Enabling blockchain innovations with pegged sidechains (2014). http://www.opensciencereviewcom/papers/123/enablingblockchain-innovations-with-pegged-sidechains
4. M. Bhargava, K. Mai, An efficient reliable PUF-based cryptographic key generator in 65 nm CMOS, in *Proceedings of the Conference on Design, Automation & Test in Europe* (European Design and Automation Association, Leuven, 2014), p. 70
5. BOSCH, Data security - how Bosch secures the camera (July 2018). http://resource.boschsecurity.com/documents/WP_TPM_WhitePaper_enUS_9007223261094667.pdf

6. V. Buterin et al., A next-generation smart contract and decentralized application platform. White paper, 2014
7. W. Che, F. Saqib, J. Plusquellic, PUF-based authentication, in *2015 IEEE/ACM International Conference on Computer-Aided Design (ICCAD)*, (IEEE, New York, 2015), pp. 337–344
8. J. Delvaux et al., Helper data algorithms for PUF-based key generation: overview and analysis. IEEE Trans. Comput.-Aided Des. Integr. Circ. Syst. **34**(6), 889–902 (2015)
9. S. Devadas et al., Design and implementation of PUF-based "Unclonable" RFID ICs for anti-counterfeiting and security applications, in *IEEE International conference on RFID, 2008* (IEEE, New York, 2008), pp. 58–64
10. W. Diffie, P.C. Van Oorschot, M.J. Wiener, Authentication and authenticated key exchanges. Des. Codes Cryptogr. **2**(2), 107–125 (1992)
11. J. Guajardo et al., Physical unclonable functions and public-key crypto for FPGA IP protection, in *International Conference on Field Programmable Logic and Applications, 2007. FPL 2007* (IEEE, New York, 2007), pp. 189–195
12. H. Handschuh, P.T. Tuyls, Device and method for obtaining a cryptographic key. US Patent App. 13/574,311, 2011
13. D.E. Holcomb et al., Power-up SRAM state as an identifying fingerprint and source of true random numbers. IEEE Trans. Comput. **58**(9), 1198–1210 (2009)
14. M.N. Islam, S. Kundu, Preserving IoT privacy in sharing economy via smart contract, in *2018 IEEE/ACM Third International Conference on Internet-of-Things Design and Implementation (IoTDI)* (IEEE, New York, 2018), pp. 296–297
15. M.N. Islam, S. Kundu, Enabling IC traceability via blockchain pegged to embedded PUF. ACM Trans. Des. Autom. Electron. Syst. **24**(3), 36:1–36:23 (2019). https://doi.org/10.1145/3315669. http://doi.acm.org/10.1145/3315669
16. M.N. Islam et al., Determining proximal geolocation of IoT edge devices via covert channel, in *2017 18th International Symposium on Quality Electronic Design (ISQED)* (IEEE, New York, 2017), pp. 196–202
17. M.N. Islam et al., A guide to graceful aging: how not to overindulge in post-silicon burn-in for enhancing reliability of weak PUF, in *2017 IEEE International Symposium on Circuits and Systems (ISCAS)* (IEEE, New York, 2017), pp. 1–4
18. M.N. Islam et al., On enhancing reliability of weak PUFS via intelligent post-silicon accelerated aging. IEEE Trans. Circ. Syst. I Reg. Pap. **65**(3), 960–969 (2017)
19. M.N. Islam et al., On IC traceability via blockchain, in *2018 International Symposium on VLSI Design, Automation and Test (VLSI-DAT)* (IEEE, New York, 2018), pp. 1–4
20. K. Iyer, C. Dannen, The ethereum development environment, in *Building Games with Ethereum Smart Contracts* (Springer, New York, 2018), pp. 19–36
21. S. Meza, Airbnb hosts are recording their guests with hidden cameras (2017). http://www.newsweek.com/airbnb-hidden-cameras-recordingguests-739709
22. Privacy in sharing economyl (August 2019). https://github.com/nazmulislam025/Privacy-Blockchain
23. Samsung, Samsung smart home hub (August 2018). https://www.samsung.com/us/smart-home/smartthings/
24. G.E. Suh, S. Devadas, Physical unclonable functions for device authentication and secret key generation, in *Proceedings of the 44th Annual Design Automation Conference* (ACM, New York, 2007), pp. 9–14
25. M. Swan, *Blockchain: Blueprint for a New Economy* (O'Reilly Media, Inc., Sebastopol, 2015)
26. N. Szabo, Formalizing and securing relationships on public networks. First Monday 2(9) (1997). https://ojphi.org/ojs/index.php/fm/article/view/548/469
27. D. Tapscott, A. Tapscott, *Blockchain Revolution: How the Technology Behind Bitcoin is Changing Money, Business, and the World* (Penguin, New York, 2016)
28. P. Tuyls, B. Škorić, Strong authentication with physical unclonable functions, in *Security, Privacy, and Trust in Modern Data Management* (Springer, New York, 2007), pp. 133–148
29. R. Wattenhofer, The Science of the Blockchain (CreateSpace Independent Publishing Platform, Scotts Valley, 2016)

Scrybe: A Second-Generation Blockchain Technology with Lightweight Mining for Secure Provenance and Related Applications

Carl Worley, Lu Yu, Richard Brooks, Jon Oakley, Anthony Skjellum, Amani Altarawneh, Sai Medury, and Ujan Mukhopadhyay

Abstract The recent popularity of cryptocurrencies has highlighted the versatility and applications of a decentralized, public blockchain. Blockchain provides a data structure that can guarantee both the integrity and non-repudiation of data, as well as providing provenance pertaining to such data. Our novel Lightweight Mining (LWM) algorithm provides these guarantees with minimal resource requirements. Our approach to blockchain-based data provenance, paired with the LWM algorithm, provides the legal and ethical framework for key classes of provenance to be managed. Contributions of this paper include the following: first, we describe the Scrybe system, including the Lightweight mining algorithm. We then note principles of secure provenance and explain how to adapt Scrybe to a series of practical use cases, such as academic integrity, forensic management of evidence, and secure logging. Finally, we explain the key features of the Scrybe system that enable secure provenance for these use cases, and we describe resilience of the system to denial of service attacks and repudiation.

C. Worley · U. Mukhopadhyay
Department of Computer Science and Software Engineering, Auburn University, Auburn, AL, USA
e-mail: crw0034@tigermail.auburn.edu; uzm0002@tigermail.auburn.edu

L. Yu · R. Brooks · J. Oakley
Department of Electrical and Computer Engineering, Clemson University, Clemson, SC, USA
e-mail: lyu@g.clemson.edu; rrb@g.clemson.edu; joakley@g.clemson.edu

A. Skjellum · A. Altarawneh · S. Medury (✉)
SimCenter & Department of Computer Science and Engineering, University of Tennessee at Chattanooga, Chattanooga, TN, USA
e-mail: tony-skjellum@utc.edu; jwh247@mocs.utc.edu; sai-medury@mocs.utc.edu

© Springer Nature Switzerland AG 2020
K.-K. R. Choo et al. (eds.), *Blockchain Cybersecurity, Trust and Privacy*, Advances in Information Security 79, https://doi.org/10.1007/978-3-030-38181-3_4

1   Introduction

Blockchain is promoted as a valuable current and future technological approach to providing currency and supporting contracts and metadata in the financial industry. Bitcoin is the most well-known of such digital currencies. As an underlying data structure, blockchain can be applied more broadly than simply to provide a virtual/digital currency.

Scrybe, the authors' blockchain technology, is primarily designed for non cryptocurrencies applications as a secure provenance system which maintain the information that explains how data were derived. This information helps with finding the sources of errors if such occur; also this information gives system users confidence in the resources and results, and maintains the integrity of the data. Although, there are various provenance tools such as Karma [1] and others that provide such information, that data still is not secure and the integrity of the data is not always guaranteed. Thus, we utilize Blockchain technology to maintain data from being corrupted or tampered by anyone. In particular, blockchain is used to guarantee integrity and non-repudiation of data, as well as to maintain provenance metadata for systems. Our innovative blockchain technology, Scrybe [2], incorporates a novel Lightweight Mining (LWM) algorithm that provides these guarantees with minimal resource requirements. The LWM algorithm departs from the resource-intensive (and time-consuming) verification approaches that cryptocurrencies, such as Bitcoin and Ethereum, use when expanding the blockchain [3] over time.

In this paper, we describe how Scrybe was designed and it's use cases in different applications: academic integrity, digital forensics, and secure logging. Also, we are providing our methodology to verify the security properties of the system; namely, data integrity, non-repudiation, and availability. We utilize Petri nets to prove that there is a path for a victim transaction to end up in a good miner pool and then be added into the blockchain.

The remainder of this paper is organized as follows. We first overview secure provenance and distributed random number generation in Sect. 2. In Sect. 3, we summarize *Scrybe*, our novel blockchain-based provenance system. We then describe a series of use cases in Sect. 4. In Sect. 5, we consider security verification, focusing on data integrity, non-repudiation, and resilience of the Lightweight Mining (LWM) algorithm to distributed denial of service (DDoS) attacks. Finally, we conclude and mention future work in Sect. 6.

2   Related Literature

In this section, we define secure provenance and mention work related to implementing blockchain-based data provenance.

2.1   Secure Provenance

Data provenance is defined as one or more artifacts of metadata that can be used to track changes to data [4] over time and ensure its integrity. Secure provenance is achieved in a system where the integrity of provenance data can be ensured, and the provenance data itself is always available for querying. Metadata collected as part of secure provenance must follow the chronological order in which events occurred and be immutable [5]; that is, once logged, the information must remain read-only and must not be susceptible to falsification. Secure provenance enforces accountability and non-repudiation, where a user cannot dispute responsibility for authoring a change [6]. Furthermore, in case of an error (or tampering), secure provenance provides the capability to chronologically trace back changes inorder to successfully identify what triggered the change responsible for the error [6] and when did that occur.

2.2   Blockchain-Based Data Provenance

Because blockchain is a highly available distributed database secured by cryptographically linked logs, it provides the perfect infrastructure for implementing secure provenance. Additionally, the provenance fields inherent to the blockchain data structure—including the timestamp, block number, and miner's signature—can be leveraged and incorporated into a secure provenance system like Scrybe.

In particular, the integrity of a cloud computing server needs to be ensured whether it is being used commercially or for a military purpose. A full compare and contrast of existing systems and technologies is beyond the scope of this paper, but we offer the following examples as relevant to our discussion of blockchain-based data provenance. Liang et al. [7] presents the design and implementation of ProvChain, a blockchain-based provenance system that enables auditing data operations while preserving privacy and ensuring integrity. Reference [8] describes a Decentralized Application (DApp) prototype that uses Ethereum blockchain technology to enable secure traceability of certifications and other salient information in supply chains. Benningfield [9] analyzes the possibility of using Hyperledger blockchain technology for supply chain traceability and avoiding counterfeit products by storing provenance data on a permissioned blockchain network.

3   Scrybe: A Blockchain-Based Provenance System

This section first provides an overview of Scrybe, our secure provenance system, through an explanation of transactions, blocks, the algorithm itself, and how servers are managed; subsequently, in Sect. 5 we introduce the LWM algorithm, a unique feature of Scrybe. The LWM algorithm is also what makes Scrybe robust against DDoS attacks; we lay out the procedure used to verify resilience and illustrate its robustness against such attacks.

3.1 Blocks

There are two main components of the Scrybe blockchain: blocks and transactions, as described in Fig. 1. A blockchain is simply a sequence of blocks, where the current block contains the cryptographic hash of the previous block (Fig. 2), that makes blockchain *immutable*. Blocks are added to the blockchain by *miners*, entities or individuals responsible for maintaining the integrity of the blockchain. Scrybe only allows authorized users to mine blocks through the secure LWM algorithm, which will be discussed in detail in Sect. 5. Miners are responsible for aggregating a list of transactions and calculating the Merkle root. The Merkle root allows other miners to quickly verify whether all transactions are included in the block. Once a miner is selected to add a block to the blockchain, the block is broadcasted to all other miners, and the block data is verified and validated (previous hash, Merkle root, and the miner's signature). At this stage, other miners will be able to detect in case a transaction is omitted from the block, or if an unauthorized miner broadcasts a block, or if the miner's signature is invalid.

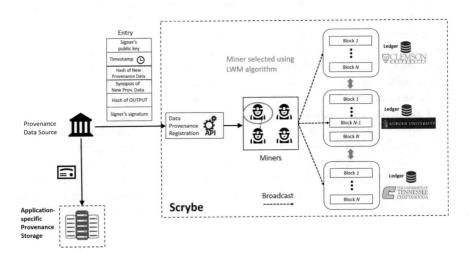

Fig. 1 Scrybe architecture

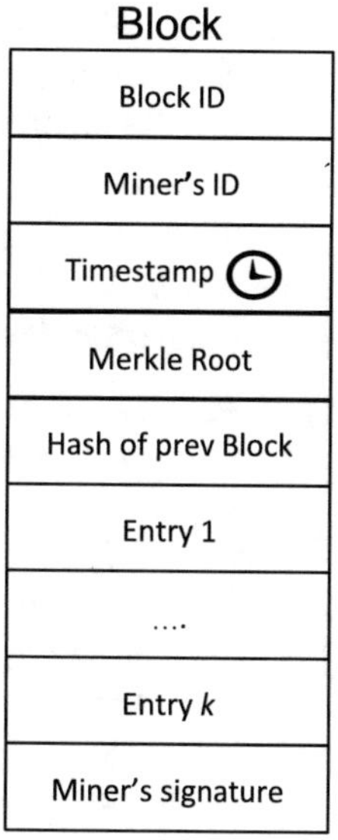

Fig. 2 Structure of a Scrybe
block

Block

Block ID
Miner's ID
Timestamp 🕓
Merkle Root
Hash of prev Block
Entry 1
....
Entry *k*
Miner's signature

3.2 Transactions

Transactions are the backbone of provenance. Conceptually, transaction input is categorized as input fields and output fields. A transaction in Scrybe comprises of input fields, output fields, and submitter's details like the name, public key, and the digital signature. The miner also adds the timestamp as part of the transaction. Transactions can also be *genesis events*, that register the acquisition of new data. The persistent URLs (PURLs) that point to the data, along with the SHA-3 hash of the data, ensure its validity. Note that while all transactions have output fields; genesis events **only** have an output with no input, whereas normal transactions have both.

By only storing the SHA-3 hash of the transaction instead of the original transaction, we can drastically reduce the size of the blockchain; consequently, there will be no penalty for an extensive number of inputs and outputs in any given transaction. The original transaction will be stored on a *transaction server*, which will be locally maintained, along with the *data server* and the *metadata server*.

3.3 Lightweight Mining

Scrybe introduces a novel way to mine new blocks in the blockchain, which is not a difficult Proof-of-Work (PoW) that is required in present-day cryptocurrency applications and needs much less computational power than what is required for traditional PoW consensus algorithm. Therefore, our LWM algorithm is a faster, more scalable, and eco-friendly alternative for a permissioned network of miners.

The LWM algorithm appears in the following frame.

***Lightweight Mining Algorithm (LWM)* Input**: The number of miners N.

Algorithm: For each miner m_i, $0 \leq i < N$,

- *Step 1*: m_i generates a random number r_i;
- *Step 2*: m_i broadcasts the SHA-3 hash of r_i, denoted by $H(r_i)$;
- *Step 3*: Once m_i has collected all N hashes $\{H(r_0), H(r_1), \cdots, H(r_{N-1})\}$, m_i broadcasts r_i.
- *Step 4*: Once m_i has collected all N random numbers $\{r_0, r_1, \cdots, r_{N-1}\}$, m_i calculates $l = \sum_j r_j \mod N$.
- *Step 5*: m_l is the selected miner to create the next block from the collected transactions. (Without loss of generality, we map $m_i = i, 0 \leq i < N$ as a simple rank ordering for the registered miners.)

The Genesis block contains the information related to initial miners, and the number of miners is fixed before the beginning of each round of miner selection. Each round has a fixed timeout for synchronization. If a miner fails to send the hash within this timeout, then that miner's hash and random number are considered to be $NULL$ for that particular round. Optimal timeout depends on the number of active participants and the desired number of transactions per round.

Considering that the network is a permissioned network, new miners wishing to join are not accepted until after the end of ongoing round. The purpose of LWM is to provide randomization of miner selection. In the case where a Denial of Service (DoS) attack is launched against Scrybe, we assume a malicious miner targets a particular user by excluding the victim's transactions from the block created. Given the randomization offered by LWM and the fact that each miner maintains their own local pool of transactions, it can be guaranteed the victim's transactions will be integrated into the blockchain as long as there is at least one honest miner.

The core idea of LWM is "sharing-hash-first." If every miner sends out the random number without sharing the hashes first, a malicious miner may hold out on sharing random number until all the other miners in the network broadcast their random number. This caveat allows a malicious miner to manipulate miner selection by choosing a number, that produces a m_l in favor of a particular miner or results in excluding a particular miner. Scrybe takes a naive approach for random number generation in a peer-to-peer service. Each node generates a random number independently before sharing the hash of that random number. This method has been proven to be robust [10]; as long as one node is generating a random number, the $\sum_j r_j \mod N$ remains random.

"Sharing-hash-first" ensures that every miner has to share his or her own number (in the form of the hash) with others before they see others' choices. Since hash values are considered impossible to invert in practice, a miner cannot change the random number after the fact. Further, the hash is signed with the sender's digital signature, which disallows a miner from equivocating. Each miner may broadcast any number they wish, and it is in the interest of each sender to broadcast a random number to avoid predictability and a pattern that can be exploited to reduce the chances of the sender being selected.

Thus, LWM can tolerate up to $N-1$ malicious miners who collude. As long as there is one miner generating a random number, the modulo operation is randomized.

The LWM consensus is one-CPU-one-vote majority, same as PoW [11], but there is no need for the concept of longest chain. In the case of a miner trying to broadcast a block containing a previous hash entry that is not the same as that of the latest block, that block will not be added to the blockchain. Furthermore, there is no chance for a fork in the blockchain for Scrybe since only one miner is chosen in each round to propose the next block.

3.4 Servers

Locally maintained transaction servers will hold the transactions comprising the ledger. An additional metadata server can be maintained along with the transaction server wherever it makes sense. The integrity of the database can be verified by generating transaction lists for each block and ensuring that these transactions and corresponding hashes accurately display the state of the database. If there is any discrepancy, the database server is deemed disreputable. The integrity of the data and metadata can be verified by comparing the SHA-3 hash of the data to the SHA-3 hash stored in the transaction: if these hashes differ, the relevant server is considered disreputable. The method for storing data on these servers is configurable and left to the end-user's discretion.

4 Use Cases

Three use cases are described in this section: Academic Integrity, Digital Forensics, and Secure Logging.

4.1 Academic Integrity

The **Datatype** of this use case is a *Published Paper*. Consider a scholarly paper, **Paper1**, produced by Alice. **Paper1** includes references to two other papers, **Paper2** and **Paper3**. **Paper1** also contains a certain experimental setup and software used to produce the results that are stored in a zip file, **container-Z**.

Alice, who is using our system, registers a transaction of Paper1 to the blockchain as follows:

- **Paper1** and zip file **container-Z** are uploaded to Git [12].
- An Entry is created, containing the following fields[1]:

  1. Timestamp
  2. Alice's Public Key Fingerprint
  3. Input Field, which consists of pointers to the hashes of all the referenced papers, public keys of their authors and a hash of the file **container-Z**
  4. Output field, which contains the output of the work:

     - Hash of **Paper1**
     - PURL to **Paper1**

  5. Alice's Signature

- The Entry is sent to the Pool.
- The selected miner produces a block that contains all the entries in his pool.
- Other miners validate the block. If they accept it as a valid block, then they add it to the blockchain by adding the hash of the previous block to the new block.
- This block is exported as XML and sent to the provenance database.
- The provenance metadata can be viewed using appropriate visualization software.

The system handles security as follows:

- **Non-Repudiation**: Austin is writing a paper, **Paper4**, that uses the results and methodology of **Paper1**. If he notices that there are some discrepancies in the results, he can easily show that Alice prevaricated about the results. Alice, on the other hand, cannot deny producing the result in **Paper1** because, when she registered **Paper1**, she signed the entries with her private key, which should always be kept secret.
- **Integrity**: If Alice changes the details of the transaction, the hash of the transaction changes. This change would imply that the hash of the whole block of which Alice's transaction comprises a part also changes. The deeper into the blockchain the transaction goes, the harder it will be to make any change to the

---

[1]One could optionally include the commit hash created by Git at the commit stage above, which is another way of definitively referencing **Paper1** in the repository. This approach would tie Git's provenance indicator for the state of all files in its repository including the state of the committed **Paper1** and **container-Z**. The provenance information is of significant interest in practice; however, since history can be rewritten in Git (through rebases, merges, git-filter-branch, and tools such as BFG [13]), and files are committed by users via login credentials vs. identities by virtue of applying their PKI infrastructure, Git provenance is insufficient in itself. Tied to the blockchain, the Git commit hash adds valuable evidence and couples blockchain metadata to Git's metadata and to the original data history. Further study of an integration scheme for Scrybe and Git appears to be a valuable undertaking for software provenance and intellectual property management.

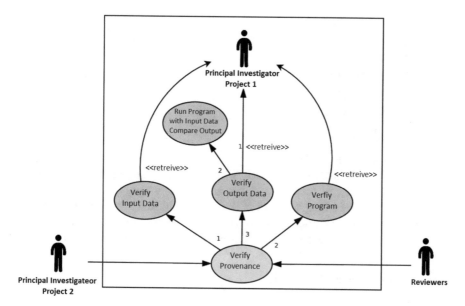

Fig. 3 Scrybe tailored to an academic integrity use case

transaction without it going unnoticed. Therefore, under normal operation of the blockchain, it becomes infeasible for Alice to make changes after the fact.

- **Detecting Plagiarism**: Assume Austin registers **Paper4** into the blockchain and fails to cite Alice for the work done in **Paper1**. If he registered **Paper4** metadata in the blockchain, it will be easy to trace the metadata and prove that he did not cite Alice. It will be impossible for Austin to change the transaction after the fact.

The workflow of this use case is shown in Fig. 3.

4.2 Digital Forensics

An example of a **Datatype** of this use case is a hard disk image. Consider the following account of a hard disk image denoted evidence **V1**, confiscated by officer Charlie, who added a transaction of the meta-data to the blockchain. Officer Charlie took it to the lab for forensic analysis. Lab technician Bob performed forensic analysis on evidence **V1** and produced evidence **V2**, a report of his findings, which was also registered to the blockchain as follows:

- Evidence **V2** is automatically uploaded to the separate data server for digital evidence.
- An Entry is created, which contains the following fields:

  1. Timestamp

2. Bob's Public Key Fingerprint
3. Input Field, which consists of pointers to the hashes of the predecessors of Evidence **V2**
4. Output field, which contains the output of the work:

   – Hash of evidence **V2**
   – PURL to evidence **V2**.

5. Bob's Signature

- The Entry is sent to the Pool.
- The selected miner produces a block, which contains all the entries in his pool.
- Other miners validate the block. If they accept it as a valid block, they add it to the blockchain by adding the hash of the previous block to the new block.
- This block is then exported as XML and sent to the provenance database.
- The provenance metadata can be viewed using appropriate visualization software.

This use case is depicted in Fig. 4.

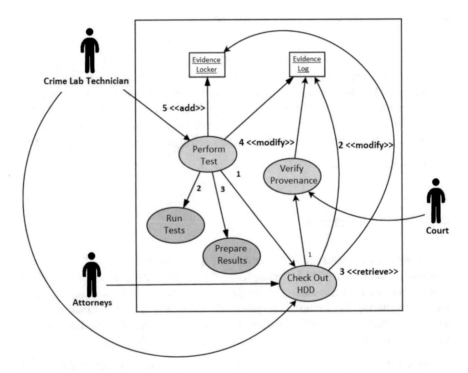

Fig. 4 Scrybe tailored to a digital forensics use case

4.3 Secure Logging

The **Datatype** of this use case is log files. Users can submit provenance metadata extracted from the output of system monitoring tools like Nagios [14] to Scrybe on a regular basis. To register a new entry to Scrybe, the user does the following:

- Upload the new log file **log-Z** a separate log database.
- Create an Entry, which contains the following fields:
  1. Timestamp
  2. User's Public Key Fingerprint
  3. Pointer/Cursor/Index to **log-Z** on the log database
  4. The hash of the log file **log-Z**
  5. User's Signature

- The Entry is sent to the Pool.
- The selected miner produces a block, which contains all the transactions in his pool.
- Other miners validate the block. If they accept it as a valid block, they add it to the blockchain by adding the hash of the previous block to the new block.
- This block is then exported as XML and sent to the provenance database.
- The provenance metadata can be viewed using appropriate visualization software.

Security is handled as follows:

- Consider the event that the computer has been compromised by an attacker for a period of time. Log files will contain traces/footprints of actions taken by the attacker, such as failed login attempts, pivoting from the compromised computer to other computers on the network, etc. The attacker might attempt to alter some of the local log files, whose metadata has been registered to the blockchain incrementally over time.
- Assuming the user notices that his or her computer has been compromised, he or she then reports the case to a security analyst, who can easily check the hash of the archived logs files and compare it to the hash registered on the blockchain. Since the attacker deleted or altered some of the log files, the hash will not match, and the analyst can easily detect which log file was modified and the accurate time at which it was modified.

This use case is depicted in Fig. 5.

Two additional Scrybe use cases are described elsewhere:

1. Secure X.509 Certificate revocation [15];
2. A novel architecture for securing IoT device identity with global and local blockchains and physically unclonable functions (PUFs) [16].

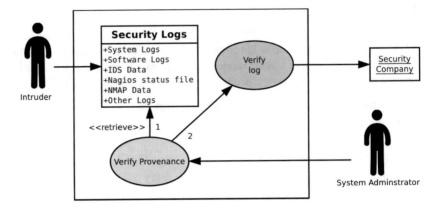

Fig. 5 Scrybe tailored to a secure logging use case

5   Security Verification

Since we replace the resource-intensive PoW mining with LWM, we needed to
conduct a comprehensive security analysis of Scrybe. Our analysis shows that
Scrybe provides data integrity, non-repudiation, availability, and strong resistance
to DDoS attacks resulting from insider threats.

5.1   Data Integrity

Integrity means that the corruption of the stored raw data can always be detected.
Scrybe uses digital signatures to ensure data integrity. All transactions are signed by
the relevant users, and all blocks are signed by the miner who created the block.
When the selected miner receives the transaction that contains the hash of the
metadata of the data such as a paper, he or she can confirm that the transaction
was signed with the user's private key and that the message was not tampered with
in transition.

5.2   Non-repudiation

In this work [17], we assume that the participants could be dishonest and that it is in
the participants' best interests not to disclose their keys or stray from the protocol
rules. Non-repudiation is concerned with protecting one participant against possible
cheating by another. We provide the parties with evidence that certain steps of the
protocol have occurred. The evidence used in this work is generated by their private
keys, which should not be disclosed to others. It is essential, therefore, that the

evidence not be modifiable by the recipient. If we can show that the miner could only have come into possession of a message of a certain form if the client had actually sent an appropriately related message to him or her, then we will have shown that the non-repudiation property holds. We use the private keys to generate digital signatures to ensure that the miner can only come into possession of such a message if the client really had previously signed and sent it to that miner.

5.3 Availability

One of the behaviors that threaten the availability of the system is when a miner chooses to drop the valid transaction, or, as described in [18], kill the transaction in his or her block. However, since the transaction has been sent to all nodes in the network, an honest miner will include the transaction in his or her block, which will be then added to the blockchain. Also, if a server decides not to add a block to the blockchain, this server will have a shorter chain that subsequently will not be the copy held in consensus on the network. We cannot allow the intruder complete control of the whole network. To prove that using LWM is sufficient in this case, we will analyze a set of properties [19] that require a system to make progress despite its concurrently executing processes using Petri net, Markov chain, and queuing theory.

In this paper we present the models to prove the lightweight mining (LMW) protocol is secure and it prevents against relevant attacks such as denial of service. We are implementing the digital signature in the LWM protocol using CSP modeling to serve three purpose. These are: authentication, integrity, and nonrepudiation. We also implement the LWM protocol in Stochastic Petri Net and Markov chain to prove the availability of the system against a DOS attack.

5.4 Communications Sequential Process (CSP) Modeling

CSP was first described by the famous British computer scientist Tony Hoare in 1978 [20]. CSP is a language that is used to describe, in real-time, the system behavior of multiple agents that communicate by passing messages. It describes two different classes: events and processes. Events represent communications, and processes represent behaviors. Each process is a set of guarded commands, where the guard is a condition that must be true for the command to execute, and the command is a transition to a new state. To achieve synchronization within a number of concurrent processes, we need to synchronize their input and output so that when one of the processes is ready to send output then the other is ready to receive input. However, if one process is not ready to communicate, the other is put on a wait queue. The system enters the non-deterministic state if more than one guard condition can be met simultaneously [20]. Ryan [18] used CSP to formalize security properties, which we will use to model the LWM security protocol. Each message that could be sent by anyone in the system is treated as a command. Messages in this paper are of two types (transactions and blocks), which have some specific structures to include encryption and signing. Work in this area will be provided in our future papers.

5.5   Resistance to Insider DoS Attacks

A key feature of LWM is its robustness to DoS attacks from malicious miners. DoS attacks are either directly by the malicious miner or through a malicious server. The malicious miner might "dislike a client," so he or she might remove such a client's transactions from the block that the client proposes; the malicious server drops targeted blocks regardless of the miners. Formal verification for the protocol's behavior under DoS threat is highly desirable. In this work, we use a Stochastic Petri net [21] to model and analyze the LWM algorithm's response to an insider DoS attack.

A Petri net is used to model, visualize, and help analyze behaviors having parallelism, concurrency, synchronization, and resource sharing [21]. A Petri net is a collection of directed arcs connecting places and transitions. Places that are represented by circles may hold an integer (positive or zero) number of tokens or marks. The marking of a net is its assignment of tokens to places. Transitions are represented by bars. Each arc is associated with a fixed weight. A transition is enabled when the number of tokens in each of its input places is at least equal to the arc weight going from the place to the transition. An enabled transition may fire at any time. When a transition is fired, the tokens in the input places are moved to output places, according to arc weights and place capacities. The input arc weights are subtracted from the input place markings, and output arc weights are added to the output place markings. Stochastic Petri nets are a form of Petri net used to calculate transitions' probabilities determined by a random value. A technique to analyze these nets is to generate all possible states in one graph that can be mapped to a Markov process. Thus, each transition firing rate λ can be mapped to its corresponding Markov state transition with probability λ. The Stochastic Petri net of three good miners is illustrated in Fig. 6. Petri net will be extend by including malicious miners who are trying to exclude the entries from a particular user. The Petri net can then be transformed into a Markov chain. We show that there always exists a path from the state representing the victim's transaction to the state where the victim's transaction gets added to the blockchain, which proves that the transaction from a victim node will eventually end up in the system as long as there is at least one honest miner. The system can thus be considered trustworthy as long as there is an active participant who is not malicious.

The Stochastic Petri net will be extended by including malicious miners who are trying to exclude the entries from a particular user. The Stochastic Petri net can be then transformed into a Markov chain [22]. We are able to show that there always

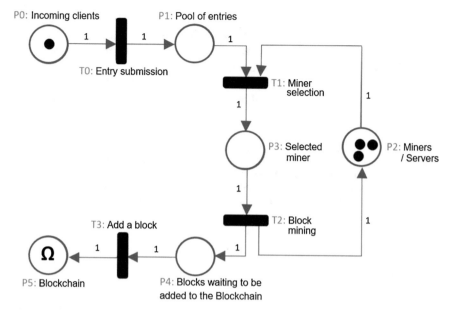

Fig. 6 Petri net of Scrybe for three good miners

exists a path from the state representing the victim's transaction to the state where the victim transaction gets added to the blockchain, which proves that the transaction from a victim node will eventually end up in the system as long as there is at least one honest miner. The system can thus be considered trustworthy as long as there is an active participant who is not malicious.

6 Conclusion

Scrybe incorporates a Lightweight Mining Algorithm (LWM), introduced to replace the resource-intensive Proof-of-Work (PoW) mining used by Bitcoin [3, 11, 23]. This design choice enables Scrybe to use fewer resources, in terms of both storage space and computation, as cpmpared to other blockchain-based tools. We presented a comprehensive security analysis of Scrybe, showing many advantageous security features including data integrity, non-repudiation, and strong resistance to DDoS attacks from insider threats.

All of these features make Scrybe a sound solution for securely storing highly sensitive metadata. We conceptualized adaptation of the Scrybe provenance system to a series of practical use cases: academic integrity, digital forensics, and secure logging. These use cases of Scrybe allow auditors to verify the integrity of the stored raw data easily. The blockchain-based ledger system guarantees data integrity and non-repudiation. We tailored the data structures of the transaction and block so that neither raw data nor the metadata is stored on the blockchain itself. This decision allows Scrybe to be entirely isolated from the data servers containing the raw data and the metadata, which are both considered highly sensitive; this approach greatly reduces the attack surface of the resulting system.

In future work, queuing theory will be utilized to verify the scalability of Scrybe, to quantify its performance and determine efficiency of the overall system for the mentioned use cases.

Acknowledgements This material is based upon work supported by the National Science Foundation under Grant Nos. 1547164, 1547245, 1049765, and 1821926, and by the NIH National Center for Advancing Translational Sciences (NCATS) through Grant No. UL1 TR001450. Any opinions, findings, conclusions, or recommendations expressed in this material are those of the authors and do not necessarily reflect the views of the National Science Foundation or the National Institutes of Health.

References

1. V. Vishnumurthy, S. Chandrakumar, E.G. Sirer, Karma: a secure economic framework for peer-to-peer resource sharing, in *Workshop on Economics of Peer-to-peer Systems*, vol. 35, 2003
2. R. Brooks, A. Skjellum, Using the blockchain to secure provenance meta-data (a CCoE webinar presentation) (2017)
3. U. Mukhopadhyay, A. Skjellum, O. Hambolu, J. Oakley, L. Yu, R. Brooks, A brief survey of cryptocurrency systems, in *2016 14th Annual Conference on Privacy, Security and Trust (PST)* (IEEE, New York, 2016), pp. 745–752
4. Technopedia, Data lineage. Online. Accessed 27 Feb 2018
5. M. Benchoufi, R. Porcher, P. Ravaud, Blockchain protocols in clinical trials: transparency and traceability of consent, F1000Research 6 (2017)
6. M. Benchoufi, R. Porcher, P. Ravaud, Traceability of consent [version 3; referees: 1 approved, 2]
7. X. Liang, S. Shetty, D. Tosh, C. Kamhoua, K. Kwiat, L. Njilla, Provchain: a blockchain-based data provenance architecture in cloud environment with enhanced privacy and availability, in *2017 17th IEEE/ACM International Symposium on Cluster, Cloud and Grid Computing (CCGRID)* (2017), pp. 468–477. http://dx.doi.org/10.1109/CCGRID.2017.8
8. Project Provenance Ltd., Blockchain: the solution for transparency in product supply chains (2015). https://www.provenance.org/whitepaper. Accessed 15 Aug 2018
9. A. Benningfield, Hyperledger - supply chain traceability: anti counterfeiting (2015). https://docs.google.com/document/d/1V0WpEggrHrBNaCL_gQrynqqmFaT3cNQw6hj1AhfkTPk/edit. Accessed 15 Aug 2018
10. B. Awerbuch, C. Scheideler, Robust random number generation for peer-to-peer systems. Theor. Comput. Sci. **410**, 453–466 (2006)
11. S. Nakamoto, Bitcoin: a peer-to-peer electronic cash system (2008)
12. Anonymous, Git. https://en.wikipedia.org/wiki/Git. Last Retrieved: 16 Mar 2018
13. Anonymous, BFG. https://rtyley.github.io/bfg-repo-cleaner/
14. Anonymous, Nagios: The industry standard in IT infrastructure monitoring. https://www.nagios.org/. Last Retrieved: 16 Mar 2018
15. S. Medury, A. Skjellum, R. Brooks, L. Yu, SCRaaPS: X. 509 certificate revocation using the Blockchain-based Scrybe secure provenance system, in *2018 13th International Conference on Malicious and Unwanted Software (MALWARE)* (IEEE, 2018), pp. 145–152

16. U. Guin, P. Cui, A. Skjellum, Ensuring Proof-of-Authenticity of IoT edge devices using Blockchain technology, in *2018 IEEE International Conference on Internet of Things, Green Computing and Communications, Cyber, Physical and Social Computing, Smart Data, Blockchain, Computer and Information Technology, Congress on Cybermatics* (2018), pp. 1042–1050

17. O. Hambolu, L. Yu, J. Oakley, R.R. Brooks, U. Mukhopadhyay, A. Skjellum, Provenance threat modeling, in *2016 14th Annual Conference on Privacy, Security and Trust (PST)* (IEEE, New York, 2016), pp. 384–387

18. P. Ryan, S.A. Schneider, M. Goldsmith, G. Lowe, *The Modelling and Analysis of Security Protocols: The CSP Approach* (Addison-Wesley Professional, Boston, 2001)

19. K. Salimifard, M. Wright, Petri net-based modelling of workflow systems: an overview. Eur. J. Oper. Res. **134**(3), 664–676 (2001)

20. C.A.R. Hoare, Communicating sequential processes. Commun. ACM **21**(8), 666–677 (1978)

21. R. David, H. Alla, Petri Nets and Grafcet: Tools for Modelling Discrete Event Systems (Prentice Hall, New York, 1992)

22. L. Yu, J.M. Schwier, R.M. Craven, R.R. Brooks, C. Griffin, Inferring statistically significant hidden Markov models. IEEE Trans. Knowl. Data Eng. **25**(7), 1548–1558 (2013)

23. Bitcoin Wiki, Proof of work (2014). https://en.bitcoin.it/wiki/Proof_of_work

Blockchain for Efficient Public Key Infrastructure and Fault-Tolerant Distributed Consensus

Melody Moh (ID), David Nguyen, Teng-Sheng Moh (ID), and Brian Khieu

Abstract This chapter consists of two major works that apply blockchain technology for improving security and trust in cyber systems. First, a cloud-based public key infrastructure (PKI) utilizing blockchain technology model is described. Enhancements over past models include the use of blockchains to establish persistent access to certificate data and certificate revocation lists. By completely decoupling the certificate authority portion of a PKI and storing certificate data inside smart contracts, the proposed method yields a sizable performance boost while decreasing the attack surface. Second, we propose a dynamic runtime sharding of Tendermint, which is an in-development state machine replication algorithm that uses the blockchain model to provide Byzantine-fault tolerance. We call this variation Randition. We incorporate recent research from blockchain consensus and replicated state machine partitioning to allow Randition users to shard their blockchain, which has greatly improved write performance at a slight cost of some Byzantine fault tolerance.

1 Introduction

Blockchain technology is a relatively new invention; it revolves around the usage of a public immutable ledger called a blockchain. Multiple parties on a network encode transactions into this ledger after going conducting a verification process. In a blockchain network, every party holds essentially the same power to verify new transactions that wish to be recorded onto the public ledger. The whole system is decentralized, and the users act as a self-policing force to ensure the integrity of every transaction that is embedded into the public ledger.

M. Moh (✉) · D. Nguyen · T.-S. Moh · B. Khieu
Department of Computer Science, San Jose State University, San Jose, CA, USA
e-mail: Melody.moh@sjsu.edu; David.nguyen16@sjsu.edu; teng.moh@sjsu.edu;
brian.khieu@sjsu.edu

© Springer Nature Switzerland AG 2020
K.-K. R. Choo et al. (eds.), *Blockchain Cybersecurity, Trust and Privacy*, Advances in Information Security 79, https://doi.org/10.1007/978-3-030-38181-3_5

1.1   Overview of Blockchain for Efficient Public Key Infrastructure

Verification of one's identity continues to be the cornerstone upon which any inter-actions or transactions between two parties lie. Every transaction or communication conducted on the internet relies upon the implicit idea that everyone knows whom he or she is conducting business. With the pervasiveness and expansion of the Internet of Things (IoT), there come new challenges for securing and authenticating the heavy flow of data generated by IoT devices. One prominent solution in the early days of the internet to authenticate the identities of various devices was the Public Key Infrastructure (PKI). However, its age has shown, and it has been unable to keep up with the demands of the IoT era [1]. Thus, a new method for identity verification over the web needs to be realized.

As of now, current traditional style PKIs are unable to keep up with the demands of new applications; in one survey, over 60% of respondents stated that their current PKI system was unable to handle new apps regardless of what the software was based in [2]. Some companies have already taken steps towards basing their PKI in the cloud; others use newer versions such as the Web of Trust (WoT) approach. However, the WoT version generally lacks speed due to its slower nature of authentication through trust based scoring.

The main issue with the currently outdated solution lies with the Certificate Authority (CA) portion of the PKI. As of now, these CAs are the main points of failure within a PKI system; once any one CA is compromised, the whole PKI crumbles [3]. Furthermore, it is currently extremely difficult for a traditional CA to revoke an old identity. However, a promising new solution marries the traditional PKI system with that of cloud and blockchain technology [4]. This new way of verifying identities can pave the way towards a safer and more secure internet.

Integrating both blockchain and cloud technologies with a public key infras-tructure system can secure certificate authorities and make them resilient against common attacks. Hosting a certificate authority on the cloud allows us to piggyback on a cloud provider's existing security measures. In addition, the auto-scaling feature that some cloud platforms offer mitigates the effectiveness of denial-of-service (DOS) attacks, attacks that center on overwhelming the provisioned resources for a web service. Blockchain technology can also bolster the defenses of a certificate authority. Previously, some denial-of-service attacks launched against certificate authorities were used to prevent requesting parties from accessing a certificate revocation lists. Holding certificate data and certificate revocation lists in a blockchain network makes this type of attack infeasible due to the shifting of the attack target to the blockchain network itself.

The objective would be to test and implement a Cloud-based blockchain PKI system, CBPKI. Our goal with the integration of blockchain and cloud technologies with the PKI model was to eliminate some of the largest weaknesses of PKIs. In addition, another goal is to determine whether such a system can outperform traditional PKI models using metrics such as complete revocation time.

1.2 Preview of Blockchain for Fault-Tolerant Distributed Consensus

Distributed consensus remains a topic of research and exploration. Three-Phase Commit was perhaps the first renown improvement over its more naive, two-phase sibling. Enhanced Three-Phase Commit (E3PC) improved upon that. Many variations and new algorithms for distributed consensus have been proposed since. The earliest research focused on tolerating failing nodes. This transitioned into overcoming network failures such as network partitioning and message delay with the proliferation of the Internet and today's modern network infrastructure. Paxos and Raft are notable algorithms in this era. Research has recently transitioned into tolerating Byzantine faults with the introduction of blockchain.

The research community has realized blockchain can address the Byzantine fault weakness in popular consensus algorithms. If a system is Byzantine fault tolerant (BFT), it can perform reliably in the face of some malicious nodes actively attempting to stop or fail consensus. Note that this tolerance also covers failing nodes, network partitions, and message delays that are the result of hardware problems—since one might not be able to distinguish the difference between a hardware failure and a Byzantine party.

A general survey of blockchain technology will reveal that blockchains are essentially distributed databases and replicated state machines. These lend themselves to participation by the general public through numerous blockchain-specific consensus protocols. This explains the terms *distributed* and *public ledger* [5–7] as common descriptors of blockchain. However, write performance in popular public blockchains are outmatched by virtually all conventional database systems—even distributed databases—available now.

2 Background and Related Studies

This section describes the background and related studies for blockchain, PKI, distributed consensus, and Tendermint.

2.1 Smart Contract and PKI

Blockchain technology revolves around the usage of a public immutable ledger called a blockchain. Within a blockchain network, miners, nodes that hold a current version of the ledger, compete with one another in an attempt to be the first to mine a new block on the ledger. They do so to receive transaction fees for their services rendered. Once a block has been mined, the data will be publicly accessible on the blockchain network.

Closely associated with blockchains, smart contracts are digital contracts typically hosted on an electronic public ledger. It comprises of an agreement between two parties and facilitates the completion of said agreement. The smart contract allows money to be deposited within it for holding and future disbursement upon successful completion of the aforementioned agreement between both parties. If a party does not abide by the terms, the money the contract holds will automatically refund the held deposit and self-terminate. Smart contracts are self-executing and can be used in a large variety of applications from legal processes to residential leases.

A public key and a private key are two mathematically and cryptographically linked strings of characters. The two of them together form a key pair; an operation conducted using one can be reversed using the other half of the key pair. In practice, encrypting a document with a public key ensures that the only feasible method of decrypting said document is by using the corresponding private key. As their names imply, a public key is the public portion of a key pair while the private key is the private portion. Key pairs help ensure the privacy and integrity of online communications.

A public key infrastructure is a system that authenticates devices and handles digital certificates; digital certificates are essentially virtual ID cards designated by the PKI to associate an identity with a public key. By relying on a public key infrastructure, users trust that any party with a digital certificate distributed by the PKI is accurate. Once a certificate is retired or deemed to be compromised, the public key infrastructure will revoke that certificate to protect other users from communicating with anything that tries to use the revoked certificate. Currently, PKIs revolve around a Certificate authority (CA) to administer and revoke certificates using the X.509 standard.

Certificate authorities certify and issue these certificates to requesting users. Since they are central to the security provided by PKIs, they often must endure more attacks. Once a certificate authority is compromised, the integrity and authenticity of every certificate within the ecosystem comes under question.

2.2   Related Studies of Blockchain-Based PKI

X509Cloud, the model proposed by Tewari et al. emphasized the storage, retrieval, and revocation of certificates [8]. In order to circumvent the associated maintenance costs of verifying identities, the model aims for mutual authentication between users and the organizations. The framework connects a cloud service to a Bitcoin inspired blockchain protocol that is used to store in newly created certificates. This approach differs from CBPKI in that instead of storing the entire certificate itself within a blockchain, mine holds all relevant certificate data within a smart contract.

A paper authored by Alexopolous et al. analyzed the merits of integrating open distributed ledgers (ODLs) [9] developed a formally defined trust management model for use with ODLs; these ODLs are the ledgers that blockchain technologies have implemented and focus on. The paper also provided an analysis of common attacks versus typical trust management systems and of certificate data in smart contracts. Both research groups utilized a Restful API implementation of a CA in order to accept and service requests for certificates. However, they did not host the CA in the Cloud; conversely, CBPKI's hosting of the CA within a cloud service such as Amazon Web Services (AWS) allows for some added security benefits. For one, AWS offers web traffic monitoring and filtering of requests to a web app. In addition, Denial of Service attacks are mitigated since AWS with its auto-scaling feature will simply continue to provision more resources in order to meet the increased demand. This change allows CBPKI to scale properly with any changes in demand by modern applications.

CBPKI also drew upon the hybridized certificate implementation from [8] and [9]; the modified certificates possess information regarding where pertinent certificate or CA information is stored in the blockchain network. In addition to the hosting of the CA on a cloud service, our proposed solution differs from the two referenced papers' approach in how certificate data is stored within the blockchain network. Instead of storing the revocation list data within a block's transaction data field, our new approach stores said data within smart contracts. This has the added benefit of lower gas cost to be mined as well as quicker mining speed as opposed to the block approach. Also of note is that this method addresses the traversal issue with the approach of [8] and [9] as put forth by [10]. Instead of having to traverse the blockchain in search of a revoked certificate, the certificate itself would contain the direct address of where to access the smart contract that contains all of the relevant data regarding said certificate. Since smart contracts can update its data fields, the CA can simply update the status of a certificate to revoked; this removes the need for CRLs and eliminates the traversal issue certificate data will be directly accessible. Instead of having to traverse the blockchain in search of a revoked certificate, the certificate itself would contain the direct address of where to access the smart contract that contains all of the relevant data regarding said certificate. Since smart contracts can update its data fields, the CA can simply update the status of a certificate to revoked; this removes the need for CRLs and eliminates the traversal issue certificate data will be directly accessible. Note that in order to use this PKI system, one needs to implement a simple verification script that matches the hash of the certificate on hand with that stored within the smart contract. This use of smart contracts helps our solution better fit the needs of Big Data applications in both terms of scalability and persistence. For one, it avoids the need for a traversal along the blockchain in order to verify the certificate. Secondly, there should be minimal persistent access issues to the data required for verification since said data is being held in a distributed network with no single point of failure.

2.3 Tendermint

Tendermint is a proof-of-stake consensus algorithm that can replicate a state machine while tolerating Byzantine failures in up to one-thirds of nodes or *validators* [11]. Developers can freely download Tendermint, attach the same deterministic state machine application to each Tendermint validator, and observe their Tendermint network replicate the application. Given at least two-thirds of validators are non-Byzantine and correct, the algorithm can guarantee safety, liveness, and even accountability. In Tendermint, validators maintain their own copy of a replicated blockchain and take turns proposing blocks (just large batches of transactions) in rounds. Two voting phases and two well-defined lock rules ensure that no correct validators accidentally fork the blockchain by getting too far ahead of the consensus, thereby providing safety. Liveness is provided in the unlock conditions that accompany the locking rules and in block proposal timeouts. Byzantine fault testing from the authors and Jepsen—a third party distributed consensus testing firm—[12] confirmed effective Byzantine fault tolerance.

Algorand's BA* is another consensus algorithm that bears close resemblance to Tendermint. To clarify, Algorand refers to a cryptocurrency and BA* refers to Algorand's consensus algorithm. Algorand tolerates up to one-thirds Byzantine nodes, nodes each maintain their own blockchain copy, and nodes propose blocks of transactions for the blockchain. However, BA*'s proposer selection and voting phases are distinct. The author utilizes a *cryptographic sortition* algorithm that uses distributed verifiable random functions (VRFs) to randomly determine one proposer out of all eligible nodes [13]. Once the proposer proposes a block, the same sortition algorithm is utilized to randomly determine voting committees of tunable size, which proceed to perform one phase of voting. There is a minimum of four of these repeated voting committees. Given an Algorand network where up to one-thirds of nodes are Byzantine, there is the negligibly small possibility of a fork if each phase repeatedly chooses voting committees that are compromised by Byzantine nodes. BA* includes logic to reach consensus on a single fork to maintain safety and liveness. Because of this consensus scheme, Algorand easily scales to tens of thousands of nodes and hundreds of transactions per second in testing.

Consensus is often the expensive operation and bottleneck for blockchains [14]. Conveniently, sharding a blockchain can also provide some of the performance benefits we observe in more classical database systems. Before blockchain, distributed state machine replication (SMR) did not scale well mainly because of synchronization (or consensus) overhead. Each node had to receive and execute all transactions. Nogueira, Casimiro, and Bessani observe that partitioning such systems into shards can achieve scalability, but note that most implementations that use partitioning don't do so in a very elastic manner [15]. They propose a modular partition transfer protocol to allow node groups to split and merge with minimal impact on performance.

Sharding is a recent development in blockchain research. For our purposes, blockchain *partitioning* can be used interchangeably with blockchain *sharding*.

However, there are subtle distinctions between the terms that are not in the scope of this chapter. ELASTICO [16] was one of the first blockchain protocols that featured sharding. In every epoch, nodes solve a proof-of-work puzzle to determine their assigned shard, each shard performs byzantine agreement to agree on a set of assigned transactions, and a *final committee* shard generates a final block from the results of all shards. Experimentation reveals transaction throughput scales almost linearly to network size. OmniLedger [17] is a recent proposal that improves upon ELASTICO by improving shard robustness, shard security, transaction atomicity, processing overhead, and transaction confirmation latency. It also takes advantage of VRFs and Algorand's cryptographic sortition as part of its security refinements. Experimentation shows OmniLedger achieves its goals for higher transaction throughput and lower confirmation latency.

3 Proposed Methodology for Blockchain-Based PKI

The following sections detail our newly proposed model for a PKI system that utilizes blockchain and cloud technologies, and they are organized as follows. Firstly, the model itself and the enhancements are explained in the next section. Afterwards, implementation details are covered, and the final section discusses the differences CBPKI possesses compare to models from related works.

3.1 Model

CBPKI consists of a stateless certificate authority that stores certificate data on the Ethereum network, a blockchain network that allows unlimited processing potential for smart contracts. The certificate authority is implemented as a Restful API; upon receiving a certificate service request posted to it, the CA generates a new certificate. Shortly following, the new certificate is embedded into a blockchain whose address is listed on the certificate itself. A python script is used to check for the certificate's appearance within the blockchain. Upon revocation of a certificate, the certificate is similarly embedded within a different blockchain for further verification purposes.

One specific enhancements over past PKI models is the transformation of the certificate authority into a stateless web service hosted on the cloud. The conversion of the certificate authority into a stateless protocol hosted on a cloud platform significantly reduces the size of the viable attack surface. Since coveted data is no longer stored within the CA itself, it also lowers the value of targeting the certificate authority for attacks. In addition, stateless web services are more conducive to relying on the protections offered by cloud platforms. For example, Amazon offers a web traffic monitoring service named AWS (Amazon Web Services) Shield to secure stateless web services. In addition, hosting the CA on a cloud platform with auto-scaling mitigates the common Denial-of-Service attack; with auto-scaling, more resources are automatically provisioned to the certificate authority so it can handle the flood of requests during a DoS attack.

The second enhancement made by CBPKI is the use of smart contracts as a storage device on the blockchain network. In general, the use of blockchains in PKI systems allows persistent certificate revocation list access and further circumvention of DoS attacks. Using smart contracts to store certificate data instead of using block transaction data fields yields the additional benefits of lowered mining times and operating costs. Also, CBPKI removes the need for CRL (Certificate Revocation List) due to the storage of certificate validity within the smart contracts. This allows for direct verification of a certificate as opposed to traversing a blockchain for a certificate's status.

3.2   Implementation

As noted earlier, CBPKI builds on the works of [8–10]. Three different PKIs were built for testing and comparison purposes: a traditional PKI and two Cloud Based PKIs utilizing blockchain technology. Both the traditional PKI and the Cloud PKIs used a remote CA in order to standardize the experiment. The overarching approach is as follows:

1. Implement a Restful API using Python and Django to act as a CA. Allow for the traditional CA to service queries for its certificate revocation lists (CRL).
2. Connect the Certificate Authority to the Ethereum Test Net Ropsten. Associate a cryptocurrency wallet with the CA in order to pay for the associated cost of embedding a certificate
3. For one of the blockchain PKIs, hash a X.509 certificate and embed it into the transaction data field of a block and send it to be mined in Ropsten. Similarly, for the new approach, set up a smart contract in which to embed the hash of an X.509 certificate and send it to be mined in Ropsten. In both cases, the X.509 certificate requires the address of where it is stored within Ethereum.
4. Implement certificate verification methods for the Blockchain PKIs. This involves searching for the hash of a certificate within a blockchain or pulling certificate information from the smart contract.

3.3   Features

The modifications to the approach created by [8] and [9] center around the hosting of the CA on the cloud as well as the embedding of certificate data in smart contracts. Both research groups utilized a Restful API implementation of a CA in order to accept and service requests for certificates. However, they did not host the CA in the Cloud; conversely, CBPKI's hosting of the CA within a cloud service such as AWS allows for some added security benefits. For one, AWS offers web traffic monitoring and filtering of requests to a web app. In addition, Denial of Service attacks are mitigated since AWS with its auto-scaling feature will simply continue to provision more resources in order to meet the increased demand.

CBPKI also drew upon the hybridized certificate implementation from [8] and [9]; the modified certificates possess information regarding where pertinent certificate or CA information is stored in the blockchain network. In addition to the hosting of the CA on a cloud service, our proposed solution differs from the two referenced papers' approach in how certificate data is stored within the blockchain network. Instead of storing the revocation list data within a block's transaction data field, our new approach stores said data within smart contracts. This has the added benefit of lower gas cost to be mined as well as quicker mining speed as opposed to the block approach. Also of note is that this method addresses the traversal issue with the approach of [8] and [9] as put forth by [10]. Instead of having to traverse the blockchain in search of a revoked certificate, the certificate itself would contain the direct address of where to access the smart contract that contains all of the relevant data regarding said certificate. Since smart contracts can update its data fields, the CA can simply update the status of a certificate to revoked; this removes the need for CRLs and eliminates the traversal issue certificate data will be directly accessible.

4 Performance Evaluation and Analysis of Blockchain-Based PKI

This section consists of the performance and results from the experiments conducted on the CBPKI model. Three different models were used for testing, and these models consisted of one traditional PKI and two variants of the CBPKI model. The section is organized as follows. First, the experimental settings subsection details the environment and testing methods used for each model. Then, the results subsection summarizes the outcomes of the tests. Finally, the last subsection evaluates each model's level of security compared to one another.

4.1 Experimental Settings

The experiments conducted on our proposed work revolved around access times and the costs associated with operating different models. Our proposed model utilized many different software tools, and two different variants were used alongside one another for the tests. As mentioned earlier, three models in total were subjected to the same conditions, and their performance was evaluated based on three metrics relating to speed, time, and cost where applicable.

4.1.1 Implementation and Resources

The following software resources are required for the implementation of our project (Table 1): Python Programming Language, Python Packages Cryptography, Hashlib, and Web3.py, Heroku, Django web framework, Django API TastyPie, Solidity Smart Contract programming language, X.509 certificates, Ethereum Test Net Ropsten, MetaMask, Ethereum IDE Remix, Etherscan, and the Infura Ethereum API. Django and the API Tastypie were used to implement the CA as a Restful API; these two technologies were available at no cost. Django web apps can be hosted by use of Heroku, a cloud platform as a service, and Heroku could also be used at no cost by use of its free tier. The Solidity smart contract programming language is available at solidity.readthedocs.io. In addition, the Python programming language is also available at python.org, and the X.509 certificates being used can be imported by installing the pyca/cryptography package for python with pip. In addition, the Hashlib python package, which is used to hash certificates, and Web3.py, which handles connections to the Ethereum network, are available through pip. Ethereum Test Net Ropsten is a test blockchain network for the cryptocurrency Ethereum. MetaMask is a free Ethereum wallet that is used to pay for the gas required to mine blocks or smart contracts. Ethereum IDE Remix is a free IDE for Ethereum smart contracts used to create and deploy said smart contracts. Also, Etherscan is a website that can monitor transactions, smart contracts, and wallets. Finally, Infura is a blockchain API that allows a connection between the Ethereum network and a python script.

Table 1 Software tools used and associated costs

Software tool	Cost
Python Programing Language	Free
Python Package: Cryptography	Free
Python Package: Hasblib	Free
Python Package: Web3.py	Free
Heroku Cloud Platform	Free tier used
Django Web Framework	Free
Django API: TastyPie	Free
X.509 Certificates	Free
Ethereum Test Net Ropsten	Free
Ethereum IDE Remix	Free
Etherscan	Free
Infura Blockchain API	Free
Solidity Smart Contract Programming Language	Free

4.1.2   Experimental Settings

Every test run used the same settings amongst each model; 50 runs were conducted for each model type. Across different models, the most similar conditions as possible to one another were used; each PKI model would be loaded with the same initial dataset of a 2 MB large certificate history list. This history list consisted of details regarding old certificates the CA had distributed in the past. Each model was also paired with a certificate revocation list that was 1 MB big; this CRL comprised of half of the distributed certificates within the certificate history list. The traditional model stored the both the history and revocation lists within cloud platform. Instead, the CBPKI block storage version held the data from both lists within two separate blockchains while the smart contract version used smart contracts as storage devices.

4.1.3   Metrics

The metrics used for judgement of both the traditional PKI and the CBPKIs will be certificate verification time. Certificate verification time within this chapter is defined as the time it takes to query the certificate authority for whether or not a given certificate has been revoked or not. In addition, the two CBPKIs will have additional metrics regarding mining time of certificate data and gas costs of mining certificate data in their different storage methods. Mining time is the time it takes the data storage method to be mined and thus publicly accessible on the blockchain network. Mining gas costs are the amount of gas or money required in order to pay miners to service the mining request.

4.1.4   PKI Models

During the experiments, three PKI models were used; these models were the traditional version, CBPKI block storage version, and the CBPKI smart contract version. The traditional version is hosted on a cloud service to limit variables, but it still holds all certificate data and certificate revocation lists together with its certificate authority. The two CBPKI models instead use a stateless CA hosted in the cloud while holding certificate data within the Ethereum blockchain network. However, they differ distinctly in how they store said data. The block storage version stores the certificate itself within the transaction data field while the smart contract version merely stores a hash of the certificate along with key certificate data inside smart contracts.

Table 2 Certificate verification times (ms)

Model	Mean
Traditional	208.52
Block storage	142.97
Smart contract	129.34

Table 3 Mining timings per certificate (ms)

Model	Mean
Block storage	325.60
Smart contract	21.36

Table 4 Mining gas cost per certificate ($)

Model	Mean
Block storage	5.95
Smart contract	0.77

4.2 Results

Overall, there is a notable improvement in each area for the Cloud PKI implementation using smart contracts to store certificate data. While both CBPKIs allow for faster CRL retrieval than that of the traditional PKI, the smart contract version is faster than the block storage version. This is mostly likely due to how the block storage version requires a traversal across the blockchain in order to find the specific certificate while the smart contract version simply pulls the relevant validity data directly from the smart contract (Table 2).

Regarding the mining times, there is a significant speedup when using smart contracts. Smart contracts are smaller and thus do not need as many resources to complete mining when compared to blocks. According to the monitoring done by Etherscan, most of the time used for mining the block was spent waiting to be serviced. Mining times are highly dependent on network congestion; this helps explain the variance between different run times (Table 3).

The final category of tests centered on the mining gas cost to embed certificate data into the Ethereum network. As the tests show, the average cost of mining a smart contract is greatly reduced in comparison to that of an entire block. This average reduction of about $5 gives significant savings in the operational costs of a PKI utilizing blockchain technology. However, it pales in comparison to the traditional PKI since there is a negligible cost associated with storing a certificate in a database (Table 4).

4.3 Security Analysis

The various public key infrastructure models covered in this chapter possess clear benefits and tradeoffs. Traditional models retain the discussed failings of certificate authorities; their large attack surface size makes them vulnerable and a target

Table 5 Qualitative comparison of PKI models

PKI model	Certificate issuance cost	CA attack surface size
Traditional	Low	High
CBPKI block storage	High	Low
CBPKI smart contract	Medium	Low

Table 6 Qualitative comparison of CBPKI variants

PKI model	CRL size	Immutable records
Block storage	High	Yes
Smart contract	Low	No

for infiltration and disruption. The weaknesses of these traditional models are well known which thus makes them quite susceptible to any attacks launched by malicious actors. However, they are cheap to operate in terms of issuing certificates, and apart from hosting and electricity costs, there is a negligible cost per certificate issuance. The CBPKIs both decrease this attack surface size significantly, and by making the CA stateless, they are able to piggyback on a cloud platform's security measures. Nevertheless, as noted in Table 5 above, this comes at a significant operating cost.

Using blockchain technology as a storage device for certificates and certificate data does not come free. Amongst the two CBPKI models, the smart contract variant outperformed the corresponding block storage version in every metric used. The smart contract version has the additional benefit of not requiring CRLs, which has resulted in measurable performance boosts over the block storage version. However, it is important to note that the smart contract version does not necessarily possess data field immutability. Depending on the implementation, the smart contract data fields could be subject to malicious alteration although in this specific version, we took care to lock any updates to the smart contract behind a SHA-256 key. While the code behind the smart contract itself is immutable, the data it holds does not possess this attribute. Thus, even though the block storage method may be more costly and slower to use than the smart contract CBPKI model, the block storage model is more secure since its records are immutable. Another thing of note is that one must be careful in programming a smart contract. Since the code itself is immutable, a bugged smart contract can run forever on the network (Table 6).

5   Randition: Blockchain-Based Fault-Tolerant Distributed Consensus with Random Sharding: Goals, Hypothesis, and Assumptions

We hypothesize that Tendermint's primary transaction processing performance bottleneck is in its consensus. As more validators join a Tendermint network, we surmise it generally takes more time to reach two-thirds majority consensus which can contend with relevant consensus timeouts the user defines at network configuration time. In other words, larger network sizes impose greater requirements to reach consensus. This bottleneck results in limitations on practical network sizes. We believe write throughput maximum is improved if Tendermint takes advantage of the concepts presented in the partition transfer protocol [15].

We propose a Tendermint variant that borrows from this partition transfer protocol, defines how it does *shard formation*, and specializes in partitionable workloads to provide significant transaction and validator scalability. Our specific goal is to observe notable improvement in mean transactions committed per second and mean blocks committed per second. Furthermore, we do not measure mean transaction commit time or validate transaction linearization. We merely focus on this variant's ability to *commit as many transactions as possible in a time frame* instead of *what it commits within a time frame*. We call this variant *Randition*.

We design Randition for users who have highly partitionable workloads within the application they wish to replicate across a network. While blockchains are very synonymous with cryptocurrencies, blockchains also lend themselves to being highly reliable distributed databases, public ledgers, and other similar applications. Tendermint provides a primitive key-value store called *kvstore* as a basic example application for users.

We understand sharding involves some safety compromises. First, allowing Tendermint's validator network to become sharded means the entire system's Byzantine-fault tolerance is based off the smallest shard's validator count. We allow this because we wish to provide additional network scaling and tuning opportunities to users whose Byzantine-fault tolerance is known more as a specific amount rather than as a ratio of total validators. Suppose we have a user who controls 64 validators. Altogether in a single Tendermint network, this network is Byzantine-fault tolerant with up to a maximum of 21 incorrect validators (less than one-thirds of 64). Now, suppose that this user could easily tolerate 5 incorrect validators at any time in any configuration. In this situation, the user could provision a Randition network of 4 16-validator shards, because one-thirds of 16 is approximately 5.3. We believe this situation would provide significantly improved transaction throughput at reasonable cost. Suppose a more extreme example in which a user controls 1000 validators. This user might decide they can tolerate far less than 333 validators experiencing Byzantine failures at any time and prefer to gain more performance at the cost of some of this high Byzantine-fault tolerance.

Second, supporting sharding means allowing a sort of network partition to occur, which completely compromises safety if a Byzantine validator is allowed to propose the sharding scheme. We resolve this issue by further proposing that Randition implement Algorand's cryptographic sortition algorithm [13] to allow the network to autonomously and safely shard itself.

Figure 1 visualizes our high-level architecture. Randition will implement shard formation logic within Tendermint round processing to allow the blockchain to randomly shard. This formation logic will take advantage of Algorand's cryptographic

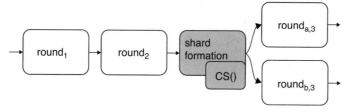

Fig. 1 High-level architecture of Randition's shard formation

sortition for safe shard formation. Discussions of safely and liveness for partition transfer by Nogueira et al. shall guide us on the correctness of our sharding scheme and logic.

Randition assumes that users will initialize the network with each validator having equal or *approximately* equal voting power. Our integration of cryptographic sortition into Tendermint has dependencies on validator voting power.

Our shard formation protocol currently requires 100% consensus, which means every validator must participate in shard formation within a network-wide time out. Of course, this is counter-intuitive in our understanding of how blockchains do and should work. Consensus should be achieved with a majority of votes instead of all of the votes. However, we put forth the notion that this is acceptable in a permissioned or private blockchain environment where initial network configuration is performed by a trusted user who also controls runtime network *reconfigurations*. In that context, consider that networks should perhaps only shard when this trusted user commands that *all* validators attempt to form shards at the same time.

6 Randition: Overview

6.1 Cryptographic Sortition

Verifiable random functions (VRFs) [18] are an essential component to Algorand's cryptographic sortition. Given a private key sk and value v as input, function F outputs a seed x and proof $proof_x$. Micali et al. prove that seed x is pseudo-random and unpredictable. Anyone who knows sk's public key pk can utilize the verification function V (consider this an inverse operation of function F) with input pk, seed x, proof $proof_x$, and value v to determine if seed x is indeed valid.

Algorand developed the cryptographic sortition algorithm to randomly and non-interactively select users based on their voting power or *weight* [13]. In order for Algorand to support this algorithm, a pseudo-random seed value must be maintained in the blockchain. Before Algorand begins, initial $seed_0$ must be selected either by a trusted agent or distributed random number generator and known to all users. At

```
procedure Sortition(sk, seed, τ, role, w, W) :
    ⟨hash, π⟩ ← VRF_sk(seed||role)
    r ← hash/2^hashlen
    p ← τ/W
    j ← 0
    // I is an interval that changes with j
    I ← [ Σ_{k=0}^{j} B(k; w, p), Σ_{k=0}^{j+1} B(k; w, p) )
    while r ∉ I do
        j++
    return ⟨hash, π, j⟩
```

Fig. 2 The cryptographic sortition algorithm [13]

every subsequent round, each block proposer (also known as user u) computes the seed for round r as follows:

$$< \text{seed}_r, \pi > \leftarrow \text{VRF}_{\text{sku}} \left(\text{seed}_{r-1} \| r \right) \tag{1}$$

where π is proof of seed_r's validity and VRF_{sku} represents the execution of the VRF with user u's secret key.

Of course, proposer u's public key is known by every other user. Proposer u includes the output seed_r and proof π in its block proposal. As part of block validation, all other users validate u's seed_r with π. If the block is approved for commit, the block is appended to the blockchain along with seed_r.

Since the VRF must be identical across the network, the same seed will be computed. Furthermore, since all correct users must have identical copies of the blockchain, all users will have access to the same seed.

Figure 2 summarizes the sortition algorithm [13]. Users input a private key sk, a pseudo-random public *seed*, the desired number of users τ, desired *role*, the user's weight w, and the network's total weight W. A pseudo-random *hash* is produced from the blockchain's public seed concatenated with the user's desired role, such as a proposer or voting committee identifier. A pseudo-random number in the interval [0, 1) is calculated by dividing the hash by the maximum numerical value of the hash. Probability p is defined as the desired number of users τ out of the total weight W between all the users and is the probability an individual unit of weight or voting power is selected by the algorithm. Counter j indicates how much of the user's weight was selected by the algorithm or "won" sortition.

The interval [0, 1) is also divided into consecutive intervals as defined by the given cumulative distribution functions. The algorithm checks if the pseudo-random

---

procedure VerifySort($pk, hash, \pi, seed, \tau, role, w, W$) :

  if $\neg$VerifyVRF$_{pk}(hash, \pi, seed\|role)$ **then**

    return 0

  $r \leftarrow \frac{hash}{2^{hashlen}}$

  $p \leftarrow \frac{\tau}{W}$

  $j \leftarrow 0$

  // I is an interval that changes with j

  $I \leftarrow \left[\sum_{k=0}^{j} B(k; w, p), \sum_{k=0}^{j+1} B(k; w, p) \right)$

  while $r \notin I$ **do**

    $j{+}{+}$

  return j

Fig. 3 The cryptographic sortition verification algorithm [13]

number falls within the defined intervals in order. As soon as the number does, the algorithm returns the amount of weight or voting power selected. Naturally, the first of the consecutive intervals is very large and has a high probability of causing the algorithm to return $j = 0$. Each following interval is smaller than the last, causing the algorithm to return a low j with high probability and vice versa. The algorithm finally outputs the number of selections j, the pseudo-random *hash* it used to determine j, and proof π of the validity of hash altogether in a *sortition message*.

Figure 3 summarizes the sortition verification algorithm [13]. If a node is selected for a role and publicly broadcasts the results of their sortition, anyone can verify the results with this algorithm along with the originating node's public key *pk*. Cumulatively, the sortition and verification algorithms are essential in providing safe and deterministic selection of committees.

6.2 Partition Transfer

Nogueira et al. iterate that modern state machine replication primarily provides fault tolerance at the cost of scalability [15] and adding replicas tends to exacerbate this tradeoff. Although recent research already propose partitioning to improve scalability, these tend to not be very *elastic* in that they don't excel at dynamically partitioning at runtime. Nogueira, Casimiro, and Bessani propose a modular *partition transfer* primitive and protocol in the state machine replication model. Their objective is to enable most state machine replication protocols to implement partitioning with minimal impact to performance and minimal requirements from the SMR protocol. Their protocol can be summarized in the following six steps [15]:

1. Group G receives a partition transfer request from a trusted agent.
2. Each replica in G sends its state S to a matching replica in new group L. During this entire stage, updates on S are logged in cache Δ.
3. Each replica in group L accepts state S when it receives and verifies matching S-hashes from enough replicas in group G.
4. Each replica in G sends its cache Δ to its matching replica in group L. From now on, group G stops serving requests that L should be handling and redirects such requests to L instead.
5. Each replica in group L accepts cache Δ when it receives and verifies matching Δ-hashes from enough replicas in group G.
6. When group G receives enough acknowledgement messages from group L, it reports the partition transfer request results back to the trusted agent.

The protocol notes that consensus is only required at the beginning of steps 1 and 4. In step 1, consensus is required for all replicas to start partitioning in a synchronized manner. In step 4, consensus is required for the replicas in group G to stop processing requests for the transferred partition in a synchronized manner.

6.3 Tendermint

While Tendermint's core design remains the same, observation of Tendermint's code repository [19] and public documentation [20] over time indicate the entire product is in a constant state of improvement and refactoring. Modifying a specific version of Tendermint alleviated problems associated with alpha and beta software updates. As such, we only worked with and discuss Tendermint version 0.24.0.

Tendermint distinguishes between *peers* and *validators*. Peers are simply the term for a node participating in the network and validators are simply peers with voting power. This means non-validator peers have zero voting power, can only observe, and keep up with consensus. After initialization, user applications can use Tendermint's API to send transactions and replicate. The *EndBlock* request is one such interface that allows user applications to execute logic at the end of every block commit.

Tendermint has a notion of *reactors*, which are concurrent processes that run alongside the main process and are responsible with helping the validator participate in the network [11]. It does so in part by utilizing a *switch* object to broadcast messages to the entire network, thereby generating *gossip*. The main reactors are the *blockchain*, *consensus*, and *mempool* reactors. The mempool reactor is responsible for caching, verifying, and gossiping application transactions in the mempool. The mempool can be considered a cache for transactions that have not been committed in a block. Tendermint's *Validator Set Update* protocol [11, 20] is integral to our effort. It is triggered when the user application specifies a new validator set at the EndBlock request.

7　Randition: Adapted Cryptographic Sortition and Adapted Shard Formation

7.1　*Adapted Cryptographic Sortition*

We modify Tendermint's consensus reactor and engine to maintain a pseudo-random seed value at every height in the blockchain. When it is time for a Proposer to propose a block, it executes Eq. 1 to obtain a candidate seed and seed proof. These are included in the proposal and the proposal is broadcast to the network for voting. Randition considers the proposal's seed and seed proof as integral to the validity of the proposal itself. Therefore, if the network determines the seed and proof as invalid, then the network will vote against the proposal and the next Proposer will be selected.

To facilitate and easily manage blockchain sharding, we define a new *shard reactor* in Randition that is responsible for tracking the validator's shard and shard status, tracking the network's shards and their status, and using sortition to attempt to form shards.

We found it necessary to define *sharding phases* so that the main process and various reactors can determine what stage of sharding a validator is in. The following phases are numbered and are set depending on the following conditions:

0: The default phase; the validator is not in a shard and sharding has not been requested.
1: The validator's user application has requested sharding and the validator is waiting for the required sortition messages to arrive.
2: The validator has received all required sortition messages and shards have formed.
3: The validator has removed all extra-shard peer validators from its peer list.
4: The validator and network is fully sharded and sharding is active.

Figure 4 illustrates the valid transitions between the phases.

We modify Tendermint's external EndBlock request to allow a user to set a new *PartitionKeys* string array with regular expressions, or *regexes*, that inform Randition which shards to sort transactions into. Let us consider these partitioning keys synonymous to those found in relational databases that support data partitioning.

For every round the *PartitionKeys* array is set, the main process will instruct the shard reactor to attempt to shard the network. Whenever the reactor receives this local sharding request, it will perform sortition using the procedure described in Fig. 2 and broadcast the results to the network. We provide the same input parameters that Algorand does into the procedure except for the *role* parameter, which is meant to be the proposer slot or voting committee a node is competing for. In Randition,

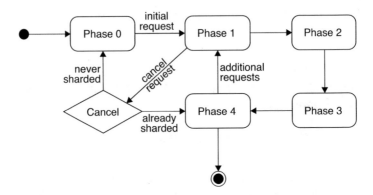

Fig. 4 Shard reactor states

the role parameter indicates which partitioning key a validator wants to form shards for. To be specific, the role parameter is actually a hash of the entire partitioning key to maintain a uniform parameter size.

Whenever the shard reactor receives sortition result broadcasts from peer validators, it will either cache the broadcast if the reactor is not aware of a sharding request or validate the broadcast using the procedure described in Fig. 3 if the reactor is waiting for consensus on shard formation. As soon as any validator has verified sortition results from every other validator (equating to 100% consensus), the reactor forms shards and instructs the main process which shard the validator is a part of. At this point, the validator communicates mainly with intra-shard validators and sharding is complete. Note that since total consensus is required, user applications should request sharding at roughly the same time or block height.

Randition uses cryptographic sortition to shard a network into sub-networks while Algorand uses it to select small committees. In Algorand's case, there are "winners" of sortition and the prize is getting to propose a block, vote on a block, etcetera. In Randition, what prizes do winners get? Presumably, there shouldn't be any *better* shard. We use cryptographic sortition for individual validators to randomly and non-interactively determine their place in a priority queue. From there, Randition can more-or-less evenly divide validators into shards by picking from the front of the queue and assigning them to shards in round-robin order. Note that formation into only 2 shards is supported at this time, although the scheme could easily be improved to support any desired number of shards.

The novel use of cryptographic sortition in shard formation is that each validator forms shards independently from each other following one phase of sortition message exchange with every other validator. Consider a Byzantine validator who wishes to trick another validator into joining the wrong shard or multiple shards. By the time this Byzantine validator determines which validators belong to which shards, the shard formation is complete, there are no additional phases or message exchanges, and no chances to influence sharding. Of course, a Byzantine validator can completely stop shard formation from occurring with our current 100%

consensus requirement by not sending any messages at all, but the key here is that they cannot corrupt shard formation and configuration.

7.2   Adapted Shard Formation

Randition is very much inspired by Nogueira et al.'s proposal and we don't precisely implement the defined protocol. Instead, we rely on it to provide valuable guidance and insight towards maintaining safety and liveness during blockchain sharding.

Consider the following Randition's shard formation protocol, inspired by Nogueira et al.'s partition transfer protocol:

I. Group G receives a sharding request from a trusted agent.
II. Group G collectively and consistently determines new groups L_1 and L_2, known as *shard formation.*
III. Groups L_1 and L_2 cease participating in consensus with each other and continue consensus locally.
IV. Groups L_1 and L_2 report the sharding request succeeded to the trusted agent.

Nogueira et al. [15] state their partition transfer protocol fulfills safety and liveness in the following ways:

- Safety 1: once partitioning completes, "the transferred partition will not be part of the source group state and will be part of the destination group state" [15]
- Safety 2: "linearizability of the service is preserved by the partition transfer" [15]
- Liveness: partitioning eventually completes

Our shard formation protocol satisfies these goals in an equivalent manner. Randition satisfies *Safety 1* due to Steps II and III. Shard formation in Step II ensures two or more independent shards. At the very least, all validators in a new shard agree they're in a shard with each other. At best, all validators in a whole network agree on which shards all other validators belong to. Step III ensures independent "group states" and data consistency, because every shard does not process extra-shard requests. Every validator in a shard will not propose or commit transactions that are rejected by their shard's partitioning key. *Safety 2* is satisfied if the protocol processes requests in total order. Randition satisfies *Safety 2* because Tendermint satisfies *state machine safety* [11] and will continue to do so after sharding completes due to Step III, where the majority of validators in any shard is expected to continue Tendermint's consensus protocol. State machine safety guarantees total order for blocks committed and transactions therein.

Randition satisfies *Liveness* because all of the Steps I through IV must terminate. In Step II of our protocol, the shard reactor will only wait as long as a round for all of the required sortition messages to arrive. If they do arrive and they are all valid, shard formation occurs and completes independently. If they do not arrive, then Randition carries on and another sharding request and sortition message gossip must be made in a future round. Steps III and IV execute independently of other intra-shard validators and rely on existing Tendermint behavior. Step III relies on execution of Tendermint's Validator Set Update protocol, which must terminate before a new block is proposed. Step IV is completed once Tendermint responds to its BeginBlock interface, which must occur before each new block commit. With our shard formation protocol and existing Tendermint behavior, Randition satisfies the safety and liveness goals outlined by Nogueira et al.

Now consider Fig. 4, where each sharding phase is represented as a state in a state machine. This begs the question regarding if state *transitions within* the shard reactor are safe and live. Can a correct validator be coerced into incorrect states or forced to not terminate? Within Randition, only the shard reactor is concerned with these phases. The rest of Randition—especially Tendermint's core and mempool reactor—is mainly concerned with whether sharding is fully activated or not.

The primary safety concerns are addressed by the definition of Phase 1: *the validator's user application has requested sharding*. More specifically, a correct validator cannot be coerced to transition outside of Phase 0 by a Byzantine entity. If the validator's user application incorrectly requests sharding, the validator will trust the user application and the validator itself can no longer be considered correct. We showed that the transition through Phase 2 by a correct validator cannot be corrupted by a Byzantine entity. Phases 3 and 4 are guaranteed to execute correctly as long as Tendermint can continue processing rounds.

The primary liveness concern lies in Phase 1, where the validator is waiting for the required sortition messages to arrive. As long as the shard reactor is in Phase 1 and 100% consensus has not been achieved, the shard reactor (and the network as a whole) will continuously execute and gossip sortition for each new round in an attempt to form shards. We purposefully allow users to constantly retry sortition and gossip since requiring 100% consensus within one or two rounds is admittedly a lofty expectation. Other than successfully transitioning to Phase 2 via 100% consensus, the only other way to guarantee termination of Phase 1 is for the user application to explicitly request cancellation. We emphasize that while the shard reactor remains in Phase 1, Randition is able to continue consensus and round execution, because Randition's core is mainly concerned with whether sharding is fully activated or not. The shard reactor does not block core processing in this regard. Phase 2 terminates because shard formation is completed independently of other validators. As long as Tendermint's round processing maintains liveness, then Phases 3 and 4 are guaranteed to terminate.

After sharding is activated, the Mempool begins distinguishing between intra- and extra-shard transactions. This is merely achieved by checking if this shard's partitioning key—which is a compiled regular expression at this point—returns a match in a transaction. Following Tendermint's design, all transactions are cached in the Mempool. However, Randition ensures transactions that are designated extra-shard are never proposed. They are retained only for gossip and gossip optimization. The gossip routine in the mempool reactor will repeatedly read the cache and broadcast each transaction to the entire network.

Note that Randition does not take additional action for extra-shard data that was already committed before sharding. Therefore, a validator in a sharded blockchain will eventually have stale data. The extra-shard data that a validator possesses will become increasingly stale as more blocks are committed to each blockchain shard. We leave handling stale data and ensuring correct query output to future work.

As a clarification, transactions in Randition are gossiped by the mempool reactor normally between all other peers a validator is connected to. What each validator does with a transaction is up to them. However, the same cannot be said for proposal, block, and vote gossip via the consensus reactor. Recall that validators are merely peers with voting power. Therefore, a validator will readily gossip messages with peers, but will only trust messages originating from other validators. In the case where a validator belongs to a shard, it will readily gossip with extra-shard validators, but will only trust messages originating from intra-shard validators. Messages that require verification are signed by the originator and this includes proposals, blocks, and votes. Tendermint's current design will only gossip signed messages after they're cached, and a validator will only cache messages after it ensures the message is trustworthy by verifying the signature or by checking if it expects the message from the originator at all.

8 Randition: Implementation and Results

8.1 Implementation

Tendermint's source code is written in Golang (also known as Go), an open source programming language whose development is led by Google [21]. Of course, our modifications were completed entirely in Golang. Our changes to Tendermint consist of approximately 1600 lines of code. Randition utilized Coniks' verifiable random function library [22]. Both Tendermint and Coniks use Ed25519 [23] as their public-private key system, but their precise implementations vary enough so that Tendermint keys cannot be used in Coniks and vice versa. As such, each validator is modified to store Coniks-compatible keys for use when calling the Coniks VRF.

8.2 Results

All experiments occur on Digital Ocean servers of size *s-2vcpu-4gb* (2 vCPU and 4 GB of memory) running 64-bit CentOS 7. All instances are located in Digital Ocean's *SFO2* (West Coast United States) region to minimize the effects of network delay. We rely on Tendermint's *tm-bench* tool to generate data and benchmark the network. Each validator is configured to execute Tendermint, Tendermint's example *kvstore* user application, and tm-bench on-demand. All validators are configured to connect directly to each other to minimize the negative effects of network topology.

Tendermint's main configuration file, the *config.toml* file, is customized by:

- setting the *moniker*, or peer name, to a unique identifier
- disabling mempool logging in the *log_level* setting
- disabling empty block commit in the *create_empty_blocks* setting
- significantly increasing the mempool *size* to 250,000
- significantly increasing the mempool *cache_size* to 500,000

We avoid tuning the remaining settings and leave them as defaults.

Each transaction in our test workload is generated by tm-bench and we selected a transaction size of 500 bytes. Each transaction is an amalgamation of pre-determined and pseudo-random hex-encoded data. New transactions are generated by mutating bytes 16 through 31 of the previous transaction with pre-determined data and by replacing bytes 40 through 89 of that transaction with new pseudo-random hex-encoded data. Our experiments rely on the 81st byte to be pseudo-random during transaction generation, because we modify the example kvstore application to shard with the following regular expression partitioning keys for 2 shards: *^.{80}[0-7]* and *^.{80}[^0-7]*. These partitioning keys will result in approximately half of the total transactions generated being committed in the first shard and remaining half becoming committed in the second shard.

We are mainly interested in observing transaction throughput *after* the blockchain shards itself. Therefore, each individual experiment is conducted after we prime the test Randition network by submitting transactions for 20 seconds, which is enough time to allow Randition to shard itself and settle network activity. We focus on committed transactions per second and committed blocks per second as calculated by tm-bench to be the basis for transaction throughput. For Randition, overall committed transactions per second is defined as the sum of transactions committed per second by all shards in the network. Since tm-bench might report slightly varying results for each validator in an individual shard, we first calculate the committed transactions per second *per shard* to be the mean average of intra-shard tm-bench outputs. We use the same definition for committed blocks per second.

Our experiments primarily vary the input transactions per second per validator in a 32-validator Randition network and compare the results to those from a 32-validator Tendermint network on the same workload. We vary the input transaction rate per validator between 25, 50, 75, 100, 150, and 200 transactions per second. That translates to 800, 1600, 2400, 3200, 4800, and 6400 input transactions per second over a whole 32-validator network. Each experiment executes for 20 seconds.

Figure 5 compares transactions committed per second between Tendermint and Randition. Note that the error bars indicate the standard deviation. Figure 6 compares blocks committed per second between Tendermint and Randition. Note that the error bars indicate the standard deviation. These results are comprised of 12 executions per input rate for Tendermint and 16 executions per input rate for Randition.

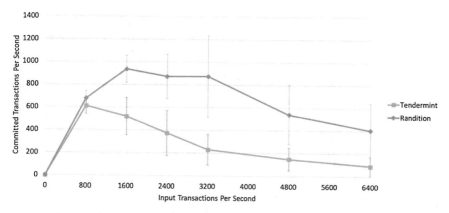

Fig. 5 Committed transactions per second

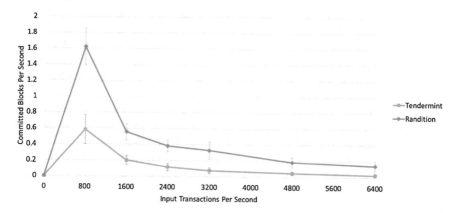

Fig. 6 Committed blocks per second

8.3 Discussion

To reiterate, this effort focuses on proving that transaction write performance is significantly improved when safely sharding a blockchain. In Fig. 5, we can observe that Tendermint and Randition output similar performance up until approximately 800 input transactions per second for a 32-validator network. However, past a threshold between 800 and 1600 transactions per second, Tendermint's performance begins to degrade. Randition reaches its peak committed-transactions-per-second past Tendermint's peak and continues to maintain better performance than that of Tendermint. In Fig. 6, we can observe that Randition commits more transactions per second mainly because the overall network can communicate and commit more blocks in a time frame.

Since our tests involve virtually the same network configuration and workload generation, we suggest this performance improvement in Randition is a direct result of blockchain sharding, dividing the cost of consensus, and parallelizing consensus. We further suggest that the performance bottleneck primarily lies in Tendermint's consensus protocol, at least for a mostly-default network configuration of 32 or more validators. In a 32-validator network, consensus between 2 networks of 16 validators—all of which remain gossiping with each other—is easier to achieve than consensus between 32 validators. Naturally, consensus requirements will tend to increase non-linearly with more participating nodes. The computations required to process proposals, blocks, and votes; and the time required for proposal, block, and vote messages to propagate sufficiently to achieve consensus are major contributors to these requirements.

Recall that Randition will only gossip messages it verifies and will not gossip extra-shard proposals, blocks, and votes. On the other hand, Tendermint will gossip these consensus messages between all validators. This translates to a notable reduction in gossip in Randition since each validator will effectively ignore—but still receive—these consensus-related messages from half of the original network if there are 2 shards. One might consider this a natural optimization of blockchain sharding, but only if one could tolerate less resilience in the face of network partitions. Of course, Randition could be modified to gossip these extra-shard messages to restore and emulate Tendermint's gossip scheme, but we leave this to future work and analysis.

While the focus of this project was to demonstrate that blockchain sharding is certainly viable in improving transaction write performance, we also reiterate that the shard formation scheme is integral in demonstrating that sharding is actually safe to use and that the network can shard with *safety and liveness*. We have demonstrated in Sect. 7 that Byzantine validators cannot coerce the network into performing incorrect shard formation or trick a validator into joining the wrong or multiple shards.

9   Conclusion

Traditional PKIs contain issues regarding its certificate authorities that inhibit their ability to properly meet the demands of the IoT era. These issues can be addressed by usage of integrating current PKIs with existing blockchain and cloud technologies. Offloading the certificate authority to the cloud allows the PKI to tap into existing security measures against common attacks such as Denial of Service. In addition, storing certificate data in the blockchain enables persistent CRL and certificate data access while avoiding potential caching issues and DOS attacks. The aforementioned qualities provide an advantage for our CBPKI model over past models in fitting the needs, scalability and availability, of modern applications and ecosystems.

The results of the conducted tests reflect a significant performance increase of blockchain PKIs over traditional PKIs. Furthermore, the proposed solution of storing certificate data in smart contracts also outperformed the block storage version in terms of CRL access time, mining speed, and mining cost. However, this mining cost is a large source of the operational costs associated with blockchain PKIs, something that traditional PKIs do not possess.

We have also shown that blockchain sharding can provide significant write performance improvements at the cost of some BFT. While the performance improvements we observe are likely unsurprising, the key to this chapter lies in our shard formation scheme and how Randition can do so safely and with liveness. Conceptually, our ideas can potentially be incorporated into any state machine replication algorithm or model that satisfies the partition transfer protocol requirements.

10   Future Research Directions

Areas for further research on Blockchain-based PKI may be based on the study conducted by [10]. As noted earlier, the group of researchers highlighted three specific issues regarding the approach taken by [8] and [9]. Additional study could be conducted in trying to resolve these issues without having to completely overhaul the PKI system as done by [10]. In addition, since there is a significant operating cost associated with storing certificate data on a blockchain network, further study in the reduction of this cost is also warranted. Additional areas for future work involve the cloud portion of the CBPKI model. Routing requests for certificates through a cloud service opens up a plethora of possibilities for the application of cloud and alternative services. One such possibility is to further merge the CBPKI model with a machine learning model to automatically verify and revoke faulty certificates, potentially before the certificate has even been issued.

Randition requires much improvement and iteration to approach becoming a useful application. This particular effort has focused on developing a prototype to demonstrate feasibility. We concede that 100% consensus is an unrealistic expectation in permissioned and perhaps even private blockchains. Tendermint's modular design allows Randition's shard formation scheme to be highly flexible and we believe a wide variety of schemes can be implemented with little additional work. Therefore, we suggest a shard formation scheme that requires only two-thirds majority consensus as a possible improvement over our current one. In Randition's current shard formation scheme, cryptographic sortition is used to randomly and non-interactively determine validators' places in a priority queue to be sorted round-robin into shards. In this situation, there are no "winners" as there are in Algorand. However, we return to Algorand's usage of cryptographic sortition by suggesting that all validators in a network perform sortition as a lottery to decide which group of validators will *secede* from a Randition sub-network and form a new shard. Informally, once a validator has received sortition results from two-thirds of the network's validators, the set of validators with the highest number of selections by sortition that form the smallest shard size might transition onto Phase 2 from Fig. 4

```
procedure Secede(sortitionResults) :
    sortByTimesSelected(sortitionResults)
    i ← 0
    min ← minimum shard size
    while i < min do
        validator ← pop(sortitionResults)
        seceders ← validator
        i ← i + validator.size
    return seceders
```

Fig. 7 The secession scheme

and form their own shard; the remaining validators must accept this and also form their own shard. Figure 7 describes this new shard formation scheme.

Validators will not have the same chance of being selected given a network with widely varying voting powers. In this scheme, validators with more voting power will have a higher likelihood of selection and winning sortition. Detailed design and analysis of such a scheme would be worthy of future research.

Acknowledgments The chapter is extended from two prior conference publications [24, 25]. M. Moh and T.-S. Moh are both supported in part by a 5-year SJSU RSCA awards (2018–2023). The authors wish to thank the Tendermint and Algorand teams for developing and publishing Tendermint and cryptographic sortition, respectively. We also thank the developers of the partition transfer protocol for their invaluable insight into replicated state machine partitioning.

References

1. T. Claeys, F. Rousseau, B. Tourancheau, Securing complex IoT platforms with token based access control and authenticated key establishment, in *2017 International Workshop on Secure Internet of Things (SIoT),* Oslo, Norway, 2017, 8 p.https://doi.org/10.1109/SIoT.2017.00006
2. J. Grimm, PKI: crumbling under the pressure. Netw Secur **2016**(5) (2016). 2 p
3. J. Zhou, Z. Cao, X. Dong, A.V. Vasilakos, Security and privacy for cloud-based IoT: challenges, in *IEEE Communications Magazine*, vol. 55(1), 2017, 7 p. https://doi.org/10.1109/MCOM.2017.1600363CMAlexander
4. A. Yakubov, W.M. Shbair, A. Wallbom, D. Sanda, R. State, A Blockchain-based PKI management framework, in *NOMS 2018–2018 IEEE/IFIP Network Operations and Management Symposium,* Taipei, Taiwan, 2018, 6 p.https://doi.org/10.1109/NOMS.2018.8406325
5. Merriam-Webster, Incorporated, Blockchain, https://www.merriam-webster.com/dictionary/blockchain. Accessed 3 Mar 2019
6. L. Fortney, Blockchain, explained, Dotdash, 10 February 2019. https://www.investopedia.com/terms/b/blockchain.asp. Accessed 3 Mar 2019

7. J. Martindale, What is a blockchain?, Designtechnica Corporation, 11 February 2019. https://www.digitaltrends.com/computing/what-is-a-blockchain/. Accessed 3 Mar 2019
8. H. Tewari, A. Hughes, S. Weber, T. Barry, X509Cloud 2014; framework for a ubiquitous PKI, in *MILCOM 2017–2017 IEEE Military Communications Conference (MILCOM)*, Baltimore, MD, 2017, 5 p.https://doi.org/10.1109/MILCOM.2017.8170796
9. N. Alexopoulos, J. Daubert, M. Mühlhäuser, S. Habib, Beyond the hype: on using blockchains in trust management for authentication, in *2017 IEEE Trustcom/BigDataSE/ICESS*, Sydney, Australia, 2017, 7 p.https://doi.org/10.1109/Trustcom/BigDataSE/ICESS.2017.283
10. J. Chen, S. Yao, Q. Yuan, K. He, S. Ji, R. Du, CertChain: public and efficient certificate audit based on blockchain for TLS connections, in *IEEE INFOCOM 2018—IEEE Conference on Computer Communications*, Honolulu, Hawaii, 2018, 8 p.https://doi.org/10.1109/INFOCOM.2018.8486344
11. E. Buchman, Tendermint: byzantine fault tolerance in the age of blockchains, 2016. https://atrium.lib.uoguelph.ca/xmlui/handle/10214/9769. Accessed 6 May 2018
12. Jepsen, Tendermint 0.10.2, 2017. https://jepsen.io/analyses/tendermint-0-10-2. Accessed 6 May 2018
13. Y. Gilad, R. Hemo, S. Micali, G. Vlachos, N. Zeldovich, Algorand: scaling byzantine agreements for cryptocurrencies, in *Proceedings of the 26th Symposium on Operating Systems Principles*, Shanghai, China, 2017.
14. T.T.A. Dinh, J. Wang, G. Chen, R. Liu, B.C. Ooi, K.-L. Tan, Blockbench: a framework for analyzing private blockchains, in *SIGMOD '17—Proceedings of the 2017 ACM International Conference on Management of Data*, Chicago, Illinois, US, 2017.
15. A. Nogueira, A. Casimiro, A. Bessani, Elastic state machine replication. IEEE Trans. Parallel Distr. Syst. **28**(9), 2486–2499 (2017)
16. L. Luu, V. Narayanan, C. Zheng, K. Baweja, S. Gilbert, P. Saxena, A secure sharding protocol for open blockchains, in *Proceedings of the 2016 ACM SIGSAC Conference on Computer and Communications Security*, Vienna, Austria, 2016
17. E. Kokoris-Kogias, P. Jovanovic, L. Gasser, N. Gailly, E. Syta, B. Ford, OmniLedger: a secure, scale-out, decentralized ledger via sharding, in *2018 IEEE Symposium on Security and Privacy (SP)*, San Francisco, California, US, 2018
18. S. Micali, M.O. Rabin, S.P. Vadhan, Verifiable random functions, in *Proceedings of the 40th Annual IEEE Symposium on Foundations of Computer Science (FOCS)*, New York, 1999
19. Tendermint, Tendermint core (BFT consensus) in Go, GitHub, 2018. https://github.com/tendermint/tendermint. Accessed 17 Aug 2018
20. Tendermint, Welcome to Tendermint!, Read The Docs, 2018, https://tendermint.readthedocs.io/en/master/. Accessed 17 Aug 2018
21. Google, The Go Project, Google, https://golang.org/project/. Accessed 24 Aug 2018
22. CONIKS Team, A CONIKS implementation in Golang, GitHub, 2018. https://github.com/coniks-sys/coniks-go. Accessed 24 Aug 2018
23. D.J. Bernstein, N. Duif, T. Lange, P. Schwabe, B.Y. Yang, High-speed high-security signatures. J. Cryptogr. Eng. **2**, 77–89 (2012)
24. B. Khieu, M. Moh, CBPKI: cloud blockchain-based public key infrastructure, in *Proceedings of 2019 Annual ACM Southeast Conference*, Kennesaw, GA, USA, 2019
25. D. Nguyen, T.-S. Moh, Randition: random blockchain partitioning for write-throughput, in *Proceedings of IEEE International Conference on High Performance Computing and Simulation*, Dublin, Ireland, 2019

Secure Blockchain-Based Traffic Load Balancing Using Edge Computing and Reinforcement Learning

Kevin Tiba, Reza M. Parizi ⓘ, Qi Zhang, Ali Dehghantanha, Hadis Karimipour, and Kim-Kwang Raymond Choo ⓘ

Abstract Congestion represents one of the major problems in constantly growing cities, and the expansion and modernization of the traffic system are a major priority to all government infrastructures. In effect, more efficient traffic represents a more efficient economy. Solving the issue of congestion by increasing the number of roads is not always the most cost-effective solution as it represents massive changes in city infrastructures that have been present for decades. Urban planning shapes the environment around us but fails to address specifically the future traffic clogging. Our research tackles the problem of traffic congestion by proposing a system for vehicle detection, identification, and count, allied with reinforcement learning for traffic congestion anticipation and prediction. The need for a real-time and efficient system led us to push the research and development onto an Edge Computing platform using IoT and secure transactions using Hyperledger Fabric blockchain. Blockchain intervenes as a security protocol in the proposed

K. Tiba
Kennesaw State University, Marietta, GA, USA
e-mail: ktiba@students.kennesaw.edu

R. M. Parizi (✉)
College of Computing and Software Engineering, Kennesaw State University, Marietta, GA, USA
e-mail: rparizi1@kennesaw.edu

Q. Zhang
IBM Thomas J. Watson Research, New York, NY, USA
e-mail: Q.Zhang@ibm.com

A. Dehghantanha
Cyber Science Lab, School of Computer Science, University of Guelph, Guelph, ON, Canada
e-mail: adehghan@uoguelph.ca

H. Karimipour
University of Guelph, Guelph, ON, Canada
e-mail: hkarimi@uoguelph.ca

K.-K. R. Choo
Department of Information Systems and Cyber Security, University of Texas at San Antonio, San Antonio, TX, USA
e-mail: raymond.choo@fulbrightmail.org

© Springer Nature Switzerland AG 2020
K.-K. R. Choo et al. (eds.), *Blockchain Cybersecurity, Trust and Privacy*, Advances in Information Security 79, https://doi.org/10.1007/978-3-030-38181-3_6

system. The native form of Internet of Things does not include security protocols which are important to a large scale implementation. Ensuring the security of transactions and permanent access control is the main reason why blockchain is rooted in our system architecture. Our project aims to reduce the traffic load on roads experiencing significant congestion, and improve overall city traffic system without costly investment into new communication infrastructures and city planning.

1   Introduction

Traffic congestion is depicted as a reduction of speed, longer commuting time and increased vehicular queuing as the use of the traffic way increases. It is an ongoing problem, especially in the United States within its large cities with populations reaching the millions. The financial cost per individuals is estimated to $1445 by Smart Cities Dive that depicted a gross total of $305 billions as a total cost to U.S. drivers in 2017 [25]. The 2018 Transport and Environment report of the European Federation for Transport and Environment AISBL [38] estimated 494.05 Kt of CO_2 solely on the European soil. The need for more efficient traffic infrastructures and reduced traffic congestion is increasing. Along with this cost can be denoted the psychological toll on drivers, stemming from the sense of helplessness. A connotation to domestic violence has been observed, as denoted in the article "Stuck and Stressed: The Health Costs of Traffic" [7], published in The New York Times most recently.

The reduction of traffic congestion appears as a must to the enhancement of living conditions for a huge part of automobile drivers. The general economy and environment would gain from such improvements [26], with a reduction of the cost per year in fuel consumption and a slowdown in the deterioration of the atmosphere by CO_2 gases. Solutions proposed concerning traffic detection and control systems focus on the efficiency of the models rather than its usability with less attention to security aspects, and many fail to address the issue of traffic pattern changes, main causes of models unsuitability [12]. The development of smart traffic control systems represent a major improvement to cities and with systems similar to SURTRAC Intelligent Traffic Signal Control [32], the reduction of traffic congestion and the enhancement of drivers safety is a reality. Nevertheless, the limitation of such systems can be depicted on the difficulty to predict congestion or maintain traffic flow to a satisfactory level. In effect, detecting congestion and reacting to it is not our main objective. Our ultimate objective is to prevent traffic congestion and maintain a cruise speed on the traffic ways equipped with our proposed system.

This research focuses on the application of reinforced learning into the observation of traffic, the understanding of the parameters (speed, traffic load, type of cars, lane occupancy, the hour of the day, temperature, humidity, rain, etc.) and their progressive combinations that lead to congestion [12]. The modeling of the different intersections and the main road of the traffic control system is an important part of the implementation. The inter-dependency of each intersection and the connection between the traffic roads needs to be considered as they greatly affect the traffic management system as a whole [30]. Issues arising from the increase in the scale of the existing systems are mainly the latency and security requirements. To counter those issues, our project uses edge-driven network and architecture to distribute the major part of the computing load to the smart nodes in the system. Edge computing shifts the paradigm from centralized to decentralized; by utilizing computers, network and storage resources that is closer to the user. It pushes the content and service away from the center nodes [10]. Other advantages proposed by edge computing are the availability of hosts for the computation of data and the data locality enabling the computation of models specific to each node or group of nodes. Enabling security over such a large scale system, which will most likely interact with other systems that are not considered as trusted, requires a security measure that is at the same time transparent and reliable [35]. This is the motivation why blockchain was devised to be integrated in our proposed system. Having a blockchain layer (implemented using enterprise-strength Hyperledger Fabric platform) enables to store security-sensitive meta-data along with the transaction information among the different nodes of the system in a distributed ledger. Our evaluation is based on the observation of traffic peaks data and their comparison with the overall predictions of our system concerning the traffic congestion. The main contributions of this paper are as follows:

- Vehicles identification, count and speed tracking operated using machine vision models.
- IoT platform for decentralized data processing as implementation of edge computing, using IoT framework and containerization.
- Prediction model for traffic clogging using reinforcement learning framework. Access control and IoT transactions security protocols using blockchain.

The rest of this paper is organized as follows. Section 2 discusses the related work. Section 3 explains the architecture of the proposed system and the step by step interactions within its inner components. Section 4 describes the uses cases and our evaluation results, and finally, Sect. 5 gives the conclusions.

2 Related Work

In this section, we discuss both published work in the academic literature along with the existing systems in the market that accomplish a similar purpose to our proposed system.

2.1 Literature Review

The capacity to ensure the security of private data is a great advantage proposed by blockchain as explained in [9, 17, 20–24, 41]. In effect, the lack of ways of communicating private patient information between third parties, and the lack of transparency in the research capacity of the different third parts using records makes it highly difficult to establish a full fledged proprietary system to store and share traffic data.

Defining an architecture relying on edge computing and sequential learning algorithm to establish a smart city system goes along with the goals of our research, which is to establish a self-sustained and self-evolving smart traffic control system that gathers, processes, analyzes and resolves data in real-time and thus ensure the reduction of traffic congestion. The capacity to develop such a grid and provide proof of its operability is what pushes us into considering such an option and analyzing the context and component used in [5].

Similar system associating the power of IoT with the security standards of blockchain has been implemented to provide new IoT standards and reduce the security breaches encounter in this domain. In effect, the interconnection and the transfer of data among IoT devices lack security standards. Most of our common IoT devices store important private data. The communication between other devices is not monitored or protected from outside actions, hence making it a potential risk of users of such devices. FogBus offers a platform-independent interface to IoT applications and computing instances for execution and interaction. It not only assists developers in building applications but also helps users in running multiple applications at a time and service providers to manage their resource [40].

The detection, identification, and counting of vehicle present on the traffic ways is the main way for us to understand the traffic data and patterns emerging from it. The work presented in [12] discusses machine vision techniques used to identify and classify the different type of vehicles on a traffic day using video detection. Those techniques interconnect with one of the objectives of our research which is vehicle count and average speed approximation. Our examination of simple and efficient models to solve this problem made us choose the machine learning framework ImageAI [4] based on OpenCV3 that enables vehicles detection.

The authors in [19] proposes a new approach concerning the security concerns of the Internet of Thing, especially in terms of privacy when dealing with access control. The paper focuses on access control in the IoT context by deriving a fully distributed security policy. Blockchain ensures the full distributed security in the context proposed and machine learning provide self-adjusted and dynamic security policy.

One of the latest studies [31] focuses on the orchestration of the edge computing platform using Hyperledger and Docker containerization. Its goal is to implement function blocks as a smart contract that will interact with edge nodes and the executive level using a micro-services architecture where Docker implements function blocks and Kubernetes orchestrates the execution of containers. Our research goes in a similar direction by providing new ground foundation for smart contracts provisions. Our goal is to generate smart contracts based on the communication information between smart nodes and operate a private ledger (residing on the blockchain) across the different nodes of the system.

2.2 Similar Systems

We established a list of systems or infrastructures using a similar or more intuitive approach to solve problems close to the one addressed in this research. Table 1 summarizes the different solutions along with the pros and cons of their implementations over ours.

The different tools listed in Table 1 represent the main functional systems that validate the notion of traffic control, management or analysis. Most of them are proprietary systems, meaning that from beginning to end, the process of data gathering, data storage, and data processing is performed solely through enterprise expensive and specialized hardware, instead of tending to rely on accessible and commonly available IoT devices. On the other hand, Calypsa is a software solution with limited action capacity, as it only provides dashboard view and alerts based on visual data collected. The system TADA of Drakewell is a pure analytic system that operates vehicles identification and counting. Each system has its own strengths but all of them fail in two major categories:

- **Network Architecture**: The different systems evaluated are cloud-based and centralized, offering more direct and controlled structure to their procedures. Nonetheless, the centralized aspect of these systems raises the issue of latency and safety. Applied to the scale of a smart city, the failure of the central decision point can lead to heavy perturbations on the traffic system. Another capital point is the ability to decentralize automated decisions that is lacking on such systems. In effect, only high latency data should reach the central server, and regular processing and decisions should be operated at the edges of the network [34].
- **Proprietary security**: Calipsa appears to be the only full fledged detection system that does not require proprietary hardware, but all systems have a proprietary security system that raises the issue of privacy and transparency of the data. The systems listed are connected to interfaces which do not affiliate with the companies. If such connections are not secure, risks of alteration or destruction of data are higher.

The goal of this research is to propose an infrastructure that suppresses the need for data reduction in an automated environment. It should also ensure the security, transparency, and privacy of the data while enabling secure transfers to third parties. The data collected and models generated from this work can be used in multiple analysis such as traffic control or vehicle detection and monitoring. Other companies can use such information to design more efficient roads and traffic systems.

Table 1 Similar systems resolving issues of traffic detection, analysis, and management

System	Description	Pros	Cons
TrafficLink [13]	Set of hardware, processing unit and detection system using machine learning for traffic detection and automated traffic control	Enhanced simulation systems and reduced information storage, Reduced workload and storage necessity	Proprietary system from detection device to the processing server, Direct link to secure server, High installation cost, No data sharing capacity, Proprietary security protocol, Lack of transparency in information collection and privacy concerns
Calipsa [2]	Deep learning powered video monitoring	Advanced detection system, Alert scheduling and storage, Easy integration without hardware required	No automation system implemented, Alert system limiting the interaction with data, No complete video data storage, Proprietary security protocol, No data sharing capacity, Lack of privacy concern, Not adequate for high traffic detection
TELEGRA [39] Smart Traffic Management	Full fledged traffic monitoring, automation and simulation system	Low Installation cost, Multi-modal detection system, Visualization tool integrated, Incident detection included	Proprietary security protocol, Data stored in-house, Use data reduction techniques
Traffic analysis data application (TADA) [8]	Traffic analysis system	Highly efficient traffic reporting system with years of available data, Respect for privacy, Large coverage of traffic data	Pure Analytic system, Traffic count system, No automation system, No complete video storage system, Fully proprietary system

3   Proposed System

3.1   System Architecture

The base architecture of our proposed system is presented in Fig. 1. The system is a combination of multiple components (devices and tools) that work in cohesion to solve the traffic congestion problem.

Our system architecture is composed of six underlying blocks whose interactions aim to contribute to the reduction of traffic congestion and constant increase in performance of the system with better security. These different blocks are the detection devices, the smart nodes, the observation system, the Hyperledger consensus system, the IoT server, and the traffic control system. Each part is

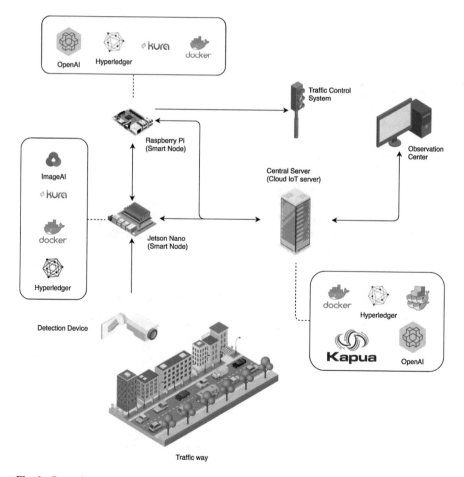

Fig. 1 General system architecture

operating as a service and provides information or action commands to the other parts of the system. The system procedure can be explained as follows:

(1) Video images are continuously collected by detection devices (IP cameras) and sent to the first layer (observation layer) of the system that is composed of our Jetson Nano. Jetson Nanos are miniature computing unit specialized for image processing. These first smart nodes of our system compute estimations of the car count and car speed every minute using ImageAI and Speed-detector [29], two machine learning models specialized respectively in object detection and speed approximation.

(2) The approximations collected enter our smart nodes network. Using Kura framework [6], our smart nodes can exchange data with other smart nodes of the system. Kura is an IoT framework providing communication gateways to smart nodes. The second layer called decision layer, receives data from the Jetson Nanos. It is composed of Raspberry Pi that are also miniature computing unit. They are in charge of collecting the data computed by the first layer and outputting predictions of the traffic flow using the reinforcement learning framework called OpenGym AI. These predictions triggers the algorithm in charge of traffic flow management.

(3) All smart nodes of the system communicate with a central cloud server. Kura enables serverless processing. Our system can operate without the help of the server as each device is already allocated the models necessary for computation. The server intervenes as a high latency computing unit. Its role is to enable the observation center to have access to the smart nodes information and provide new models to each smart nodes after specific model training. Running Kapua IoT server, the central server proposes an interface to communicate and assess the interaction of all devices present in our Kura powered network.

(4) The different communications operated within the system (smart-node to smart-node and smart-node to server) are supervised through Hyperledger Fabric. All devices present on the system network are peers of the ledger and store crucial communication information. This is specifically designed to ensure no external attacks or penetration to the system. On top of the security defined by Kura, Hyperledger ensures that the communication ends are secure from attacks.

All of the above components along with their inner workings are explained in the following sections.

3.2 Vehicle Detection

The vehicle detection system presented in Fig. 2 uses a simple two devices module using an IP Camera (more likely to be Pi Camera in case the road does not have CCTV cameras available at that particular point) and a Jetson Nano running an ImageAI model within a Docker Container.

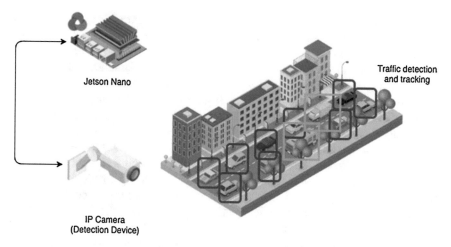

Jetson Nano

Traffic detection
and tracking

IP Camera
(Detection Device)

Fig. 2 Vehicle detection

The model used by the Jetson Nano takes advantage of the GPU core of the device to power efficient vehicle count, identification and tracking. The power of the model resides in its capacity to detect a different kind of vehicles and assess the overall traffic composition. The speed of the cars can be assessed with a satisfying amount of precision using the module Speed-detector [29]. Having this information, we can generate a traffic clogging score—the traffic clogging score is a proportion of the amount of car and the average speed of the traffic a higher number of cars along with a really low speed will be assessed as congestion as both elements interact in the traffic congestion phenomena. Setting thresholds accordingly can help set up a reliable infrastructure for our prediction and decision model. The locality of the prediction models enables to define clogging thresholds for each region observed. The occupancy of the section of the road observed also gives information on how the threshold should be set. We, therefore, have four main elements that will affect the reward definition of our prediction and decision model:

- The number of cars
- The average speed of the cars
- The speed limit of the zone observed
- The maximal occupancy of the road observed

3.3 Data Transmission over Kura

Cloud computing, in spite of its maturity and commercial advancement, has its disadvantages. Some of the limitations are WAN latency, bandwidth and application response time. Data and applications are processed in the cloud where every bit of data is transferred over the network [10]. In the context of IoT, edge refers to the computing infrastructure that exists close to the sources of data, for example, industrial machines (e.g. wind turbine, magnetic resonance (MR) scanner, undersea blowout preventers), industrial controllers such as SCADA systems, and time series databases aggregating data from a variety of equipment and sensors. These edge computing devices typically reside away from the centralized computing available in the cloud. In our case, edge computing refers to the computing of the sensor data at the "edge" of the network using specific smart nodes [3].

Edge computing reduces the latency time and enables faster response to localized issues within the traffic system. In effect, rather than pushing all data to a central server for computation, with latency and non-locality, having a node with a model adapted to its locality can enable faster response in case of eventual congestion.

The implementation of our edge platform goes through the use of an OSGi communication framework called Kura, working in combination with an IoT cloud service called Kapua. Both are Eclipse product running on Java OSGi platform and enabling the communication and exchange of data among IoT devices. With the help of an open-source tool called Kura Wires [14], the design of the system architecture and procedures is made simpler by using data-flow programming. The environment at the edges may consist of low-end devices that are not comparable, e.g. performance or capacity to servers in data center. Personal PC, laptops, mobile devices are some of the common computer power at the edges. Geo-distributed computation at edges requires a platform to be flexible enough to handle application or service deployment and management. The flexibility of candidate platform, i.e. Docker, requires it to be able to deploy reusable service without dependency on heterogeneous devices [10].

The data transmission operated on the system enables fluid communication between the nodes at the edge of the system and the central server. This system is set up to reduce the latency of our operations, allowing at the same time the locality of the models. As presented in Fig. 3, the different smart nodes of the system operate the Kura framework and can therefore interconnect and exchange information over MQTT. MQTT is a machine-to-machine (M2M)/"Internet of Things" connectivity protocol. It was designed as an extremely lightweight publish/subscribe messaging transport. It is useful for connections with remote locations where a small code footprint is required and/or network bandwidth is at a premium [15]. The data collected over one of the Jetson Nano is sent to the Raspberry Pi to orchestrate a hierarchical network, whose operations and authorities are defined by how the Kura network is organized. Each node is allocated processes directly through Kura framework and optionally conveys data to the central server.

The interaction of each device with other devices is defined using Kura Wires as presented in Fig. 4. This software module enables to define the assets and modules accessed and used by each node of the system, along with the timing, storage, and connection to the server. The data collected by each node is accessible through the API framework of the server or directly through the volume of each device. The server access will be important to the observation and control center whereas

Fig. 3 Simple Kura network
architecture

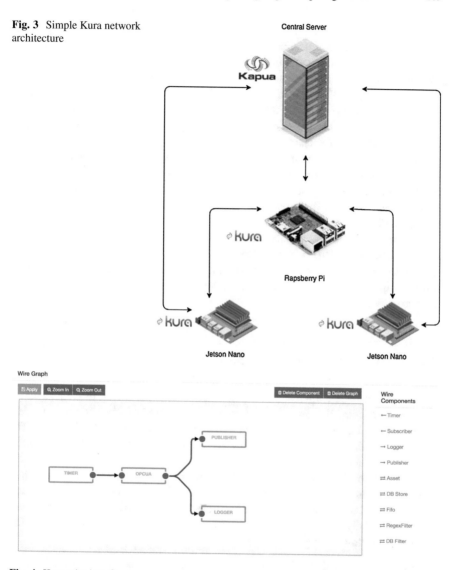

Fig. 4 Kura wire interface

the direct volume access will be important to the prediction and decision model
containers that will require those data. The containers in device proceed to actions
based on the data fed to the device. Similar systems such as Node-RED [16] and
FLOGO [37] provide services close to our needs but Kura gets to the top for its ease
to use and is a tool developed by the company Oracle, hence making it a top option
in term of quality and stability.

One main advantage of Kura is the fact that its operations have a low impact
on the computing performance of the device it is running on. The use of MQTT as

communication protocol reduces the need for large bandwidth or processing power from the device. Kura enables to define how data will be transmitted, produced and consumed by devices. In effect, through Apache Camel Consumer and Apache Camel Producers [36], we are able to define how data will be processed in node and what output data will be sent out of the node. We are able to setup the computing instances within devices, store the results in volume and transmit those results and data to other members of the network. Processing is done in nodes, at the edge of the network through the use of Kura framework. The main disadvantage of Kura is the inability to directly train the data over the smart nodes. This operation would be computationally inefficient based on the nature of the devices. Raspberry Pi and Jetson Nano device do not have the computing capacity to operate training over large clusters of data. This is why data collected is sent to central server to compute training and generate new models.

Kapua is an IoT cloud service that enables the communication and management of Kura devices over the network. Kura devices can be connected to the server and this server gives access to all the data about the devices and the data they provide through direct communication with the server, defined in the Kura Wires structure of each device.

3.4   Docker Swarm Model Deployment

The different models available on our smart nodes are generated by the central server [1]. Due to latency, the central server is only in charge of computing new models for the different devices by following an iterative model as presented in Fig. 5. The computation of models is a high latency operation, thus it is assigned to our central server.

The deployment of prediction and decision models to smart nodes is separated into three main phases which end in the availability of a brand new and more efficient model in our smart nodes. After training of the model operated on server using OpenAI Gym [18], each model is transferred to its corresponding smart node through the following steps:

(1) **Container creation**: Each model generated by the server is pushed into a container using Docker. The YAML description file is created and within it the model newly created. The stack created using docker compose is pushed into the registry and then deployed using Docker Swarm.
(2) **Swarm deployment**: Using the Kapua API, the server has access to each device IP address. That address is the deployment target of the model. The deployment of the stack to each node is operated using Docker Swarm. Each device is equipped with Docker to run the containers provided.

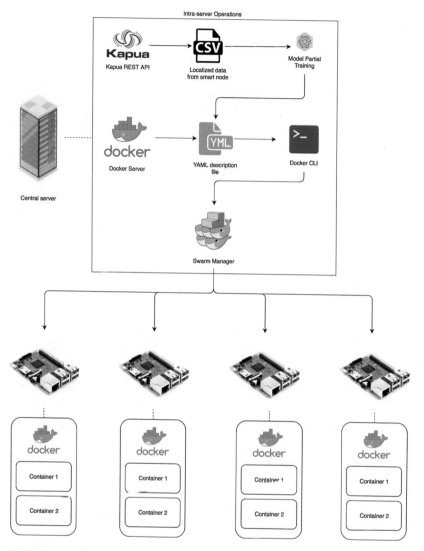

Fig. 5 Model deployment infrastructure

3.5 *Observation System*

The observation system displayed in Fig. 6 is composed of our general flow from detection device to server, with a observation center connected to the server via the Kapua REST API. In effect, Kapua proposes an API to assess the performance, data and tasks completed by the different smart nodes. The observation center is a web interface enabling the user to assess the traffic density, average speed and clogging on a user friendly dashboard using Kapua REST API, AngularJS and PatternFly

Fig. 6 Observation system

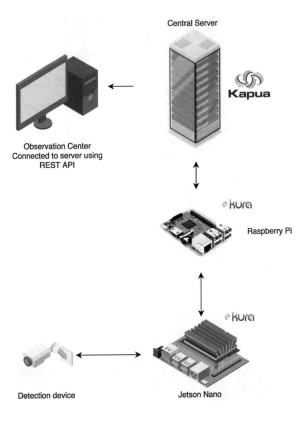

[27]. The control center does not allow direct operation over the devices but enable to user to assess the traffic evolution and the data flow of the system. The observation will display information gathered by each smart node of the system in real-time.

3.6   Reinforcement Learning Prediction and Decision Model

The count and distinction of vehicles, along with the estimation of their average speed is a must in order to understand the traffic flow. Deep Learning algorithms are widely employed in the field of object detection [12]. Using ImageAI, we are able to distinguish, count and track vehicles, along with approximating their average speed at any time. This information is highly important as it will feed our deep reinforced learning decision model.

3.6.1 Data Collection

The detection devices and Jetson Nano smart nodes enable to access the speed and count of the traffic over particular area. Once these two values are computed, the traffic clogging is calculated and represent the main input of our reinforcement learning algorithm. The traffic clogging is given by the formula:

$$tClogging = tCount/tSpeed. \tag{1}$$

3.6.2 Model Training

As defined in Fig. 5, the models of the system are trained in the server. Using the real data collected by the smart nodes and the predictions provided by the models present in those smart nodes, the server can update the utility function of the model and provide a new model to the smart node. This method is used contrarily to continuously updating the model from the node because of the nature of the smart nodes. They do not have enough resource to monitor the performance and continuously train their models.

Reinforcement learning is converges to an optimum. This is mathematically proven in the paper [33], Hence the reason why we use it to train our prediction model. The model is train using the utility function defined in Eq. 2.

$$Util(s_t, a) = E\left\{Reward(s_t, a) + max_{policies} \sum_{j=1}^{N-1} Reward_{t+j}\right\} \tag{2}$$

where s_t is the state at time step t. $Reward(s_t, a)$ is the immediate reward of executing action in state s_t. N is the number of steps in the lifetime of the agent, and $Reward_t$ is the reward at time step t. The operator $E\{\ \}$ stands for taking an expectation over all sources of randomness in the system [28]. Our reward function is defined in Eq. 3.

$$Reward_t = \frac{\log_2 (1 + threshold)}{\left|tClogging_{observed} - tClogging_{predicted}\right| * 10^3} \tag{3}$$

where $\left|tClogging_{observed} - tClogging_{predicted}\right| * 10^3$ is the distance between the observed clogging value and the predicted clogging value, $threshold$ represent the threshold of the observed area and $Reward_t$ represents the reward at time step t.

Using OpenAI Gym, we are able to define our environment structure, with the observation, reward, and parameters necessary to predict the event and generate decision models for our system. Based on the average speed and number of vehicles present during observation, we can define thresholds that will be considered as congestion and will affect the reward of our system. The system predicts congestion

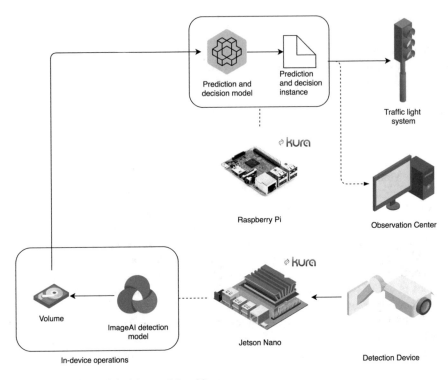

Fig. 7 Prediction and decision model architecture

based on previous conditions and is rewarded based on how close its suggestions are to the real-time traffic clogging.

3.6.3 Model Operation

The decision model presented in Fig. 7 takes advantage of the preprocessing operated through our detection model. In our smart nodes volume are stored data concerning the average speed of the cars along with the current count of cars. That volume data is shared to the authoritative Raspberry Pi through Kura. The decision model and prediction model present in one container access and process the data, with parameters such as the speed limit and the maximal occupancy of the traffic way observed. The models run on the Raspberry Pi present in the network.

Each run of the model will be extended to the next 24 h, giving the prediction a one day heads up. The result is then compared to the current hourly traffic clogging. Based on the comparison results, we establish as reward to the model and define a new training for the next day with the total rewards score. The prediction and decisions are made available to the observation center. The traffic light system is represented using a graph diagram, with each edge given a maximum load (maximal occupancy) and a node representing intersections. Using flow algorithm, we can assess what will be the most efficient way to modify traffic pattern to reduce congestion probabilities [30] over a particular road.

3.7 Blockchain Ledger Operations

Authentication and access control technologies are known as the main elements to address the security issues in the Internet of Things. Blockchain is a distributed ledger technology for secure transaction processing. All transactions in a blockchain are stored into a single ledger [31]. The operations surrounding the blockchain technology in use are oriented toward the overall security of the system and of the ongoing transaction within the different members of the system. Our project uses a private ledger development framework called Hyperledger Fabric. The main goals of the blockchain are to identify and store every communication between the devices part of our system along with the deployment smart contracts that allow the storage of the hash of the latest firmware update on the network [19].

The main weakness of IoT resides in the lack of security in the communication protocol of devices. In the case one hacker would be to use an exploit, he would usually just require the IP address of the device to proceed to alteration of the data. In effect, the data stored in volume can be corrupted if the access to the devices and internal operations are not supervised. This is the reason why blockchain intervenes. Any communication to a sensible port of the device is controlled through consensus. In the case the machine trying to access the device is not validated, the access is denied. With the same design in mind, data computations are controlled and their meta-data is stored on the ledger. As computation can only be realized by models in containers, any signature different than the one of the container currently running will be denied. Such control over access ensures that no unauthorized command or action affects the integrity of the system.

3.7.1 Blockchain Information

Nodes are set up using Docker containers and chaincode to the peers (users of the nodes) to create transactions between themselves. The transactions send key information between the nodes and gets added to the chain. Those information are the Kura identifiers of the two nodes in communication, the identifier of the Kura Envelope, and the timestamp of the transaction as shown in Fig. 8. At this point the information is immutable and may only be appended. In the hyperledger network, all peers can view previous transactions, this provides a transparent and accountable network for the users. As transactions happen between nodes, the system must periodically reach a consensus. A consensus is the point in which all transactions are confirmed between all nodes and become synced.

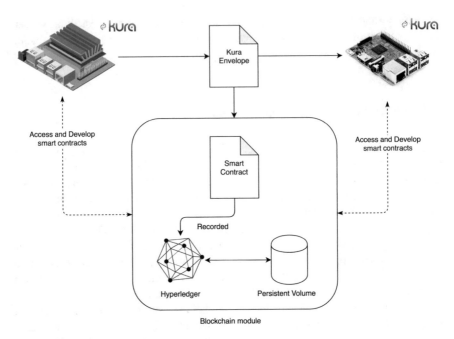

Fig. 8 Hyperledger communication operations

3.7.2 Instantiating the Network

Starting the file titled "docker-compose-simple.yam": This instantiates the chain-code network and brings up the docker containers required to begin the transactions. One of the important one is the CLI container as presented in Fig. 9. This manages the containers and works to bring the network into consensus. In the sample network of 2 nodes (one smart node + server) used for our experiment, the consensus is always reached fast.

3.7.3 Instantiating the Transaction

The transactions are performed by actions from one peer to another by using the command "Invoke" to send data and the command "Query" to check the data. In the CLI, the command is:

```
Peer chaincode invoke
    −n mycc −c '{"Args":
        ["set",
        "envelope_ID",
        "wire_envelope_identifier"]}'
    −C myc
```

```
peer          | 2019-05-24 16:45:07.321 UTC [msp] GetDefaultSigningIdentity -> DE
BU 1ec Obtaining default signing identity
peer          | 2019-05-24 16:45:07.321 UTC [msp.identity] Sign -> DEBU 1ed Sign:
 plaintext: 0A09706565723A37303531
peer          | 2019-05-24 16:45:07.321 UTC [msp.identity] Sign -> DEBU 1ee Sign:
 digest: D18B553283AFC791A71A1AB3F379E85F4599DAAE3CE5B43F6A912E5BFD23E73D
peer          | 2019-05-24 16:45:07.321 UTC [gossip.discovery] periodicalSendAliv
e -> DEBU 1ef Sleeping 5s
peer          | 2019-05-24 16:45:08.507 UTC [gossip.election] waitForInterrupt ->
 DEBU 1f0 f3cfe41cabf0f6322f7e4c6b27c3bc597cac47379afa9a77ccb84a227a349f47 : Exi
ting
peer          | 2019-05-24 16:45:08.507 UTC [gossip.election] IsLeader -> DEBU 1f
1 f3cfe41cabf0f6322f7e4c6b27c3bc597cac47379afa9a77ccb84a227a349f47 : Returning t
rue
peer          | 2019-05-24 16:45:08.508 UTC [msp] GetDefaultSigningIdentity -> DE
BU 1f2 Obtaining default signing identity
peer          | 2019-05-24 16:45:08.508 UTC [msp.identity] Sign -> DEBU 1f3 Sign:
 plaintext: 12036D79631804A201320A20F3CFE41C...120C08A9B6A48FED86EBD01510031801
peer          | 2019-05-24 16:45:08.508 UTC [msp.identity] Sign -> DEBU 1f4 Sign:
 digest: AC46497F7523B10415DDA60D32E892522A8F4D67CA2C99A08B70E5544239B5A3
peer          | 2019-05-24 16:45:08.508 UTC [gossip.election] waitForInterrupt ->
 DEBU 1f5 f3cfe41cabf0f6322f7e4c6b27c3bc597cac47379afa9a77ccb84a227a349f47 : Ent
ering
```

Fig. 9 Docker composer network CLI

The data store in a transaction in the case of this chaincode is a string, which allows for any type of data to be stored with in. Upon a successful query the "wire_envelope_identifier" string would be retrieved when querying for "envelope_ID". The chaincode docker-compose network stores the information, but the network can be run with different chaincode codes by mounting a different image of code when instantiating the CLI.

4 Evaluation and Results

In this part, we evaluated different uses cases and discussed relevant solutions to critical issues that will be solved by our system. We then explained our experimental setup and presented the main results of our analysis.

4.1 Use Cases

The two use cases used in the study are examples of congestion prone areas experiencing high congestion periods that can be solved by our proposed system. We first assess one intersection close to a populated point of interest. Then we look at a highway crossing a heavily populated area. Solving the traffic congestion issues linked to such areas is a major goal for our research.

Fig. 10 Google Maps view of the intersection between South Marietta Parkway SE and Technology Parkway SE

4.1.1 Technology Parkway SE, KSU Marietta Campus

Our very first observation was done over the main entrance of the Marietta Campus of the Kennesaw State University, as shown in Fig. 10.

We observe four 2-way axis coming through our observed intersection presented in Fig. 11. Our prioritized way was Technology Parkway SE with the Traffic ID TPSE01. We had the occupancy and speed limit data provided by TADA traffic control system presented in Table 1, to enable the understanding of the road structure and assess its congested state. This representation makes it easy to assess the traffic flow and define actions oriented toward the reduction of congestion. A one day observation of the traffic occupancy and average speed per hour captured is given in Fig. 12.

The most important analytics for our system is the traffic clogging presented in Fig. 13. The higher the value, the higher the probability of congestion. For this particular area, we set the threshold to be 3 to be considered a congestion. This value defines congestion from 7:30 AM to 9:15 AM and 5:30 PM to 6:15 PM. These are most likely the rush hours of the campus and it explains the congestion at those hours of the day.

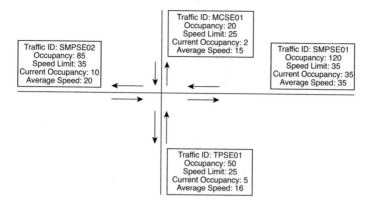

Fig. 11 Graph diagram of the intersection showing the main attributes of the graph

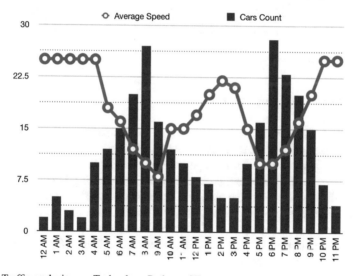

Fig. 12 Traffic analysis over Technology Parkway SE

With a test-bed observing the four main axis of the system in their 2-way design, along with a knowledge of the roads occupancy and speed limits, we are able to train a decision and prediction model that will assess the time and duration of congestion, and provide resolution through traffic light changes.

Limiting incoming traffic from SMPSE01 during the morning and allowing more traffic to exit TPSE01 during the evening will reduce the congestion on the system. This is the objective of the system during the training phase.

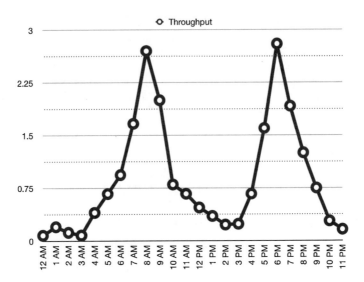

Fig. 13 Traffic clogging on Technology Parkway SE

4.1.2 I-75/I-85 Merging Point, Downtown Atlanta

Contrarily to the previous case axed around an intersection, this problem deals with the congestion of a portion of a highway HWI8575S presented in Fig. 14. In effect, both highways meet with a huge amount of traffic into a single parkway. The limiting agent in this case are the different exits and entering lanes throughout the portion of the highway from the margin point to exit 246. In Fig. 15, we observe that the maximal occupancy of those exits is really small, compared to the occupancy of the highway. Plus, the occupancy of the surrounding roads is also small, making it hard to dissipate highway traffic in the downtown area. Figure 16 gives an insight of the traffic flow in the observed area.

The traffic clogging presented on Fig. 17 shows two major peaks of traffic in the downtown area. For this case, the congestion is set above a traffic clogging of 10. The first one happens in the morning from 6:20 AM to 10 AM and the second one occurs from 3:30 PM to 8PM. These are the main rush hours of the city as they represent the moments when people either get to work or leave work. The bottleneck is the different exits used by the different drivers exiting the highway. Increasing the duration of exits traffic signals to liberate the highway is a solution that our model training so converge toward.

4.2 Experimental Setup

4.2.1 Dataset

The dataset used for our experiment is a 4 h video sequence of a traffic intersection provided by urbantracker of the René-Levesque road [11]. The dataset was evaluated

Fig. 14 Google Maps view of the merging point between I-75 South and I-85 South

Fig. 15 Graph diagram of the highways merging and neighbor exit

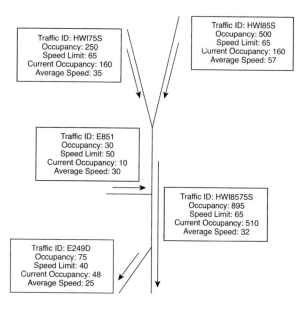

Traffic ID: HWI75S
Occupancy: 250
Speed Limit: 65
Current Occupancy: 160
Average Speed: 35

Traffic ID: HWI85S
Occupancy: 500
Speed Limit: 65
Current Occupancy: 160
Average Speed: 57

Traffic ID: E851
Occupancy: 30
Speed Limit: 50
Current Occupancy: 10
Average Speed: 30

Traffic ID: HWI8575S
Occupancy: 895
Speed Limit: 65
Current Occupancy: 510
Average Speed: 32

Traffic ID: E249D
Occupancy: 75
Speed Limit: 40
Current Occupancy: 48
Average Speed: 25

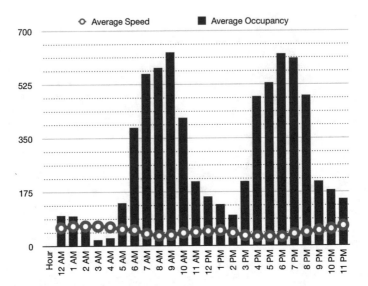

Fig. 16 Traffic analysis over Highway I-85S/I-75S

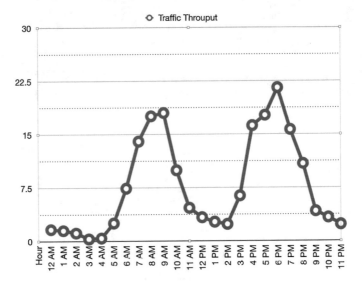

Fig. 17 Traffic clogging for Highway I-85S/I-75S

using ImageAI and Yolo pre-trained model to assess the number of vehicles. With a speed set at 35 mph and an occupancy fixed at 30, we set the value 4 as the threshold for our traffic clogging. The observation provided using ImageAI are displayed in Fig. 18.

Fig. 18 Traffic observation on the Rene-Levesque road

4.2.2 Experimental Environment

The experiment was completed using a single smart node connected to one Kapua server. The main software and hardware configurations of the experiment are as follows:

- Smart Node: Raspberry Pi 3 B+, CPU: ARM Cortex-A53 4-core 1.4 GHz, Wi-Fi: Dual-band 2.4 and 5 GHz, 802.11b/g/n/ac (Broadcom BCM43438), Memory: 1 GB LPDDR2, OS: Raspbian, Kura Version: 4.1.0, Docker version: 2.0.0.3 (31259)
- Server: MacBook Pro, CPU: 2.7 GHz Intel Core i5, Memory: 8 GB 1867 MHz DDR3, OS: Mac OS High Sierra 10.13.6 (17G65), Kapua version: 1.0.4, Docker version: 2.0.0.3 (31259)

4.3 Results and Analysis

We first collected car count and average speed values for the 4 h of observation and organized them over intervals of 10 min. Coupled with the base truth provided by the dataset, we were able to check the accuracy of our detection model. The model is

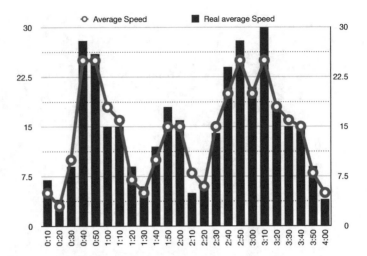

Fig. 19 Speed comparison chart for the Rene-Levesque road

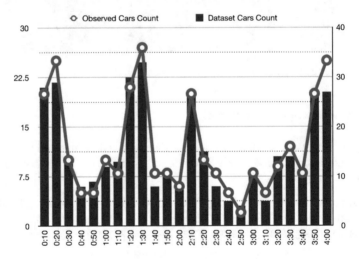

Fig. 20 Cars count comparison chart for the Rene-Levesque road

stored on a container deployed on our Raspberry Pi using Docker Swarm. Figures 19 and 20 show the comparative results.

We decided to train our prediction model based on the clogging of the first 3 h. We then generated the next hour of clogging using our model generated through OpenAI Gym. Figure 21 shows the comparison between the last minutes of our calculated clogging and the predicted clogging.

The prediction proved to be close from the reality but failed as we progressed toward the end of the dataset. Better results can be attained with longer repeated

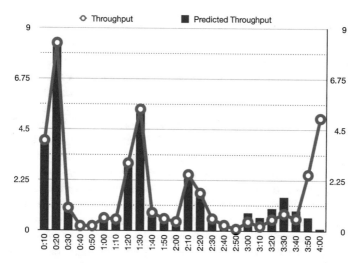

Fig. 21 Clogging comparison for the Rene-Levesque road

Table 2 System benchmarking

Operation observed	Proposed	Benchmark
Prediction model training	16 min	16 min
Docker Swarm model deployment	8.140 s	0 s
Prediction model estimate for next hour	9.610 s	4.871 s
Deployment smart contract	0.643 s	0 s
End to End data transmission	0.827 s	0.030 s

training phases. For a model with high prediction capacity, a better training time is estimated around a week worth of data.

We benchmark our proposed system to assess the time complexity of the main operations of our system. Table 2 gives the results with respect to the time complexity.

To give estimate for the different time complexity, we used the same experimental setup as the one defined in Sect. 4.2 for the proposed system and a single server unit as the benchmark system. The different time complexities for both the proposed and the benchmark systems were evaluated over the same set of data and under similar circumstances for both systems. We observe that the prediction estimate takes a longer time in the smart node + server configuration as the prediction is solely operated on the smart node. Its lack of processing resource compared to the server makes it slow to compute.

One main advantage of our architecture is the load of computation assigned to each smart node. In the case of a 20 points experiment, in which our system includes 20 detection cameras, the load on the server will be higher and each latency will be multiplied by the number of devices operating on the system. While the deployment time for our system increases, the estimate time will not change, along with the data transmission from one end to another.

5 Conclusion

In this paper, we discussed a major economic issue that is traffic congestion and proposed a technological solution. The research conducted on each part of the solution pushed new implementation designs and new concepts whose association could reduce traffic congestion in the observed zones. Our effort to generate a predictive model and ensure a constant evolution of the predictive model is one of the main active aspect of this solution. Using the IoT framework Kura and the IoT cloud server Kapua, we were able to define an edge computing architecture, enabling low latency computations and locality for our models. Blockchain intervene as a security feature of the project by limiting the access to the network devices and preventing alteration of the data transmission. The experimental results gathered show capacity of the system to translate problems into a simpler case, and proceed with prediction results close from reality. The predictions are then used as starting point for the decision model and observation. The future work will focus on the capacity to scale the architectures and take advantage of the containerization and locality. In effect, Docker Swarm enables to configure localized deployments, enabling a node to receive a specific model that is better suited for the area controlled.

References

1. P. Bellavista, A. Zanni, Feasibility of fog computing deployment based on docker containerization over RaspberryPi, pp. 1–10 (2017). https://doi.org/10.1145/3007748.3007777
2. Calipsa (2019), Calipsa. Retrieved April 30, 2019 from http://calipsa.io/
3. J. Cao, Q. Zhang, W. Shi, Challenges and opportunities in edge computing. Springer Briefs in Computer Science (2018), pp. 59–70.https://doi.org/10.1007/978-3-030-02083-5_5 arXiv:arXiv:1609.01967v1
4. DeepQuestAI (2019), ImageAI. Retrieved May 16, 2019 from http://imageai.org/
5. A. Dorri, S.S. Kanhere, R. Jurdak, Blockchain in internet of things: challenges and Solutions. (2016). arXiv:1608.05187 http://arxiv.org/abs/1608.05187
6. Eclipse Foundation (2019), Kura Framework. Retrieved May 10, 2019 from https://www.eclipse.org/kura/
7. A. Frakt (2019), Stats and Analysis. Retrieved April 15, 2019 from https://www.nytimes.com/2019/01/21/upshot/stuck-and-stressed-the-health-costs-of-traffic.html
8. GDOT (2019), Traffic Analysis Data Application. Retrieved May 10, 2019 from https://gdottrafficdata.drakewell.com/publicmultinodemap.asp
9. S. Homayoun, A. Dehghantanha, R.M. Parizi, K.-K.R. Choo, A blockchain-based framework for detecting malicious mobile applications in app stores, in *Proceedings of the 32nd IEEE Canadian Conference of Electrical and Computer Engineering (IEEE CCECE'19)* (2019)
10. B.I. Ismail, E.M. Goortani, M.B. Ab Karim, W.M. Tat, S. Setapa, J.Y. Luke, O.H. Hoe, Evaluation of Docker as edge computing platform. *ICOS 2015 - 2015 IEEE Conference on Open Systems* (2016), pp. 130–135.https://doi.org/10.1109/ICOS.2015.7377291
11. J.-P. Jodoin, G.-A. Bilodeau, N. Saunier, Urban tracker: multiple object tracking in urban mixed traffic, in *IEEE Winter conference on Applications of Computer Vision (WACV14), Steamboat Springs* (2014)

12. S. Li, J. Lin, G. Li, T. Bai, H. Wang, Y. Pang, Vehicle type detection based on deep learning in traffic scene. Proc. Comput. Sci. **131**, 564–572 (2018).https://doi.org/10.1016/j.procs.2018.04.281

13. MIOVISION (2019), Miovision TrafficLink. Retrieved April 20, 2019 from https://miovision.com/trafficlink/

14. A.K. Mondal. [n.d.]. Kura Wires : Design and Development of a Component for managing Devices and Drivers in. (n. d.)

15. MQTT (2019), MQTT. Retrieved May 03, 2019 from http://mqtt.org/

16. Node-RED (2019), Node-RED. Retrieved May 03, 2019 from https://nodered.org/

17. E. Nyaletey, R.M. Parizi, Q. Zhang, K.-K.R. Choo, BlockIPFS - blockchain-enabled inter-planetary file system for forensic and trusted data traceability, in *Proceedings of 2nd IEEE International Conference on Blockchain (IEEE Blockchain-2019)* (2019)

18. OpenAI (2019), OpenAI Gym. Retrieved May 08, 2019 from http://gym.openai.com/

19. A. Outchakoucht, H. ES-Samaali, J. Philippe, Dynamic access control policy based on blockchain and machine learning for the internet of things. Int. J. Adv. Comput. Sci. Appl. **8**(7), 417–424 (2017).https://doi.org/10.14569/ijacsa.2017.080757

20. R.M. Parizi, A. Dehghantanha, On the understanding of gamification in blockchain systems, in *2018 6th International Conference on Future Internet of Things and Cloud Workshops (FiCloudW)* (2018), pp. 214–219. https://doi.org/10.1109/W-FiCloud.2018.00041

21. R.M. Parizi, Amritraj, A. Dehghantanha, Smart contract programming languages on blockchains: an empirical evaluation of usability and security, in *Blockchain – ICBC 2018*, ed. by S. Chen, H. Wang, L.-J. Zhang (Springer, Cham, 2018), pp. 75–91

22. R.M. Parizi, A. Dehghantanha, K.-K.R. Choo, A. Singh, Empirical vulnerability analysis of automated smart contracts security testing on blockchains, in *Proceedings of the 28th Annual International Conference on Computer Science and Software Engineering (CASCON '18)* (IBM Corp., Riverton, NJ, 2018), pp. 103–113. http://dl.acm.org/citation.cfm?id=3291291.3291303

23. R.M. Parizi, S. Homayoun, A. Yazdinejad, A. Dehghantanha, K.-K.R. Choo, Integrating privacy enhancing techniques into blockchains using sidechains, in *Proceedings of the 32nd IEEE Canadian Conference of Electrical and Computer Engineering (IEEE CCECE'19)* (2019)

24. K. Peterson, R. Deeduvanu, P. Kanjamala, K. Boles, A blockchain-based approach to health information exchange networks. Colleaga (Jan 2018). https://www.colleaga.org/tools/blockchain-based-approach-health-information-exchange-networks

25. K. Pyzyk, Stats and Analysis (2018). Retrieved May 2, 2019 from https://www.smartcitiesdive.com/news/gridlock-woes-traffic-congestion-by-the-numbers/519959/

26. M.A. Quddus, C. Wang, S.G. Ison, Road traffic congestion and crash severity: an econometric analysis using ordered response models. J. Transp. Eng. **136**(5) 424–435 (Jan 2010). https://ascelibrary.org/doi/10.1061/%28ASCE%29TE.1943-5436.0000044

27. Red Hat (2019), PatternFly. Retrieved May 14, 2019 from https://www.patternfly.org/v4/

28. S. Singh, P. Norvig, D. Cohn, How to make software agents do the right thing: an introduction to reinforcement learning, in *Adaptive Systems Group* (1996)

29. R. Sinha, Speed-Detector (2018). Retrieved May 10, 2019 from https://github.com/ronitsinha/speed-detector

30. D. Srinivasan, M.C. Choy, R.L. Cheu, Neural networks for real-time traffic signal control. IEEE Trans. Intell. Transp. Syst. **7**(3), 261–272 (2006).https://doi.org/10.1109/TITS.2006.874716

31. A. Stanciu, Blockchain based distributed control system for edge computing, in *Proceedings - 2017 21st International Conference on Control Systems and Computer, CSCS 2017* (2017), pp. 667–671.https://doi.org/10.1109/CSCS.2017.102

32. SURTRAC (2018), SURTRAC Intelligent Traffic Control System. Retrieved May 4, 2019 from https://www.rapidflowtech.com/surtrac

33. C. Szepesvári, The asymptotic convergence-rate of Q-learning, in *Advances in Neural Information Processing Systems*, vol. 10, ed. by M.I. Jordan, M.J. Kearns, S.A. Solla (MIT Press, 1998), pp. 1064–1070. http://papers.nips.cc/paper/1383-the-asymptotic-convergence-rate-of-q-learning.pdf

34. B. Tang, Z. Chen, G. Hefferman, W. Tao, H. He, Q. Yang, A hierarchical distributed fog computing architecture for big data analysis in smart cities, in *Proceedings of the ASE Big Data and Social Informatics 2015*, October 2015, p. 6. https://doi.org/10.1145/2818869.2818898

35. P.J. Taylor, T. Dargahi, A. Dehghantanha, R.M. Parizi, K.-K.R. Choo, A systematic literature review of blockchain cyber security. Digit. Commun. Netw. (2019).https://doi.org/10.1016/j.dcan.2019.01.005

36. The Apache Software Foundation (2015), Apache Camel. Retrieved May 05, 2019 from https://camel.apache.org/

37. TIBCO Software Inc. 2019. FLOGO. Retrieved May 02, 2019 from https://www.flogo.io/

38. Transport & Environment (T&E) (2014), CO2 emissions from Cars: The Facts. Technical Report August, https://www.dbresearch.de/PROD/DBR_INTERNET_EN-PROD/PROD0000000000346332/CO2+emissions+from+cars:+Regulation+via+EU+Emissio.pdf

39. TELEGRA (2018), Smart Traffic Management. Retrieved April 18, 2019 from https://www.telegra-europe.com/

40. S. Tuli, R. Mahmud, S. Tuli, R. Buyya, FogBus: A blockchain-based lightweight framework for Edge and Fog computing. J. Syst. Softw. **154**, 22–36 (2019).https://doi.org/10.1016/j.jss.2019.04.050

41. A. Yazdinejad, R.M. Parizi, A. Dehghantanha, K.-K.R. Choo, Blockchain-enabled authentication handover with efficient privacy protection in SDN-based 5G networks. CoRR abs/1905.03193 (2019). arXiv:1905.03193 http://arxiv.org/abs/1905.03193

Blockchain Applications in Power Systems: A Bibliometric Analysis

Hossein Mohammadi Rouzbahani, Hadis Karimipour, Ali Dehghantanha, and Reza M. Parizi ⓘ

Abstract Power systems are growing rapidly, due to ever-increasing demand for electrical power. These systems require novel methodologies and modern tools and technologies, to better perform, particularly for communication among different parts. Therefore, power systems are facing new challenges such as energy trading and marketing and cyber threats. Using blockchain in power systems, as a solution, is one of the newest methods. Most studies aim to investigate innovative approaches of blockchain application in power systems. Even though, many articles published to support the research activities, there has not been any bibliometric analysis which specifies the research trends. This paper aims to present a bibliographic analysis of the blockchain application in power systems related literature, in the Web of Science (WoS) database between January 2009 and July 2019. This paper discusses the research activities and performed a detailed analysis by looking at the number of articles published, citations, institutions, research area, and authors. From the analysis, it was concluded that there are several significant impacts of research activities in China and USA, in comparison to other countries.

1 Introduction

Power systems are experiencing swift changes due to the rapid growth of electricity demand, which is expected to grow further by around 30% in 2035 [1, 2]. While, power systems are facing challenges because of new technology developments,

H. M. Rouzbahani · H. Karimipour (✉)
University of Guelph, Guelph, ON, Canada
e-mail: hmoham15@uoguelph.ca; hkarimi@uoguelph.ca

A. Dehghantanha
Cyber Science Lab, School of Computer Science, University of Guelph, Guelph, ON, Canada
e-mail: adehghan@uoguelph.ca

R. M. Parizi
College of Computing and Software Engineering, Kennesaw State University, Marietta, GA, USA
e-mail: rparizi1@kennesaw.edu

© Springer Nature Switzerland AG 2020
K.-K. R. Choo et al. (eds.), *Blockchain Cybersecurity, Trust and Privacy*, Advances in Information Security 79, https://doi.org/10.1007/978-3-030-38181-3_7

Fig. 1 Power system changes and challenges

security concerns, new market patterns, consumer demand changes, etc. [3, 4]. There are some permanent challenges such as stability, reliability, environmental concerns, and costs [5].

Various type of methods have been employed over the years for solving problems in different sections and improving the performance of the power systems [3, 6–15], but some of these problems are related to the growing network and its integration. Due to using distributed generation in power systems (which is one of the main reasons for network growth) and using communication tools and smart meters, marketing and communication in power networks require new and up-to-date methods. It should be noted power systems are on the edge of entering the digital era by a massive deployment of in most countries in the world [3, 16]. Figure 1 shows the summary of the content discussed.

Central management and operation are becoming ever more challenging because of the need for an advanced communication and data exchanges among different parts of the power network [17]. On the other hand, the decentralization of the property, and the decision-making process are complex which are evolving the Information Technologies [8, 9, 18]. Thus, to accommodate these decentralization and digitalization trends, local distributed control and management techniques are in need [19]. The importance of this issue has led many researchers to seek new methodologies and concepts to improve the performance and security of the power systems [13, 15, 20, 21]. Application of blockchain is one of the newest ones.

Blockchain, also called distributed ledger, is a technology, by a set of nodes that do not fully trust each other, which first was proposed in 2008 [22, 23]. This technology is designed to secure data storage and transfer through decentralized, trustless, peer-to-peer systems with no participation of a third party which records transactions of value using a cryptographic signature [22, 24, 25]. Blockchain started from cryptocurrency, grew in assets and credit field, and increasingly found its place in information and communication field. Various industries have realized the value of the blockchain and how this technology is secure and reliable as a technical solution. This technical solution allows users to contribute jointly in data computing, storage, authenticity verification and the preserving the reliable database [26, 27].

Early research shows that blockchain technology could potentially provide solutions to some of the challenges faced by power systems and it can be used for different concepts of the power system due to the decentralized structure (e.g.

privacy and security, energy trading and marketing, using new communication and smart tools). Regarding privacy and security in power systems, Dorri et al. [28] applied blockchain to Direct Load Control to protect user privacy and security of communications. Yang et al. [29] proposed an algorithm, applied to a self-organized cyber-physical power system, which has short blockchain construction time and achieves better data block exchange performance. Liang [30] showed how blockchain technology can be used to enhance the robustness and security of the power grid.

In terms of energy trading and marketing, recently, blockchain has been an interesting topic for many researchers and companies. Aitzhan and Svetinovic [31] proposed using blockchain to build a decentralized energy trading system. To secure the energy trading transactions in their token-based system, multi-signatures and anonymous encrypted message propagation streams were used. Mannaro et al. [32] developed a blockchain-based platform to recommend the best trading strategy for prosumers in the renewable energy market.

In addition, some blockchain projects have focused on energy trading, especially renewable energy, and smart tools. It should be noted, most of these projects are still in the testing phase or under development. The PWR Company developed Ethereum-based solutions for trading renewable energy and installed deep cycle batteries for consumers for power storage to stabilize the grid, instead of selling the energy immediately. SolarCoin, PowerLedger, Key2Energy and TheSunExchange aim is to increase solar energy production and facilitate the trade of this type of energy [33]. NRGcoin [34] is currently at the conceptual stage, uses smart contracts framework which is based on Ethereum for trading an energy-based cryptocurrency. Regardless of the retail value of electricity, one NRGcoin is equivalent to 1 kWh. Share & Charge [35] developed a network of electric vehicle (EV) charging stations and owners of charging stations can register their station and set tariffs for charging. Finally, some projects are focused on smart metering tools for increasing the performance of power systems in fields of energy trading and privacy and security such as Bankymoon [36] and the Electron company [37]. These examples demonstrate that the research activities conducted in this field are significant. However, no bibliometric analysis has been done to report the impacts and trends of such researches.

Bibliometric allows researchers to understand the characteristics, structure, and patterns of research activities. Also, the research activities are combined into a realistic trend of a research domain by this statistical analysis. This involves literature studies of scientific activities in different contexts such as publications, authors, institutions, citations, and countries. Moreover, this method reports on the comprehensive evaluation of the expansion of research fields [38].

The purpose of this study is to well understand the state-of-the-art application of blockchain in power systems. It is vital to identify top-tier researchers, organization and institutes, and collaboration amongst them as well as hot topics. To address these questions, we aim to make a bibliometric analysis on relevant papers published in the Web of Science from 2009 to 2019.

The outline of this paper is as follows. We present the research method in Sect. 2. Thereafter in Sect. 3 findings and information about using blockchain in power systems are presented. Section 4 is the conclusion to the study.

2 Methodology

The citation analysis in academic papers was initiated by Garfield [39]. Bibliometrics was defined by Pritchard as the application of mathematics and statistical methods to books and other media of communication and is the oldest research methods in library and information science [40]. Bibliometric contains various applications from information science, sociology and history of science to research evaluation [41]. This method is used to evaluate, monitor and visualize the structure of scientific fields [42]. Bibliometric methods can be divided in two parts: general instructions and publication analysis. For general instructions, researchers show how to avoid possible sources of error in the search process by showing how to search article using a search engine. However, the evaluation of publication such as impact factor, citations, publisher, and country described in publication analysis [38]. In general, citation analysis and content analysis are two widely used bibliometric methods. Citation analysis helps to identify core literatures, journals, countries, etc., and shows a relationship between citing and cited works in a research area [43]. For examples Dabbagh [44] studied the Evolution of Blockchain, and analyzed scientific production of Geographical Information System (GIS) in Web of Science, and WL. Woon and Zeineldin [45] presented a bibliometric based study on distributed generation. Three main bibliometrics data sources for searching the literature are Web of Science, Scopus, Google Scholar. These sources are generally used to rank journals in terms of their productivity and the total citation received to indicate the journal impact, prestige or influence. In this paper, the WoS data is selected to complete the bibliometric analysis based on the following reasons.

Web of science is the most famous tool for bibliometrics analysis and until the creation of Scopus and Google Scholar in 2004 [46], and it used to be the only tool and contains great features. This bibliometrics tool has over 12,000 titles of journals since 1900–present, covers 45 Languages, and provides citation analysis by author, country, document type, institution, language, publication year, source title, subject area and funding information. Web of Science contains citation maps which helps to visualize the result of the citing references. The cited reference search in WOS is a unique feature that cannot be found in any other databases [47]. In addition, 94% of Scopus highest impact factor journals were indexed in WoS [48].

After using Web of Science as the search engine of this study, we identified some related keywords to start the process of extracting papers. There are some equivalent for Blockchain such as distributed ledger and cryptocurrency [49]. Also, the power network sometimes named by power network or electrical power system [50]. So, the inquiry to collect the data for bibliometric analysis was as follows: (TS = ((Blockchain OR Distributed ledger OR Cryptocurrency) AND (Power System OR Power Network OR Electrical Power Network))). The time

Fig. 2 The schematic of data collection process

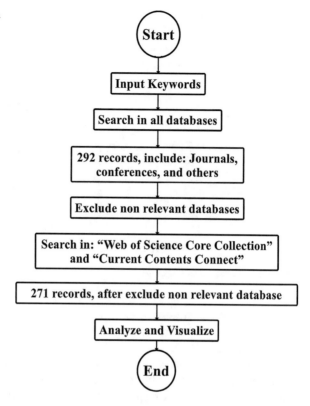

period for this study, was limited to the past decade (between 2009 and 2019). As a result, we detected a total of 291 publications from various journals, books, conferences, and patterns. For this analysis, two following databases were selected: "Web of Science Core Collection" and "Current Contents Connect". To remove unrelated publications such as patterns and non-English publications, we excluded other databases. As a result, 271 articles were secured for this analysis' purposes. This process is shown in Fig. 2. The criteria of this bibliometric analysis are: (a) productivity, (b) research areas, (c) institutions, (d) authors, (e) Impact Publishers, (f) highly cited articles and (g) keyword frequency. Figure 2 is provided for illustration. It should be noted, there is no result before 2014. So, in the rest of this research, presented results will be limited to 2014–2019.

3 Findings

In this section, we discuss the finding of the bibliometric analysis for blockchain application in power systems. The results detect high-quality research to support researchers enhancing research in this field. Finding section is divided into 7 sub-

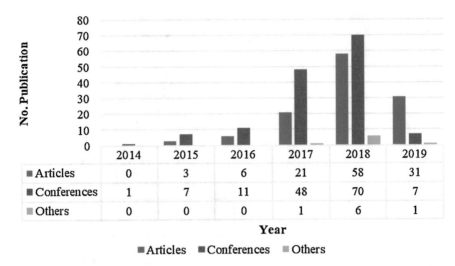

Fig. 3 The number of publications

topics: productivity, research areas, institutions, impact journals, authors, highly cited articles and keyword frequency. Figure 3 shows the number of publications between 2014 and 2019.

Figure 3 shows three categories of publications including journals, conferences, and other types (reviews, editorials and abstracts) which are extracted from various studies related to blockchain application in power systems. The conference category has the highest proportion of the total publications by 56.16% in this time period. However, in 2019, as of 21 Jun 2019, the share of articles has been about 79.5% (30 of 39) which shows a significant increase in this type of documents. This value for 2018 was 43.2%. It is more likely that the journal publications would increase even more in the remaining of 2019.

As it mentioned previously, citation analysis is used to recognize the frequency of the journals and to evaluate researchers' performance. Also, this analysis provides an overview of the topic studied and information about researchers to other researchers using common references. It has been realizing that there are two major types of publications in the academic research study. These publications focusing on originality and developers of the contents to show the significance of research.

The citation is a way of showing the evidence of material in the publications to illustrate the increasing number of research activities that contributed to the high impact of publications. Figure 4 demonstrates the citations received bythe publications over the last 6 years. As the number of publications has increased the number of citations has been also increased. The earlier publication which stays in the database for a longer period of time, has the higher chance to be cited. The average number of citations is about 218 annually during 2014–2018. The number of annual citations shows a positive trend with a distinct peak occurring in 2018. The citation has increased by about fivefold in 2018 when compared to 2017. Given that

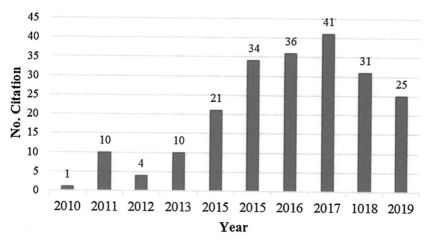

Fig. 4 The number of citation

the study was conducted in June 2019, it is expected to see the number of citations to be higher than 2018 for 2019.

3.1 Productivity

The productivity of the countries, which refers to the frequency or the number of publications, is presented in this section. A study of productivity growth of articles reflects the attentions and overall strength of different countries in the related research fields. It also shows strengthen of the research mechanisms while leading research involving analysis on blockchain application in power systems. The focus on productivity analysis helps to enhance and improve the production efficiency of the publications. This also assesses which countries have produced more publications.

Figure 5 shows that China and the United States are the lead countries in the number of publications and data show these two countries contributed to almost half of the entire publications related to blockchain application in power systems. As Table 1 shows, this is followed by South Korea, England, and Australia.

3.2 Research Areas

To measure the research performance based on citation and publication rates, researchers use research areas which shows the trend of the publication over time. Research areas develop a logical understanding of explicit research areas and how these challenge other areas in different sectors of the industries. Table 2 shows more details about research areas.

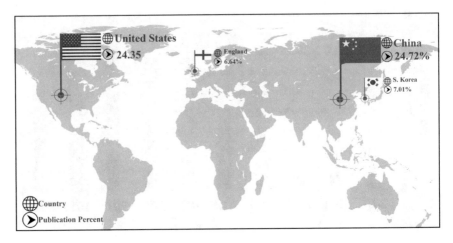

Fig. 5 The most productive countries

Table 1 Productivity

Country	Publication (No)	Publication (%)
China	67	24.72
United States	66	24.35
South Korea	19	7.01
England	18	6.64
Australia	16	5.90
Italy	15	5.54
Singapore	15	5.54
Germany	14	5.16
India	12	4.48
France	10	3.79
Canada	9	3.32
Romania	9	3.32
Japan	8	2.95
Norway	6	2.21
Austria	5	1.84
Poland	5	1.84
Russia	5	1.84
Scotland	5	1.84
Switzerland	5	1.84
United Arab Emirates	5	1.84

Table 2 shows that the majority of the publications fall under computer science and engineering areas. In this regard, computer science and engineering are the two main research areas for blockchain application in power systems.

Table 2 Research areas

Research areas	Publication (No)	Publication (No)
Computer science	187	69.00
Engineering	154	56.82
Energy fuels	97	35.79
Telecommunication	64	23.61
Business economics	60	22.14
Communication	47	17.34
Mathematics	26	9.59
Automation control systems	25	9.22
Science technology	17	6.27
Instrument instrumentation	10	3.69
Government law	4	1.47
Physics	4	1.47
Educational research	3	1.10
Materials science	3	1.10
Robotics	3	1.10
Transportation	3	1.10
Optics	2	0.74
Social work	2	0.74
Development studies	1	0.37
Mechanics	1	0.37
Nuclear science technology	1	0.37

3.3 Institutions

This section discusses the number of publications noted according to various institutions and measures different institution's quality according to their publications. Also, it identifies which of these institutions are currently active. Table 3 lists the institutions which conducted research related to blockchain application in power systems. The table shows that institutions in China in total have the highest number of publications. According to this table, the Chinese Academy of Sciences and Nanyang Technological University have the highest number of publications. The most prominent institutions in Asia are located in China. It seems that the speed of publication about using blockchain in power systems, in China is much faster than the other countries in the world. This evidence suggests that there is keen competition among institutions across China in terms publications.

3.4 Authors

This section discusses the number of publications noted according to authors in various countries to identify who is the most active in terms of authorship. Table 4 lists the findings for authors who are the most productive. As the table illustrates, the majority of the authors are from China, Australia, Denmark, Italy, and Singapore. It

Table 3 Institution

Institution	Publication (No)	Publication (%)	Country
Chinese Academy of Sciences	10	10	China
Nanyang Technological University	10	10	Singapore
National University of Singapore	6	6	Singapore
University of California	6	6	United States
Beijing University of P&T	5	5	China
Politehnica University of Bucharest	5	5	Romania
Shanghai Jiao Tong University	5	5	China
UESTC	5	5	China
UNSW Sydney	5	5	Australia
University of Aalborg	4	4	Denmark
Chung-Ang University	4	4	South Korea
NUDT	4	4	China
Tsinghua University	4	4	China
United States Department of Energy	4	4	United States
University of Illinois	4	4	United States
The University of Newcastle	4	4	Australia
Chongqing University	3	3	China

Table 4 List of authors

Authors	Publication (No)	Publication (%)	Country
Yan Chen	4	1.47	China
Pietro Danzi	4	1.47	Denmark
Aggelos Kiayias	4	1.47	Greece
Petar Popovski	4	1.47	Denmark
Prateek Saxena	4	1.47	Singapore
Cedomir Stefanovic	4	1.47	Denmark
Jun Wang	4	1.47	Australia
Xiaonan Wang	4	1.47	Singapore
Yong Yuan	4	1.47	China
Yan Zhang	4	1.47	Norway
Ryosuke Abe	3	1.11	Japan
Matthew Davison	3	1.11	Australia
Maria Di Silvestre	3	1.11	Italy
Fei Yue Wang	3	1.11	China
Nikos Leonardos	3	1.11	Greece
Yang Li	3	1.11	Canada
Loi Luu	3	1.11	Singapore
Cristina Roscia	3	1.11	Italy
Eleonora Sanseverino	3	1.11	Italy
Terrence Summers	3	1.11	Australia
Christopher Townsend	3	1.11	Australia
Ping Wang	3	1.11	Canada
Hui Yang	3	1.11	China
Xiaosong Zhang	3	1.11	China
Gaetano Zizzo	3	1.11	Italy

appears some other countries such as Greece, Canada, Norway, and Japan are also able to contribute to many publications.

3.5 Publishers

This section discusses the list of publishers which published the most publications about blockchain application in power systems. This section is important as it shows the most leading journals, conferences, and book series in publications and the ones which have the highest citations. This information helps researchers to identify the high-quality journals and conferences to strengthen their work by publishing in them. Table 5 lists some publishers titles with the greatest number of publications in the field. It shows that the greatest number of publications belongs to the IEEE Access journal and Lecture Notes in Computer Sciences book series and followed by other journals such as Energies and Sensors.

Table 5 demonstrates that IEEE Journals and Conferences are major publishers in terms of blockchain application in power systems. It shows that Lecture Notes in Computer Science received 67,051 citations over the years followed by Applied Energy and Sensors with 42,891 and 25,150 citations respectively. This table also illustrates that journals with dominant citations per document by a remarkable difference from the rest, are IEEE Internet of Things Journal, Applied Energy, and IEEE Transactions on Industrial Informatics. As a whole, the quality of high impact journals attracts researchers to publish their articles because it widely read by the other researcher and increases their citations.

Table 5 List of publishers

Title	Type	P	TC	CD	CPD
IEEE access	Journals	12	19,132	3277	4.944
Lecture notes in computer science	Book Series	12	67,051	25,610	1.120
Energies	Journals	8	12,160	3202	3.178
Sensors	Journals	6	25,150	5692	3.715
ICRERA	Conferences	5	251	99	1.873
Applied energy	Journals	4	42,891	4416	9.593
IEEE ICSGC	Conferences	3	210	90	1.680
Future generation computer systems	Journals	3	4600	658	6.897
IEEE internet of things journal	Journals	3	4529	369	11.613
IEEE spectrum	Journals	3	383	133	0.934
IEEE transactions on industrial informatics	Journals	3	6348	676	8.878
ICPADS	Conferences	3	256	134	0.959
Sustainability	Journals	3	13,827	3781	3.029

P publication No, *TC* total cites, *CD* cited documents, *CPD* citations per document (2015–2018)

3.6 Highly-Cited Articles

This section illustrates the quality and influence of research done in using blockchain in power systems by assessing the number of citations received by each publication. Table 6 lists the top 15 most cited publications, number of times cited, type to about 5.53% of the total publications. Moreover, the top highly-cited publication was published 4 years ago, showing compliance with the concept that the longer the publications have been in the database, the higher the number of citations accumulated. Even though the blockchain is a new advent technology and

Table 6 Top 15 highly-cited publications

Title	Times cited
The Bitcoin backbone protocol: analysis and applications	116
Blockchain technology in the chemical industry: machine-to-machine electricity market	63
Security and privacy in decentralized energy trading through multi-signatures, blockchain and anonymous messaging streams	61
Enabling localized peer-to-peer electricity trading among plug-in hybrid electric vehicles using consortium blockchains	60
Blockstack: a global naming and storage system secured by blockchains	52
A secure sharding protocol for open blockchains	51
Industry 4.0: state of the art and future trends	45
A blockchain-based smart grid: towards sustainable local energy markets	41
Blockchain based decentralized management of demand response programs in smart energy grids	38
Analyzing the Bitcoin network: the first four years	26
Consortium blockchain for secure energy trading in industrial internet of things	25
Research on the technology and economic calculation model of power transmission line considering environmental benefits	22
Citizen utilities: the emerging power paradigm	21
Privacy-preserving and efficient aggregation based on blockchain for power grid communications in smart communities	20
Cryptocurrencies without proof of work	20

there is no publication about blockchain application in power systems prior to 2014, the number of citations for publications in this field is high.

Of the articles published, the most cited was "Blockchain technology in the chemical industry: Machine-to-machine electricity market". This paper investigated blockchain application and presented a scenario including two electricity producers and one electricity consumer trading with together based on blockchain. It can be concluded that highly cited articles are high quality research in which the researcher recognizes other author's findings, ideas, methods, and influence in certain fields. As a whole, if the topic in articles is more interesting, it increases journal citations particularly when the subject is more special.

3.7 Keywords Frequency

This section discusses the type of keywords which are frequently used by researchers. These keywords could be used to analyze and identify research trends and gaps. Table 7 provides a list of unique keywords and title occurrences. This list was derived from a total of 5958 keywords and 701 titles that had appeared in 271 publications between 2014 and 2019.

Table 7 shows that the most relevant title and keyword is blockchain. This table also shows that blockchain and power system are consistently used in the literature.

To provide an in-depth analysis, Fig. 6 presents a word map based on a content analysis of the publications. According to this map, the keywords are divided into 3 clusters in which two clusters are more specific. One of these clusters highlighted by key terms which are related to "cryptocurrency", "bitcoin", "protocol", "attack", "reward" and another one contains keywords such as "microgrid", "energy", "market", "electric vehicle". In addition, "power system", "blockchain", and "energy" were noted as terms that act as links between the research topics.

Table 7 Frequency of keywords in titles and abstracts

Titles	Frequency	Keywords	Frequency
Blockchain	93	Blockchain	364
System	33	Power system	136
Bitcoin	21	Protocol	95
Analysis	12	Energy	90
Microgrid	12	Market	84
Application	11	Miner	75
Attack	10	Block	58
Power system	10	Cost	55
Cryptocurrency	9	Smart contract	46
Mining	8	Vehicle	46
Security	8	Mining	43
IOT	7	Management	40
Smart grid	6	Privacy	40
Energy trading	6	Method	38
Privacy	5	Grid	36

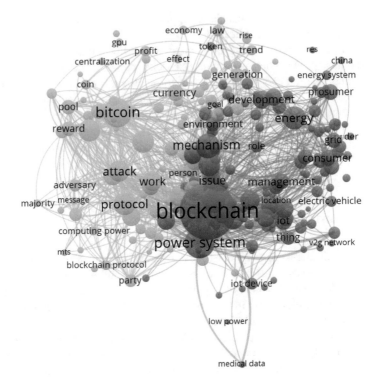

Fig. 6 Keywords map

4   Conclusions

In this paper, we used WoS as the literature source for the bibliometric analysis of blockchain application in power system from January 2014 to June 21, 2019. Seven criteria including productivity, research areas, institutions, authors, impact publishers, highly cited articles, and keyword frequency have been used in this study. Using these criteria, we uncovered the global trends and frontiers related to our subject. Between 2014 and 2018, it was noted that the number of publications related to blockchain application in power system had increased with an average annual growth rate of 418%. The analysis also indicated that the trend of blockchain publications experienced speedy progress with increased article publications and citations during this time period.

It was noted that China and the United States are the lead countries with the most publications produced in academic research. Then, we showed that the majority of the publications fall under computer science and engineering.

Our analysis had indicated that IEEE Journals and Conferences are the major publishers in terms of blockchain application in power systems. This study also highlighted the active authors in terms of publications in different countries. Among the top 15 most active authors, there are 10 authors with 4 publications in this field. Finally, a map analysis of keyword frequencies had been used to describe the trends and research directions for future studies in blockchain application in power system field.

References

1. L. Abdallah, T. El-Shennawy, Reducing carbon dioxide emissions from electricity sector using smart electric grid applications. J. Eng. **2013**, 1–8 (2013). https://doi.org/10.1155/2013/845051
2. H.M. Ruzbahani, H. Karimipour, Optimal incentive-based demand response management of smart households. in *2018 IEEE/IAS 54th Industrial and Commercial Power Systems Technical Conference (I&CPS)* (2018), pp. 1–7. https://doi.org/10.1109/ICPS.2018.8369971
3. H. Karimipour, A. Dehghantanha, R.M. Parizi, K.-K.R. Choo, H. Leung, A deep and scalable unsupervised machine learning system for cyber-attack detection in large-scale smart grids. IEEE Access **7**, 80778–80788 (2019). https://doi.org/10.1109/ACCESS.2019.2920326
4. D. Tan, Energy challenge, power electronics & systems (PEAS) technology and grid modernization. CPSS Trans. Power Electron. Appl. **2**(1), 3–11 (2017). https://doi.org/10.24295/CPSSTPEA.2017.00002
5. H. Rouzbahani, Smart households demand response management with micro grid (n.d.). Arxiv.Org. Retrieved from https://arxiv.org/abs/1907.03641
6. V. Dinavahi, H. Karimipour, Parallel relaxation-based joint dynamic state estimation of large-scale power systems. IET Gener. Transm. Distrib. **10**(2), 452–459 (2016). https://doi.org/10.1049/iet-gtd.2015.0808
7. F. Ghalavand, I. Al-Omari, H. Karimipour, Hybrid islanding detection for ac/dc network using DC-link voltage (n.d.). Ieeexplore.Ieee.Org. Retrieved from https://ieeexplore.ieee.org/abstract/document/8499479/
8. F. Ghalavand, B. Alizade, H. Gaber, H. Karimipour, Microgrid islanding detection based on mathematical morphology. Energies **11**(10), 2696 (2018a). https://doi.org/10.3390/en11102696
9. F. Ghalavand, B. Alizade, H. Gaber, H. Karimipour, F. Ghalavand, B.A.M. Alizade, H. Karimipour, Microgrid islanding detection based on mathematical morphology. Energies **11**(10), 2696 (2018b). https://doi.org/10.3390/en11102696
10. H. Karimipour, International, On false data injection attack against dynamic state estimation on smart power grids (n.d.). Ieeexplore.Ieee.Org. Retrieved from https://ieeexplore.ieee.org/abstract/document/8052831/
11. H. Karimipour, Power, Accelerated parallel WLS state estimation for large-scale power systems on GPU (n.d.). Ieeexplore.Ieee.Org. Retrieved from https://ieeexplore.ieee.org/abstract/document/6666827/
12. H. Karimipour, Power, On detailed synchronous generator modeling for massively parallel dynamic state estimation (n.d.). Ieeexplore.Ieee.Org. Retrieved from https://ieeexplore.ieee.org/abstract/document/6965417/
13. H. Karimipour, V. Dinavahi, On false data injection attack against dynamic state estimation on smart power grids. in *2017 IEEE International Conference on Smart Energy Grid Engineering (SEGE)* (2017), pp. 388–393. https://doi.org/10.1109/SEGE.2017.8052831
14. H. Karimipour, V. Dinavahi, Robust massively parallel dynamic state estimation of power systems against cyber-attack. IEEE Access **6**, 2984–2995 (2018). https://doi.org/10.1109/ACCESS.2017.2786584

15. J. Sakhnini, H. Karimipour, A. Dehghantanha, Smart grid cyber attacks detection using supervised learning and heuristic feature selection (2019). Retrieved from http://arxiv.org/abs/1907.03313
16. S. Zhou, M.A. Brown, Smart meter deployment in Europe: a comparative case study on the impacts of national policy schemes. J. Clean. Prod. **144**, 22–32 (2017). https://doi.org/10.1016/j.jclepro.2016.12.031
17. A.J. Goldsmith, S.B. Wicker, Design challenges for energy-constrained ad hoc wireless networks. IEEE Wirel. Commun. **9**(4), 8–27 (2002). https://doi.org/10.1109/MWC.2002.1028874
18. R. Mijumbi, J. Serrat, J.-L. Gorricho, N. Bouten, F. De Turck, R. Boutaba, Network function virtualization: state-of-the-art and research challenges. IEEE Commun. Surv. Tutorials **18**(1), 236–262 (2016). https://doi.org/10.1109/COMST.2015.2477041
19. U. Ahsan, A. Bais, Distributed big data management in smart grid. in *2017 26th Wireless and Optical Communication Conference (WOCC)* (2017), pp. 1–6. https://doi.org/10.1109/WOCC.2017.7928971
20. E. Dovom, A. Azmoodeh, D.-J. Karimipour, Fuzzy pattern tree for edge malware detection and categorization in IoT. Elsevier (n.d.). Retrieved from https://www.sciencedirect.com/science/article/pii/S1383762118305265
21. S. Mohammadi, Cyber intrusion detection by combined feature selection algorithm. Elsevier (n.d.). Retrieved from https://www.sciencedirect.com/science/article/pii/S2214212618304617
22. M. Parizi, A. Dehghantanha, On the understanding of gamification in blockchain systems. in *2018 6th International Conference on Future Internet of Things and Cloud Workshops (FiCloudW)* (2018), pp. 214–219. https://doi.org/10.1109/W-FiCloud.2018.00041
23. R.M. Parizi, A. Amritraj, Dehghantanha, smart contract programming languages on blockchains: an empirical evaluation of usability and security (2018). https://doi.org/10.1007/978-3-319-94478-4_6
24. S. Aggarwal, R. Chaudhary, G.S. Aujla, A. Jindal, A. Dua, N. Kumar, EnergyChain. in *Proceedings of the 1st ACM MobiHoc Workshop on Networking and Cybersecurity for Smart Cities - SmartCitiesSecurity'18* (2018), pp. 1–6. https://doi.org/10.1145/3214701.3214704
25. P.J. Taylor, T. Dargahi, A. Dehghantanha, R.M. Parizi, K.-K.R. Choo, A systematic literature review of blockchain cyber security. Digital Commun. Netw. (2019). https://doi.org/10.1016/j.dcan.2019.01.005
26. F. Dai, Y. Shi, N. Meng, L. Wei, Z. Ye, From Bitcoin to cybersecurity: a comparative study of blockchain application and security issues. in *2017 4th International Conference on Systems and Informatics (ICSAI)* (2017), pp. 975–979. https://doi.org/10.1109/ICSAI.2017.8248427
27. R.M. Parizi, S. Homayoun, A. Yazdinejad, A. Dehghantanha, K.-K.R. Choo, Integrating privacy enhancing techniques into blockchains using sidechains (2019). Retrieved from http://arxiv.org/abs/1906.04953
28. A. Dorri, F. Luo, S.S. Kanhere, R. Jurdak, Z.Y. Dong, A secure and efficient direct power load control framework based on blockchain (2018). Retrieved from http://arxiv.org/abs/1812.08497
29. T. Yang, F. Zhai, J. Liu, M. Wang, H. Pen, Self-organized cyber physical power system blockchain architecture and protocol. Int. J. Distrib. Sens. Netw. **14**(10), 155014771880331 (2018). https://doi.org/10.1177/1550147718803311
30. G. Liang, S.R. Weller, F. Luo, J. Zhao, Z.Y. Dong, Distributed blockchain-based data protection framework for modern power systems against cyber attacks. IEEE Trans. Smart Grid **10**(3), 3162–3173 (2019). https://doi.org/10.1109/TSG.2018.2819663
31. N.Z. Aitzhan, D. Svetinovic, Security and privacy in decentralized energy trading through multi-signatures, blockchain and anonymous messaging streams. IEEE Trans. Dependable Secure Comput. **15**(5), 840–852 (2018). https://doi.org/10.1109/TDSC.2016.2616861
32. K. Mannaro, A. Pinna, M. Marchesi, Crypto-trading: blockchain-oriented energy market. in *2017 AEIT International Annual Conference* (2017), pp. 1–5. https://doi.org/10.23919/AEIT.2017.8240547

33. M. Meisel, S. Wilker, A.G. Goranovic, L. Fotiadis, T. Sauter, Blockchain applications in microgrids an overview of current projects and concepts Thilo Sauter TU Wien blockchain applications in microgrids an overview of current projects and concepts (n.d.). https://doi.org/10.1109/IECON.2017.8217069

34. M. Mihaylov, I. Razo-Zapata, A. Nowé, NRGcoin—a blockchain-based reward mechanism for both production and consumption of renewable energy. Transforming climate finance and green investment with blockchains (2018), pp. 111–131. https://doi.org/10.1016/B978-0-12-814447-3.00009-4

35. F. Vanrykel, D. Ernst, M. Bourgeois, Fostering share & charge through proper regulation. Compet. Regul. Netw. Ind. 19(1–2), 25–52 (2018). https://doi.org/10.1177/1783591718809576

36. R. Chitchyan, J. Murkin, Review of blockchain technology and its expectations: case of the energy sector (2018). Retrieved from http://arxiv.org/abs/1803.03567

37. A.V. Vladimirova, Blockchain revolution in global environmental governance: too good to be true? (2019). https://doi.org/10.1007/978-3-030-17705-8_18

38. M.F.A. Razak, N.B. Anuar, R. Salleh, A. Firdaus, The rise of "malware": bibliometric analysis of malware study. J. Netw. Comput. Appl. 75, 58–76 (2016). https://doi.org/10.1016/J.JNCA.2016.08.022

39. H.D. White, Pennants for garfield: bibliometrics and document retrieval. Scientometrics 114(2), 757–778 (2018). https://doi.org/10.1007/s11192-017-2610-9

40. Information, Formalized curiosity: reflecting on the librarian practitioner-researcher. Ejournals.Library.Ualberta.Ca (n.d.). Retrieved from https://ejournals.library.ualberta.ca/index.php/EBLIP/article/download/18901/14819

41. P. Mongeon, A. Paul-Hus, The journal coverage of web of science and scopus: a comparative analysis. Scientometrics 106(1), 213–228 (2016). https://doi.org/10.1007/s11192-015-1765-5

42. J. Koskinen, M. Isohanni, H. Paajala, E. Jääskeläinen, P. Nieminen, H. Koponen, J. Miettunen, How to use bibliometric methods in evaluation of scientific research? An example from Finnish schizophrenia research. Nord. J. Psychiatry 62(2), 136–143 (2008). https://doi.org/10.1080/08039480801961667

43. A. Pilkington, J. Meredith, The evolution of the intellectual structure of operations management—1980–2006: a citation/co-citation analysis. J. Oper. Manag. 27(3), 185–202 (2009). https://doi.org/10.1016/J.JOM.2008.08.001

44. M. Dabbagh, M. Sookhak, N.S. Safa, The evolution of blockchain: a bibliometric study. IEEE Access 7, 19212–19221 (2019). https://doi.org/10.1109/ACCESS.2019.2895646

45. W. Woon, H. Zeineldin, Bibliometric analysis of distributed generation. Elsevier (n.d.). Retrieved from https://www.sciencedirect.com/science/article/pii/S0040162510002039

46. I.S. Adriaanse, C. Rensleigh, Comparing web of science, scopus and google scholar from an environmental sciences perspective. South Afr. J. Libr. Inf. Sci. 77(2), 58 (2011). https://doi.org/10.7553/77-2-58

47. J. Li, J.F. Burnham, T. Lemley, R.M. Britton, Citation analysis: comparison of Web of Science®, Scopus™, SciFinder®, and Google Scholar. J. Electron. Res. Med. Libr. 7(3), 196–217 (2010). https://doi.org/10.1080/15424065.2010.505518

48. C. López-Illescas, F. de Moya-Anegón, H.F. Moed, Coverage and citation impact of oncological journals in the web of science and scopus. J. Informet. 2(4), 304–316 (2008). https://doi.org/10.1016/J.JOI.2008.08.001

49. S. Miau, J.-M. Yang, Bibliometrics-based evaluation of the Blockchain research trend: 2008 – March 2017. Tech. Anal. Strat. Manag. 30(9), 1029–1045 (2018). https://doi.org/10.1080/09537325.2018.1434138

50. E. Hache, A. Palle, Renewable energy source integration into power networks, research trends and policy implications: a bibliometric and research actors survey analysis. Energy Policy 124, 23–35 (2019). https://doi.org/10.1016/j.enpol.2018.09.036

A Systematic Literature Review of Integration of Blockchain and Artificial Intelligence

Ala Ekramifard, Haleh Amintoosi, Amin Hosseini Seno, Ali Dehghantanha, and Reza M. Parizi

Abstract Blockchain and artificial intelligence (AI) have gain the most research attention during recent years. Blockchain is a distributed ledger of trustworthy digital records shared by a network of participants. Blockchain technology has the potential capacity in many fields such as international payment, secure data sharing and marketing, and supply chain management. On the other side, Artificial Intelligence (AI) is used to develop the creation of machines capable of performing tasks that need intelligence.

This paper aims to determine the current state of the art within the field of AI with Blockchain technology. In particular, we investigated the latest articles on this integration and carried out an analysis to determine what applications can benefit from it. We identified 23 articles that comply with the assessment criteria. The review research demonstrates that distributed management, security and efficiency improvement, prediction and decision making are among the most popular types of applications that benefit from the integration of AI and Blockchain, while security is the hottest topic. In general, AI algorithms can improve Blockchain design and operation. The combination of these two technologies increases security, efficiency and, productivity of applications.

A. Ekramifard · H. Amintoosi (✉) · A. H. Seno
Computer Engineering Department, Faculty of Engineering, Ferdowsi University of Mashhad, Mashhad, Iran
e-mail: ekramifard@um.ac.ir; amintoosi@um.ac.ir; hosseini@um.ac.ir

A. Dehghantanha
Cyber Science Lab, School of Computer Science, University of Guelph, Guelph, ON, Canada
e-mail: adehghan@uoguelph.ca

R. M. Parizi
College of Computing and Software Engineering, Kennesaw State University, Marietta, GA, USA
e-mail: rparizi1@kennesaw.edu

© Springer Nature Switzerland AG 2020

K.-K. R. Choo et al. (eds.), *Blockchain Cybersecurity, Trust and Privacy*, Advances in Information Security 79, https://doi.org/10.1007/978-3-030-38181-3_8

1 Introduction

Blockchain is the secure decentralized ledger that underlies cryptocurrencies like Bitcoin and future infrastructures for distributed computing with consensus truth states. It evolves from the white paper [1] that describes how the Bitcoin cryptocurrency could be constructed. Recently, the Blockchain system has become popular in a wide range of applications due to its dominance in terms of security, decentralization, and reliability [2].

The Blockchain is a list of connected blocks which contain a hash, a link to the previous block, a timestamp, and transaction data [3]. Once a valid transaction is done, the details are distributed among other parties in order to be verified (via a mining process) before being added to the chain. A block is then constructed containing a set of verified and cryptographically signed transactions. In order to ensure the security, integrity and tamper-resistance of the transactions, a hashing process is carried out on the block until a satisfactory hash value is determined. The block is then appended to the chain of previously constructed blocks.

The above description demonstrates the independence of Blockchain from a trusted third party as all transactions are being processed without the need for a central authority. In fact, Blockchain technology has paved the way for implementing the transactions while ensuring data immutability and ascertaining trust between unknown parties [4]. Such improvements result in the emergence of a large number of applications such in healthcare [5], banking [6] and smart contracts [7] that are shaping the Internet of Value, while bringing major changes as those brought by the traditional Internet [8]. It is expected for Blockchain to become an essential part of many businesses in the coming years [9].

Artificial Intelligence (AI), another prominent research field attracting great amount of attention, is the simulation of human intelligence processes by computer systems, which has led to an automated world powered by machine-2-machine interconnection [10]. AI is used in a wide range of applications like daily life activities [11], financial and banking services [12], healthcare [5], and transportation [13]. Recent news predict that by the year 2030, AI will reach 13 trillion dollars in value[1].

AI can learn on its own by analyzing and discovering patterns from massive amounts of data via various deep learning techniques [8]. However, AI is based on centralized storage and management which may lead to data tampering, manipulation, or privacy leakage due to the single source of failure problem [14]. Moreover, there is no guarantee regarding the provenance of the data and authenticity of the data sources [15]. This may result in erroneous and risky decision results that can be dangerous for applications handling sensitive data (e.g., AI-based healthcare applications) [14].

---

[1]https://www.zdnet.com/article/mckinsey-ai-will-create-13-trillion-in-value-by-2013/.

The integration of AI and Blockchain is estimated to have various advantages and benefits. It provides a secure, trusted and distributed platform for sharing huge volumes of data for the purpose of analysis, learning and decision making between parties, without the need to the central authority or intermediaries [16]. It can also lead to the innovation and introduction of several large scale applications [17]. Blockchain ability to guarantee the accuracy of data, makes it useful for feeding data into AI systems and recording results from them [18].

To date, there appear to be no systematic literature review in cross use of Blockchain and AI. This study focuses on existing literature convergence of Blockchain with artificial intelligence and outlines the key benefits brought via this integration. Open research challenges related to the adaptation and utilization Blockchian capabilities for AI applications are also discussed.

The rest of the paper is structured as follows. Section 1 defines the research goals and contributions as well as questions that are going to be answered. Section 2 expresses the research methods that lead to the selection of primary studies. The analysis results of the selected studies are presented in Section 3. In Section 4, research findings are discussed, and answers to research questions are expressed. Section 5 concludes the paper and provides suggestions for further research.

1.1 Research Goals

In this research, we aim to analyze existing works, and find and summarize the research done on the cross use of Blockchain and AI. For this purpose, we developed three research questions as follows:

- *RQ1*: What are the latest studies on the integration of Blockchain and AI?
- *RQ2*: What are the AI use cases in Blockchain?
- *RQ3*: What applications can benefit from the integration of AI and Blockchain?

The contributions of this article are as follows:

1. We identified 69 primary studies relating to Blockchain use case mixed with AI until early 2019. These articles can be used in further studies for comparative analysis in this specific field.
2. We selected 23 studies for a comprehensive review and expressed the research ideas and contributions in the fields of Blockchain use cases mixed with AI.
3. We present the state of the art methods and contributions in which, integrating AI and Blockchain improves various types of applications.
4. We provide guidelines to support further work in this area.

2   Research Methodology

2.1   Selection of Primary Studies

To answer the research questions, we applied the systematic literature review as described by Kitchenham and Charters [19] in three review phases: planning, conducting, and reporting. In the following, we express the process of searching and selection of primary studies. To obtain the collection of relevant studies, we made a combination of keywords in the search string and passed it to particular search engines. The searches were run against the title, keywords, and abstract. The search was conducted on the 14th of January 2019.

The search strings were: ("Blockchain" OR "distributed ledger" OR "smart contract") AND ("machine learning" OR "AI" OR "neural network" OR "artificial intelligence" OR "fuzzy").

Databases include: IEEE Xplore Digital Library, ACM, ScienceDirect, Springer, Scopus, and Google Scholar. Duplicate studies were removed, then the results were filtered through the inclusion/exclusion criteria, as shown in Table 1. Forward and backward snowballing iterations were also applied to assure that all papers matching the inclusion criteria have been included.

Figure 1 illustrates the selection process. At first, 1689 studies identified from searches against the selected database. Abstract and conclusion of all papers were read and based on inclusion/exclusion criteria, the number of remaining papers was 69. To answer the research questions, these 69 papers were read in full to extract more detailed information, and the inclusion/exclusion criteria were re-applied, leaving 19 articles. Forward and backward snowballing identified an additional two and two papers respectively. Finally, 23 papers were included in this SLR.

The data from each study were extracted, categorized, and stored in a spreadsheet. The extracted data consists of three parts:

- *Context Data*: Information about the aim of the research, domain of the applications, size and sources of data.
- *Qualitative Data*: A summary of findings and conclusions for each primary study.

Table 1 Inclusion and exclusion criteria

Inclusion criteria
1. The paper must be an empirical study about the integration of Blockchain and AI
2. The paper must emphasize on the improvements obtained on applications by the integration of Blockchain and AI
3. The paper must be a reviewed product published in a conference proceeding or journal
Exclusion criteria
1. Studies just focusing on smart devices and do not use AI literally
2. The conference version of a study that has an extended journal version
3. Grey or non-English language papers

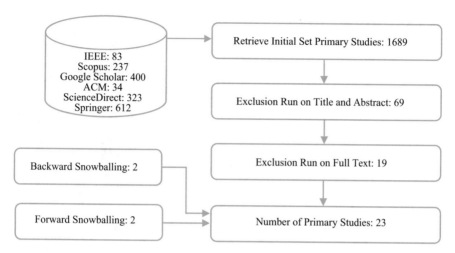

Fig. 1 The process of primary studies selection

Fig. 2 Number of papers published over time

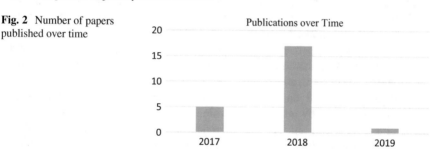

- *Quantitative Data*: The majority of the results applicable to the study, data observed by experimentation.

2.2 Data Analysis

We conducted a meta-analysis of final selected studies and did the data extraction process. Figure 2 shows the number of papers published each year. As can be seen, the idea of combining BC and AI technologies has been formed over the last past two years and has been growing. Since our study was conducted at the beginning of 2019, not much has been published yet.

A keyword analysis was performed across 23 of the primary studies. Table 2 shows the number of times specific words appeared in paper keywords. As shown in this table, "Blockchain" is the most repeated word is all article. "Machine learning", "Neural network", and "Deep learning" are the next most repeated words; all referred to the concept of artificial intelligence.

Table 2 Primary study
keyword count

Keywords	Count
Blockchain	19
Machine learning	5
Neural network	3
Deep learning	3
Bitcoin	3
Health care	3
Mining	2
Smart contract	2
IoT	2
Classification	2

3   Findings

Each primary study was read in full and relevant data was extracted and summarized in Table 3. Each of the studies was determined to have a focus on specified category. Extracted data and categories are recorded in Table 3.

Figure 3 shows the percentage of themes for primary studies that are categorized into seven parts: Classification, Security, Efficiency, Prediction, Decision making, Distributed management, and Marketing. The themes identified highlight that 43% of studies are focused on security that is the inherent nature of Blockchain. Blockchain governed by intelligent machine learning algorithms can lead to automatic attack detection and defense approaches. The second most popular theme with 17% is classification. Various machine learning methods have been proposed to formulate the problem of classification based on features or behavior patterns in Blockchain applications. Efficiency, Prediction, Distributed management, and Marketing have all 9% and at last Decision making has 4%. Difference neural networks algorithms utilize to model and forecast the Bitcoin prices. Single point of failure and trust management are two major problems in data sharing and decision making systems which Blockchain can be a suitable solution in these scenarios.

4   Discussion

Blockchain is a hash-based linked data structure that is kept by every node on the peer-to-peer network. Due to its nature, Blockchain can provide security, privacy, decentralization, anonymity, and immutability. Artificial Intelligence, which has been used for a couple of decades, can help to introduce an automated and intelligent world powered by machine to machine or machine to human interconnection. It seems we can get a great advantage by combining AI and Blockchain.

By conducting the survey, we divided the studies into two distinct parts. The first part covers studies that use AI algorithms to improve Blockchain design and

Table 3 Key findings from primary studies

Primary study	Key qualitative and quantitative data reported	Category
[20]	Classifying the Blockchain peers into categories with respect to their behavior patterns by a novel deep learning based approach	Classification, security
[21]	Improving security of the Blockchain-based medical data management. Proposal of a rootkit detection system that utilizes machine learning prediction to detect unknown root exploit	Security
[22]	Proposal of a traceability chain algorithm instead of consensus in the Blockchain using deep learning concept	Improve efficiency
[23]	A practical analysis on modeling and predicting of the Bitcoin pricing process by employing a Bayesian neural network	Prediction
[24]	Applying supervised machine learning algorithms and algorithmic game Theory to identify majority attack (51%) in Blockchain network	Security
[25]	Providing a Blockchain-based decentralized resource management system to minimize the total energy cost in cloud datacenters. Models the request migrations with an embedded smart contract and Markov decision process cost saving	Decision making
[26]	Proposal of a credit evaluation system based on Blockchain in the food supply chain to ensure food safety. Using deep learning for supervision and management of traders by analyzing the credit evaluation	Security, credit evaluation
[27]	Proposing a biometric authentication system based on nail images analysis that can be effectively used to predict and prevent disease Blockchain technology is used to record the nail information of each user and deep neural network algorithm is used for data classification	Classification, security
[28]	Proposal of an intelligent manufacturing system based on Blockchain distributed ledger and data mining. A huge amount of data collect, integrate, and topic mining proses is done to help predict production line failure, extract health information on human resources, and provide personalized health service	Classification, security
[29]	Proposal of a crowdsensing platform to reveal hidden information about user behavior. It uses Blockchain to achieve security and reliability, also uses clustering and fuzzy theories to evaluate the quality of the collected data	Quality evaluation, security
[30]	Proposing a fair data trading environment in a big data market, based on Blockchain smart contract. It sues distance metric learning to evaluate the content of data and decided if the data provider provided the trustful data or not	Data trading, security
[31]	Presents a Blockchain-based platform for healthcare marketplace, provides security and transparency in personal data utilizing deep learning	Security and privacy
[32]	Presents incident reports manager for cyber threats based on deep neural network and smart contracts technique	Security
[33]	Proposes hardware management (governance) platform to address faults, security and performance issues based on BC. It uses AI method to analysis and classify collected data and fault prediction	Distributed manage-ment
[34]	Modeling the malware detection engine using Blockchain and deep learning technology	Security

(continued)

Table 3 (continued)

Primary study	Key qualitative and quantitative data reported	Category
[35]	Proposes decentralized face recognition platform based on Blockchain and machine learning which can be used for identity management in cloud-based IoT applications	Distributed management
[36]	Proposes an easy to use and secure personal health data sharing system based on Blockchain and cloud storage. Data providers sell and researchers or data consumers can buy necessary required data. Quality of the data is evaluated by deep learning	Data market, quality validation
[37]	Develops an arrhythmia (irregular heartbeats) classifier Blockchain. Blockchain used as access control manager that verifies patient identities and records transactions; Stacked Denoising Auto-encoder (SDA) makes the classifier and anomaly detector	Classification
[38]	Develops a secure model in a smart home to create personal profile for IoT devices. Personal information for each user and each device is stored in the Blockchain. The personalization parameters are computed using association rule mining	Security
[39]	Proposes an optimal mining process in mobile Blockchain environment based on deep learning	Optimization
[40]	Proposes Bitcoin address clustering based on Bitcoin Blockchain information like input addresses of one transaction and transaction changes	Classification, clustering
[41]	Presents an anomaly detection for Blockchain with a machine learning core	Security
[42]	Bitcoin volatility prediction using financial time series and machine learning	Prediction

Fig. 3 Chart of primary study themes

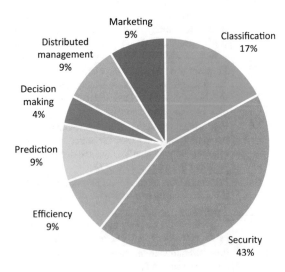

operation. The second part introduces the works concentrating on the combination of these two technologies to increase security, efficiency, and productivity in a particular application.

The researchers used conventional classification and decision making approaches such as neural networks, deep learning based methods, boosting in machine learning, and Bayesian neural networks. Some works that rely on Blockchain have only introduced their models, without dealing with real implementations. There are several decentralized Blockchain application platforms, such as Ethereum, Hyperledger, and others. Some researchers proposed their architecture using Hyperledger fabric, which is open source permission based Blockchain.

4.1   RQ1: What Are the Latest Studies on the Integration of Blockchain and AI?

Various types of AI applications are known as classification, prediction, decision making, and optimization. Also, Blockchain is known as a secure, distributed leger that can be used in trading ecosystems. We divided all studies into these specified categories: Classification or Clustering, Distributed management, Improve Security or Efficiency, Prediction or Decision making.

- Classification or Clustering: Classify the behavior patterns of peers via deep learning method, can help to get accurate understanding of Blockchain network and know malignant behavior [20, 40]. By exploring and analyzing big data, we can find meaningful rules and relations from data that lead to intelligent systems [27, 28].
- Distributed management: Centralization of the service causes the bottleneck and point of failure that can disrupt the whole operations. A decentralized solution could be more reliable, secure, and faster [33, 35].
- Improve Security or Efficiency: Security is the major achievement of AI and Blockchain convergence. Some studies are detecting fraud behavior [24, 26, 29, 30, 38, 41] and malware [21, 34] or reporting incident and attacks [24, 32]. Also this convergence leads to improve efficiency [22, 39].
- Prediction or Decision making: That contains Predicting Bitcoin price [23, 42] and deciding on resource management [25].

4.2   RQ2: What Are the AI Use Cases in Blockchain?

There are several issues and challenges in the Blockchain such as security and performance that can be addresses by applying AI techniques. Deep learning approaches can automatically classify the behavioral patterns of Blockchain peers. It also helps to identify strange behavioral patterns of malicious peers [20]. To increase the security of Blockchain-based healthcare applications, machine learning prediction is used to detect unknown root exploit [21]. Furthermore, the supervised machine learning algorithm can detect and stop the Majority attack [24] or anomaly behaviors [41] in the Blockchain network.

AI can also be used to manage Blockchain and improve its performance. Examples are using the deep learning concept instead of consensus [22] or using neural networks in edge computing to optimize the mining process in mobile Blockchain [39].

Bitcoin as the popular cryptocurrency has an important role in distributed marketing. Its exchange rate and volatility makes high-risk challenges in trading and requires more detailed evaluation before making any decision. Predicting the Bitcoin pricing process has also been done using machine learning techniques [23]. A prediction model for the volatility of Bitcoin returns proposes by [42] using USD/BTC (price analysis) hourly log returns with various time series models. Anonymity is one of the Bitcoin properties, so real owners of them are not known. Based on behavior pattern analysis, Bitcoin address can be classified and each cluster is controlled by the same user [40].

4.3   RQ3: What Applications Can Benefit from the Integration of AI and Blockchain?

Integration of AI and Blockchain can empower difference types of applications. It helps management, making decisions, and providing security and privacy for different types of applications in the domain of health, trading, security, and IoT.

Different types of smart and wearable devices collect various personal health data. These great amounts of data are valuable resources for healthcare research and applications. The combination of AI and Blockchain technology enhances the progress in health care sciences. AI and Blockchain-based systems provided in [31] simplify data acquisition, upload and grant access permission to personal data by guaranteeing privacy and security. Zheng et al. [36] proposes a personal health data sharing system using Blockchain with the considerations of security and transparency. It also uses machine learning techniques to control data quality. Also, Blockchain with Stacked Denoising Auto-encode provided an application of patient classification and anomaly detection for arrhythmia illness [37]. The Blockchain technology as decentralized data recording system combined with neural network for image clustering is proposed in [27].

Converging of Blockchain and AI can provide intelligent marketplaces and production lines. Exchanging of data between the data provider and consumer leads to a new context of trading. Smart contract addition machine learning-based system ensures secure and fair marketing [30]. In the manufacturing industry, a distributed ledger that is combined with topic mining process that improves productivity and quality control [28].

To identify and defeat cyber-attacks, Graf and King [32] proposes an automatically cyber incident classification system based on the smart contract. Instead of human involvement, a deep auto-encoder has been developed to analyze a large number of cyber incidents.

IoT Devices help to collect people and surrounding environments data. The analysis of these data can help to reveal hidden information about user behavior. Blockchain combined with clustering algorithms can be applied to control the quality of data [29]. Singla et al. [38] proposes a Blockchain-based system in smart home to predict the user activity and store the device profiles. Rule mining technique is used to compute preferred parameters for each user and device type. Kundu et al. [33] proposes a decentralized platform to collect technical data from the chip vendor and analyses it for fault detection.

To improve decentralizing identity management in IoT-cloud applications, Ahmad et al. [35] proposed the face recognition system to strengthen the printer security in a campus. A smart contract is used to record every printing transaction and apply printing service agreements and the face matching process in the Blockchain, which is implemented by using Local Binary Pattern Histogram (LBPH).

5   Conclusion and Future Work

We conducted a systematic literature review on cross uses of Blockchain and AI in various types of applications. We defined three research questions and performed searching in knowledge databases to answer these questions. This research has focused on studies that used artificial intelligence or machine learning algorithm to add intelligence to applications, and at the same time used Blockchain as a hyper leger to add automation, security, and truth. Distributed management, security and efficiency improvement, prediction and decision making are the most popular types of applications.

As the review shows, security is the hottest topic in recent studies. Blockchain governed by machine learning algorithms can detect and prevent attacks and improve security and privacy in different applications. It also shows that integrated features of AI and Blockchain can play an important role in the medical field, including various stages such as gathering, analytics, and decision making on healthcare dataset.

In future, the convergence of Blockchain and AI can provide lots of innovations to improve human life; however, it is still in the first of the road, and there are many research challenges to be addressed, e.g. scalability, lack of standards, issues in consensus protocols, etc. It is a great opportunity for future research to be conducted in this area.

References

1. S. Nakamoto, Bitcoin: a peer-to-peer electronic cash system (2018), https://bitcoin.org/bitcoin.pdf
2. S. Homayoun, A. Dehghantanha, R.M. Parizi, K.K.R. Choo, A blockchain-based framework for detecting malicious mobile applications in app stores, in *32nd IEEE Canadian Conference of Electrical and Computer Engineering (IEEE CCECE'19)*. Canada (2019)
3. Q. Zhang, R.M. Parizi, K.K.R. Choo, A pentagon of considerations towards more secure blockchains, in *IEEE Blockchain Technical Briefs* (2018)
4. A. Yazdinejad, R.M. Parizi, A. Dehghantanha, K.K.R. Choo, Blockchain-enabled authentication handover with efficient privacy protection in SDN-based 5G networks. arXiv:1905.03193 (2019)
5. P. Mamoshina, L. Ojomoko, Y. Yanovich, A. Ostrovski, A. Botezatu, P. Prikhodko, A. Zhavoronkov, Converging blockchain and next-generation artificial intelligence technologies to decentralize and accelerate biomedical research and healthcare. Oncotarget **9**(5), 5665–5690 (2017)
6. Y. Guo, C. Liang, Blockchain application and outlook in the banking industry. Financ. Innov. **2**, 24 (2016)
7. H. Watanabe, S. Fujimura, A. Nakadaira, Y. Miyazaki, A. Akutsu, J. Kishigami, Blockchain contract: securing a blockchain applied to smart contracts, in *IEEE International Conference on Consumer Electronics (ICCE)*, Las Vegas, NV, pp. 467–468 (2016)
8. S. Makridakis, A. Polemitis, G. Giaglis, S. Louca, Blockchain: the next breakthrough in the rapid progress of AI, in *Artificial Intelligence-Emerging Trends and Applications* (IntechOpen, 2018)
9. R.M. Parizi, A. Dehghantanha, On the understanding of gamification in blockchain systems, in *6th IEEE International Conference on Future Internet of Things and Cloud (FiCloud'18)*, Barcelona, Spain (IEEE Computer Society, 2018)
10. M. Koch, Artificial intelligence is becoming natural. Cell **173**(3), 531–533 (2018)
11. G. Dermody, R. Fritz, A conceptual framework for clinicians working with artificial intelligence and health-assistive smart homes. Nursing Inquiry **26**, e12267 (2018)
12. P. Agarwal, Redefining banking and financial industry through the application of computational intelligence, in *2019 Advances in Science and Engineering Technology International Conferences (ASET)*, Dubai, United Arab Emirates, pp. 1–5
13. A. Horzyk, Introduction to artificial intelligence (2018), http://home.agh.edu.pl/~horzyk/lectures/ai/aiintro.php
14. K. Salah, M.H.U. Rehman, N. Nizamuddin, A. Al-Fuqaha, Blockchain for AI: review and open research challenges. IEEE Access **7**, 10127–10149 (2019)
15. Y. Qi, J. Xiao, Fintech: AI powers financial services to improve people's lives. Commun. ACM **61**(11), 6569 (2018)
16. R.M. Parizi, A. Dehghantanha, Smart contract programming languages on blockchains: an empirical evaluation of usability and security, in *1st International Conference on Blockchain (ICBC'18)*, Seattle, USA. LNCS (Springer, 2018)
17. R.M. Parizi, A. Dehghantanha, K.K.R. Choo, A. Singh, Empirical vulnerability analysis of automated smart contracts security testing on blockchains, in *28th ACM Annual International Conference on Computer Science and Software Engineering (CASCON'18),* Ontario, Canada (IBM, 2018)
18. K. Rabah, Convergence of AI, IoT, big data and blockchain: a review. Lake Inst. J. **1**(1), 1–18 (2018)
19. B. Kitchenham, S. Charters, Guidelines for performing systematic literature reviews in software engineering. Engineering **1051**(2), 1051 (2017)

Primary Studies

20. H. Tang, Y. Jiao, B. Huang, C. Lin, S. Goyal, B. Wang, Learning to classify blockchain peers according to their behavior sequences. IEEE Access **6**, 71208–71215 (2018)
21. A. Firdaus, N.B. Anuar, M.F. Ab Razak, I.A.T. Hashem, S. Bachok, A.K. Sangaiah, Root exploit detection and features optimization: mobile device and blockchain based medical data management. J. Med. Syst. **42**(6), 112 (2018)
22. R.Y. Chen, A traceability chain algorithm for artificial neural networks using T–S fuzzy cognitive maps in blockchain. Futur. Gener. Comput. Syst. **80**, 198–210 (2018)
23. H. Jang, J. Lee, An empirical study on modeling and prediction of bitcoin prices with Bayesian neural networks based on blockchain information. IEEE Access **6**, 5427–5437 (2018)
24. S. Dey, A proof of work: securing majority-attack in blockchain using machine learning and algorithmic game theory. Int. J. Wirel. Microwave Technol. **5**, 1–9 (2018)
25. C. Xu, K. Wang, M. Guo, Intelligent resource management in blockchain-based cloud datacenters. IEEE Cloud Comput. **4**(6), 50–59 (2017)
26. D. Mao, F. Wang, Z. Hao, H. Li, Credit evaluation system based on blockchain for multiple stakeholders in the food supply chain. Int. J. Environ. Res. Public Health **15**(8), 1627 (2018)
27. S.H. Lee, C.S. Yang, Fingernail analysis management system using microscopy sensor and blockchain technology. Int. J. Distrib. Sens. Netw. **14**(3), 1550147718767044 (2018)
28. K. Chung, H. Yoo, D. Choe, H. Jung, Blockchain network based topic mining process for cognitive manufacturing. Wirel. Pers. Commun. **105**, 583–597 (2018)
29. J. An, D. Liang, X. Gui, H. Yang, R. Gui, X. He, Crowdsensing quality control and grading evaluation based on a two-consensus blockchain. IEEE Internet Things J. **6**(3), 4711–4718 (2019)
30. Y. Zhao, Y. Yu, Y. Li, G. Han, X. Du, Machine learning based privacy-preserving fair data trading in big data market. Inf. Sci. **478**, 449–460 (2019)
31. P. Mamoshina, L. Ojomoko, Y. Yanovich, A. Ostrovski, A. Botezatu, P. Prikhodko, I.O. Ogu, Converging blockchain and next-generation artificial intelligence technologies to decentralize and accelerate biomedical research and healthcare. Oncotarget **9**(5), 5665–5690 (2018)
32. R. Graf, R. King, Neural network and Blockchain based technique for cyber threat intelligence and situational awareness, in *2018 10th International Conference on Cyber Conflict (CyCon)* (IEEE, 2018), pp. 409–426
33. A. Kundu, Z. Sura, U. Sharma, Collaborative and accountable hardware governance using blockchain, in *2018 IEEE 4th International Conference on Collaboration and Internet Computing (CIC)* (2018), pp. 114–121
34. S. Raje, S. Vaderia, N. Wilson, R. Panigrahi, Decentralised firewall for malware detection, in *2017 International Conference on Advances in Computing, Communication and Control (ICAC3)* (IEEE, 2017), pp. 1–5
35. N.M. Ahmad, S.F.A. Razak, S. Kannan, I. Yusof, A.H.M. Amin, Improving identity management of cloud-based IoT applications using blockchain, in *2018 International Conference on Intelligent and Advanced System (ICIAS)* (IEEE, 2018), pp. 1–6
36. X. Zheng, R.R. Mukkamala, R. Vatrapu, J. Ordieres-Mere, Blockchain-based personal health data sharing system using cloud storage, in *2018 IEEE 20th International Conference on e-Health Networking, Applications and Services (Healthcom)* (IEEE, 2018), pp. 1–6
37. A. Juneja, M. Marefat, Leveraging blockchain for retraining deep learning architecture in patient-specific arrhythmia classification, in *2018 IEEE EMBS International Conference on Biomedical & Health Informatics (BHI)* (IEEE, 2018), pp. 393–397
38. K. Singla, J. Bose, S. Katariya, Machine learning for secure device personalization using blockchain, in *2018 International Conference on Advances in Computing, Communications and Informatics (ICACCI)* (IEEE, 2018), pp. 67–73
39. N.C. Luong, Z. Xiong, P. Wang, D. Niyato, Optimal auction for edge computing resource management in mobile blockchain networks: a deep learning approach, in *2018 IEEE International Conference on Communications (ICC)* (IEEE, 2018), pp. 1–6

40. D. Ermilov, M. Panov, Y. Yanovich, Automatic bitcoin address clustering, in *2017 16th IEEE International Conference on Machine Learning and Applications (ICMLA)* (IEEE, 2017), pp. 461–466
41. A. Bogner, Seeing is understanding: anomaly detection in blockchains with visualized features, in *Proceedings of the 2017 ACM International Joint Conference on Pervasive and Ubiquitous Computing and Proceedings of the 2017 ACM International Symposium on Wearable Computers* (ACM, 2017), pp. 5–8
42. N.N. Vo, G. Xu, The volatility of bitcoin returns and its correlation to financial markets, in *2017 International Conference on Behavioral, Economic, Socio-cultural Computing (BESC)* (IEEE, 2017), pp. 1–6

The Future of Blockchain Technology in Healthcare Internet of Things Security

Gautam Srivastava, Reza M. Parizi ⓘ, and Ali Dehghantanha

Abstract The recent emergence of Internet of Things (IoT) brings a whole new class of applications and higher efficiency for existing areas of services. One such popular service that is trying to reap the benefits of IoT is the Healthcare sector. Application-specific requirements, as well as connectivity and communication ability of devices have introduced new challenges for these Healthcare IoT applications. Specifically, we have seen a surge of healthcare IoT applications that have manifested in recent years. Almost simultaneously to the surge in IoT, there has been potential venues for Blockchain Technology to find a home outside of the financial sector in many different applicable scenarios, including those in Healthcare. This chapter provides an overview of IoT health technologies with a specific emphasis on those proposed making use of Blockchain Technology. We investigate both the positive aspects of such implementations for the future, as well the shortcomings of known designs and tackle future challenges of this novel area of research. This chapter surveys the latest works in this very specific field, and gives an unbiased vantage point to assist researchers navigate this new horizon for Healthcare, IoT, and Blockchain Technology towards the future.

G. Srivastava (✉)
Department of Mathematics and Statistics, Brandon University, Brandon, MB, Canada

Research Center for Interneural Computing, China Medical University, Taichung, Taiwan, Republic of China
e-mail: srivastavag@brandonu.ca

R. M. Parizi
College of Computing and Software Engineering, Kennesaw State University, Marietta, GA, USA
e-mail: rparizi1@kennesaw.edu

A. Dehghantanha
Cyber Science Lab, School of Computer Science, University of Guelph, Guelph, ON, Canada
e-mail: adehghan@uoguelph.ca

© Springer Nature Switzerland AG 2020
K.-K. R. Choo et al. (eds.), *Blockchain Cybersecurity, Trust and Privacy*, Advances in Information Security 79, https://doi.org/10.1007/978-3-030-38181-3_9

1 Introduction

The use of wireless sensor networks (WSN) in healthcare applications started growing at a fast pace around 2010 (See Fig. 1). Numerous applications such as heart rate monitors, blood pressure monitors and endoscopic capsules are already in common use. Now, these devices are seeing themselves connected to the internet as well. To address the growing use of sensor technology in general, a new area called Internet of Things has emerged rapidly [8, 21]. As most devices and their applications are wireless in nature for the Internet of Things, security and privacy concerns are among major areas of interest to resolve. Due to the direct involvement of humans in the use of such devices also increases the sensitivity. Whether the data gathered from patients in healthcare or individuals in other scenarios where data is obtained with the consent of the person or without it due to the need by the system, misuse or privacy concerns may restrict people from taking advantage of the full benefits of such a system. People may not see these devices as safe for daily use. There may also be the possibility of serious social unrest due to the fear that such devices may be used for monitoring and tracking individuals by government agencies or other private organizations. In this chapter, we will discuss these issues and analyze in detail the problems and their possible solutions for a secure healthcare IoT.

One solution for the growing security and privacy concerns in Healthcare IoT that has been proposed recently is the use of blockchain technology [29]. Blockchain technology has shown its considerable adaptability in recent years as a variety of

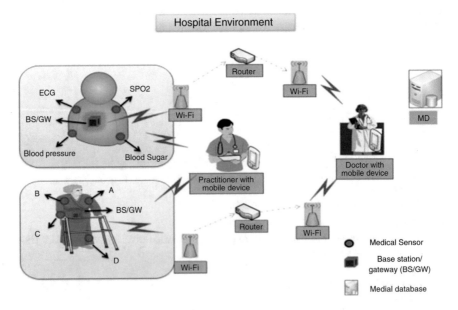

Fig. 1 Overview of Healthcare IoT [18]

different market sectors have sought ways of incorporating its abilities into their operations [30, 31]. While so far most of the focus has been on the financial services industry, several projects in other service related areas such as healthcare show this is beginning to change.

In this chapter, we will survey the security requirements of healthcare IoT and try to see how blockchain technology may be the answer to these concerns. We will investigate some recent designs of how blockchain technology has been proposed to function inside a blockchain IoT system.

The rest of this chapter is organized as follows. In Sect. 2, we give a summary of security requirements for IoT systems in general. Next, we focus our attention of healthcare IoT security in Sect. 3. We give a blockchain technology overview in Sect. 4 for those readers unfamiliar with it. Finally, in Sect. 5 we present three healthcare IoT systems that incorporate blockchain technology and discuss their strengths and weaknesses. Lastly, we give some concluding remarks in Sect. 6.

2 Security Requirements for Healthcare IoT

IoT security is concerned with safeguarding connected devices and networks. IoT involves adding internet connectivity to a system of interrelated computing devices, mechanical and digital machines, objects, animals and/or people. Each "thing" is provided a unique identifier and the ability to automatically transfer data over a network. Allowing devices to connect to the internet opens them up to a number of serious vulnerabilities if they are not properly protected.

IoT security has become the subject of scrutiny after a number of high-profile incidents where a common IoT device was used to infiltrate and attack the larger network. Implementing security measures is critical to ensuring the safety of networks with IoT devices connected to them.

2.1 IoT Security Challenges

A number of challenges prevent the securing of IoT devices and ensuring end-to-end security in an IoT environment. Because the idea of networking appliances and other objects is relatively new, security has not always been considered top priority during a product's design phase. Additionally, because IoT is a fairly new market, many product designers and manufacturers are more interested in getting their products to market quickly, rather than taking the necessary steps to build security in from the start.

A major issue with IoT security is the use of hardcoded or default passwords, which can lead to security breaches. Even if passwords are changed, they are often not strong enough to prevent infiltration.

Another common issue facing IoT devices is that they are often resource-constrained and do not contain the compute resources necessary to implement strong security. As such, many devices do not or cannot offer advanced security features. For example, sensors that monitor humidity or temperature cannot handle advanced encryption or other security measures. Plus, as many IoT devices are "set it and forget it"—placed in the field or on a machine and left until end of life—they hardly ever receive security updates or patches. From a manufacturer's viewpoint, building security in from the start can be costly, slow down development and cause the device not to function as it should.

Connecting legacy assets not inherently designed for IoT connectivity is another security challenge. Replacing legacy infrastructure with connected technology is cost-prohibitive, so many assets will be retrofitted with smart sensors. However, as legacy assets that likely have not been updated or ever had security against modern threats, the attack surface is expanded.

In terms of updates, many systems only include support for a set timeframe. For legacy and new assets, security can lapse if extra support is not added. And as many IoT devices stay in the network for many years, adding security can be challenging.

IoT security is also plagued by a lack of industry-accepted standards. While many IoT security frameworks exist, there is no single agreed-upon framework. Large companies and industry organizations may have their own specific standards, while certain segments, such as industrial IoT, have proprietary, incompatible standards from industry leaders. The variety of these standards makes it difficult to not only secure systems, but also ensure interoperability between them.

The convergence of IT and operational technology (OT) networks has created a number of challenges for security teams, especially those tasked with protecting systems and ensuring end-to-end security in areas outside their realm of expertise. A learning curve is involved, and IT teams with the proper skill sets should be put in charge of IoT security.

Organizations must learn to view security as a shared issue, from manufacturer to service provider to end user. Manufacturers and service providers should prioritize the security and privacy of their products, and also provide encryption and authorization by default, for example. But the onus does not end there; end users must be sure to take their own precautions, including changing passwords, installing patches when available and using security software.

2.2 Known IoT Breaches of Security

Security experts have indicated the potential risk of large numbers of unsecured devices connected to the internet since the IoT concept first originated in the early 2000s. A number of attacks subsequently have made headlines. It is important to note that many of the IoT hacks do not target the devices themselves, but rather use IoT devices as an entry point into the larger network.

In 2010, researchers revealed that the Stuxnet virus was used to physically damage Iranian centrifuges, with attacks starting in 2006 but the primary attack occurring in 2009 [11]. Often considered one of the earliest examples of an IoT attack, Stuxnet targets supervisory control and data acquisition (SCADA) systems in industrial control systems (ICS), using malware to infect instructions sent by programmable logic controllers (PLCs).

Attacks on industrial networks have only continued, with malware such as CrashOverride/Industroyer, Triton and VPNFilter targeting vulnerable OT and industrial IoT systems [16, 19].

In December 2013, a researcher at enterprise security firm Proofpoint Inc. discovered the first IoT botnet [24]. According to the researcher, more than 25% of the botnet was made up of devices other than computers, including smart TVs, baby monitors and household appliances.

In 2015, security researchers Charlie Miller and Chris Valasek executed a wireless hack on a Jeep, changing the radio station on the car's media center, turning its windshield wipers and air conditioner on, and stopping the accelerator from working [37]. They said they could also kill the engine, engage the brakes and disable the brakes altogether. Miller and Valasek were able to infiltrate the car's network through Chrysler's in-vehicle connectivity system, Uconnect.

Mirai, one of the largest IoT botnets to date, first attacked journalist Brian Krebs' website and French web host OVH in September 2016 [2]. The attacks clocked in at 630 gigabits per second (Gbps) and 1.1 terabits per second (Tbps), respectively. The following month, domain name system (DNS) service provider Dyn's network was targeted, making a number of websites, including Amazon, Netflix, Twitter and The New York Times, unavailable for hours. The attacks infiltrated the network through consumer IoT devices, including IP cameras and routers.

A number of Mirai variants have since emerged, including Hajime, Hide 'N Seek, Masuta, PureMasuta, Wicked botnet and Okiru, among others [10, 28].

In a January 2017 notice, the Food and Drug Administration (FDA) warned the embedded systems in radio frequency-enabled St. Jude Medical implantable cardiac devices, including pacemakers, defibrillators and resynchronization devices, could be vulnerable to security intrusions and attacks [21].

2.3   Common IoT Security Solutions

Common IoT security measures include:

- **Incorporating security at the design phase**. IoT developers should include security at the start of any consumer-, enterprise- or industrial-based device development. Enabling security by default is critical, as well as providing the most recent operating systems and using secure hardware.
- **Hardcoded credentials should never be part of the design process**. An additional measure developers can take is to require credentials be updated by

a user before the device functions. If a device comes with default credentials, users should update them using a strong password or multifactor authentication or biometrics where possible.

- **PKI and digital certificates**. Public key infrastructure (PKI) and 509 digital certificates play critical roles in the development of secure IoT devices, providing the trust and control needed to distribute and identify public encryption keys, secure data exchanges over networks and verify identity.
- **API security**. Application performance indicator (API) security is essential to protect the integrity of data being sent from IoT devices to back-end systems and ensure only authorized devices, developers and apps communicate with APIs.
- **Identity management**. Providing each device with a unique identifier is critical to understanding what the device is, how it behaves, the other devices it interacts with and the proper security measures that should be taken for that device.
- **Hardware security**. Endpoint hardening includes making devices tamper-proof or tamper-evident. This is especially important when devices will be used in harsh environments or where they will not be monitored physically.
- **Strong encryption** is critical to securing communication between devices. Data at rest and in transit should be secured using cryptographic algorithms. This includes the use of key lifecycle management.
- **Network security**. Protecting an IoT network includes ensuring port security, disabling port forwarding and never opening ports when not needed; using anti-malware, firewalls and intrusion detection system/intrusion prevention system; blocking unauthorized IP addresses; and ensuring systems are patched and up to date.
- **Network access control**. NAC can help identify and inventory IoT devices connecting to a network. This will provide a baseline for tracking and monitoring devices.
- **IoT devices** that need to connect directly to the internet should be segmented into their own networks and have access to enterprise network restricted. Network segments should be monitoring for anomalous activity, where action can be taken, should an issue be detected.
- **Security gateways**. Acting as an intermediary between IoT devices and the network, security gateways have more processing power, memory and capabilities than the IoT devices themselves, which provides them the ability to implement features such as firewalls to ensure hackers cannot access the IoT devices they connect.
- **Patch management/continuous software updates**. Providing means of updating devices and software either over network connections or through automation is critical. Having a coordinated disclosure of vulnerabilities is also important to updating devices as soon as possible. Consider end-of-life strategies as well.
- **IoT and operational system security**. This is new to many existing security teams. It is critical to keep security staff up to date with new or unknown systems, learn new architectures and programming languages and be ready for new security challenges. C-level and cybersecurity teams should receive regular training to keep up with modern threats and security measures.

- **Integrating teams**. Along with training, integrating disparate and regularly siloed teams can be useful. For example, having programming developers work with security specialists can help ensure the proper controls are added to devices during the development phase.
- **Consumer education**. Consumers must be made aware of the dangers of IoT systems and provided steps they can take to stay secure, such as updating default credentials and applying software updates. Consumers can also play a role in requiring device manufacturers to create secure devices, and refusing to use those that don't meet high security standards.

3 Healthcare IoT Security

This section presents healthcare IoT architecture environments and gives potential adversary attack models for healthcare applications.

3.1 *Healthcare IoT Architecture*

A patient healthcare IoT architecture is depicted in Fig. 2, where usual patient monitoring devices connected to patients are then shared with other IoT devices wirelessly. When a patient needs care, he/she can get some sort of suitable medical

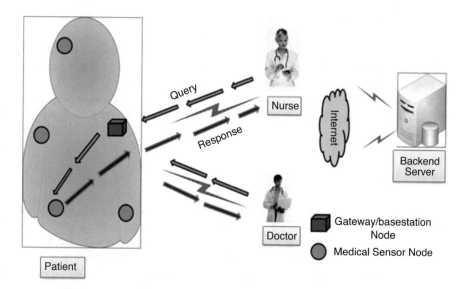

Fig. 2 Overview of Healthcare IoT [18]

sensor device, deployed strategically on the patient's body. These sensors sense the health parameters, (e.g., blood pressure, movement, breathing, ECG etc.) and sends physiological parameters to professional's who monitor or store the data for future observations. A medical professional may store patient data on a backend server for further processing, which is currently outside the scope of this chapter. It is obvious that a professional can access the patient's health parameters directly from the medical sensor, in an ad-hoc manner.

As shown in Fig. 2, healthcare IoT architecture has three active entities, namely, patient, medical sensors device and base-station/gateway. We assume a real-time scenario in most instances however it may be possible to analyze the data after collection. Based on the above scenario, we describe some known adversarial attacks for Healthcare IoT.

3.2 Adversary Attack Models

The patient's physiological information is very sensitive and may attract many attackers, such as insurance companies, corrupt media persons, individual enemies, etc. Furthermore, the patient's medical sensors and the professionals' hand-held devices are wireless in nature. So, these wireless devices may attract unauthorized users or thieves, more especially. For example, they (unauthorized users or thieves) can roam to the hospital ward and easily eavesdrop on the patients locally, so we have categorized the attack models as follows.

3.2.1 Eavesdropping on Wireless Medical Data

As the medical sensors sense the patient's body data, they transmit it over the radio communication channel. The wireless transmission ranges are not confined to hospital wards and these wireless channels are highly susceptible. As a result, an attacker may eavesdrop air messages (i.e., a patient's physiological information), and can disclose the patient's physiological information. Hence, the patient privacy is breached.

3.2.2 Active Attack

In an active attack scenario, the capability of an attacker depends on his/her skill (i.e., ability to monitor all the communication versus only a portion of communication). An attacker may inject bogus messages into the wireless channel and may alter the wireless medical sensor data during the communication. Any spurious messages injection into the healthcare network could cause mistreatment. Furthermore, an attacker may replay the old messages again and again, which could cause overtreatment (i.e., medicine overdose). Thus, active attacks endanger and may pose a life-threatening risk to the patients.

3.3   Security Requirements for Healthcare IoT

Based on the above attack model and literature surveys [6, 17, 20, 23, 34, 36] , this sub-section sketches out the paramount security requirements for healthcare IoT.

3.3.1   Strong User Authentication

The major problem in wireless healthcare environments is the vulnerability of wireless messages to access by unauthorized users, so it is desirable that strong user authentication be considered, where each user must prove their authenticity before accessing the patient's physiological information. Furthermore, strong user authentication, also known as two-factor authentication, provides greater security for healthcare application using wireless medical sensor networks [35].

3.3.2   Mutual Authentication

In real-time healthcare applications, the user and the medical sensor must authenticate each other; hence, they can ensure the communication is established between the authenticated user and the medical sensors.

3.3.3   Confidentiality

The patient health data are highly sensitive and medical sensors are wireless in nature, therefore patient physiological data should remain confidential from passive attacks such as eavesdropping or traffic analysis. Thus, patient's health data is only accessed or used by authorized professionals.

3.3.4   Session Key Establishment

A session key should be established between a user/professional and a medical sensor node, so that subsequent communication could take place securely.

3.3.5 Low Communication and Computational Cost

Since wireless medical sensors are resource constrained devices, and the healthcare application's functions also need room for executing their tasks, the protocol must be efficient in terms of communication and computational cost.

3.3.6 Data Freshness

Generally, professionals need patient physiological data at regular intervals, so there must be guarantee that patient health data is recent or fresh. Furthermore, it (data freshness) also ensures that an adversary cannot replay the old messages.

3.3.7 Secure Against Popular Attacks

In real-time healthcare environments the protocol should be defensive against different popular attacks, such as replay attack, impersonation attack, stolen-verifier attack, password guessing attack, and information-leakage attack. As a result, the protocol can be easily applicable to the real-time wireless healthcare applications.

3.3.8 User-Friendliness

The healthcare IoT architecture should be easy to deploy as well as user-friendly; such as, a user can update his/her password securely, whenever he/she needs to.

4 Blockchain Overview

Blockchain is a sequence of blocks, which holds a complete list of transaction records like conventional public ledger [26, 38, 39]. Figure 5 illustrates an example of a blockchain. With a previous block hash contained in the block header, a block has only one parent block. It is worth noting that uncle blocks (children of the block's ancestors) hashes would also be stored in Ethereum blockchain [3]. The first block of a blockchain is called genesis block which has no parent block. We then explain the internals of blockchain in details.

4.1 Block

A block consists of the block header and the block body as shown in Fig. 3. In particular, the block header includes:

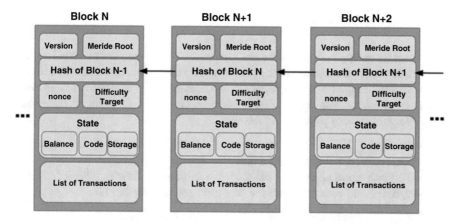

Fig. 3 Blockchain overview [15, 39]

Fig. 4 Blockchain blocks [39]

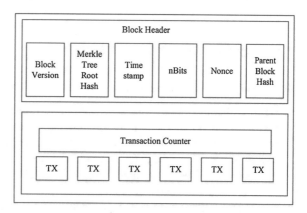

- Block version: indicates which set of block validation rules to follow.
- Merkle tree root hash: the hash value of all the transactions in the block.
- Timestamp: current time as seconds in universal time since January 1, 1970.
- nBits: target threshold of a valid block hash.
- Nonce: an 4-byte field, which usually starts with 0 and increases for every hash calculation
- Parent block hash: a 256-bit hash value that points to the previous block.

The block body is composed of a transaction counter and transactions. The maximum number of transactions that a block can contain depends on the block size and the size of each transaction. Blockchain uses an asymmetric cryptography mechanism to validate the authentication of transactions [25, 33, 40]. Digital signature based on asymmetric cryptography is used in an untrustworthy environment. We next briefly illustrate digital signature (Fig. 4).

4.2 Digital Signature

Each user owns a pair of private key and public key. The private key that shall be kept in confidentiality is used to sign the transactions. The digital signed transactions are broadcasted throughout the whole network. The typical digital signature is involved with two phases: signing phase and verification phase. For instance, an user Alice wants to send another user Bob a message.

1. In the signing phase, Alice encrypts her data with her private key and sends Bob the encrypted result and original data.
2. In the verification phase, Bob validates the value with Alice's public key. In that way, Bob could easily check if the data has been tampered or not.

The typical digital signature algorithm used in blockchains is the elliptic curve digital signature algorithm (ECDSA) [13].

4.3 Key Characteristics of Blockchain

In summary, blockchain has following key characteristics.

- **Decentralization**. In conventional centralized transaction systems, each transaction needs to be validated through the central trusted agency (e.g., the central bank), inevitably resulting to the cost and the performance bottlenecks at the central servers. Contrast to the centralized mode, third party is no longer needed in blockchain. Consensus algorithms in blockchain are used to maintain data consistency in distributed network.
- **Persistency**. Transactions can be validated quickly and invalid transactions would not be admitted by honest miners. It is nearly impossible to delete or rollback transactions once they are included in the blockchain. Blocks that contain invalid transactions could be discovered immediately.
- **Anonymity**. Each user can interact with the blockchain with a generated address, which does not reveal the real identity of the user. Note that blockchain cannot guarantee the perfect privacy preservation due to the intrinsic constraint.
- **Auditability**. Bitcoin blockchain stores data about user balances based on the Unspent Transaction Output (UTX-O) model [22]: Any transaction has to refer to some previous unspent transactions. Once the current transaction is recorded into the blockchain, the state of those referred unspent transactions switch from unspent to spent. So transactions could be easily verified and tracked.

5 Healthcare IoT Security Preserving Models Using Blockchain

In this section we detail and examine some proposed healthcare IoT models that use blockchain and discuss their security implications.

5.1 Healthcare Blockchain System Using Smart Contracts for Patient Monitoring

In [12], Griggs et al. mention that as Internet of Things (IoT) devices and other remote patient monitoring systems increase in popularity, security concerns about the transfer and logging of data transactions arise. In order to handle the protected health information (PHI) generated by these devices, we propose utilizing blockchain-based smart contracts to facilitate secure analysis and management of medical sensors. Using a private blockchain based on the Ethereum protocol, they created a system where the sensors communicate with a smart device that calls smart contracts and writes records of all events on the blockchain. This smart contract system would support real-time patient monitoring and medical interventions by sending notifications to patients and medical professionals, while also maintaining a secure record of who has initiated these activities. This would resolve many security vulnerabilities associated with remote patient monitoring and automate the delivery of notifications to all involved parties in a Privacy Rule of the Health Insurance Portability and Accountability Act (HIPAA) of 1996 compliant manner.

5.1.1 System Overview

The authors outline the system as follows. A patient remotely monitored by a doctor is equipped with various medical devices, such as an insulin pump or blood pressure monitor. The raw data is sent to a master "smart device," typically a smartphone or tablet, for aggregation and formatting by the application. Once complete, the formatted information is sent to the relevant smart contract for full analysis along with customized threshold values as in Fig. 5. In the Ethereum protocol, the source for the information fed to the smart contracts is known as the "Oracle" [4]. In this case, the Oracle is the smart device, which communicates directly to the smart contracts. The smart contract will then evaluate the provided data and issue alerts to both the patient and healthcare provider, as well as automated treatment instructions for the actuator nodes if desired as in Fig. 6.

No confidential medical information will be stored on the blockchain or in the smart contracts because of HIPAA compliance reasons. They propose to only record the fact that events occurred and using the blockchain technology as a ledger. The measurements themselves will be forwarded to a designated EHR storage

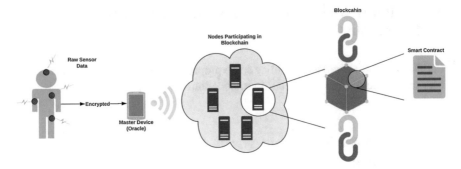

Fig. 5 System overview [12]

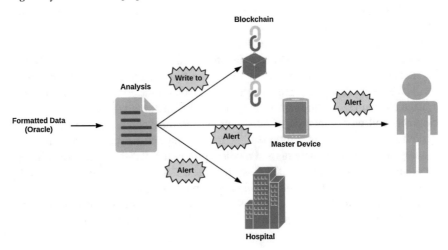

Fig. 6 Nodes of model [12]

database, while a new transaction will be added to the blockchain stating that the data was successfully processed. The system will integrate with EHR APIs and send data directly to the EHR for storage. Similarly, all treatment commands from the smart contract and healthcare provider will be recorded as complete in a blockchain transaction. These blockchain transactions can then be linked to the EHR in order to provide authentication of the data in the patient's medical history as a comprehensive record of care. This authentication will help to prevent and detect alterations of a patient's EHR, whether it be on purpose or accidental.

This system will have a private and consortium-led blockchain, meaning that only authorized viewers can read the blocks and only designated nodes can execute smart contracts and verify new blocks. Limiting the viewers to only invested parties such as care providers, device manufacturers, and patients themselves will help to reduce excess exposure of information by requiring authentication to access the application. In the consortium style of blockchain management, a set of pre-approved members operate the nodes in the blockchain, and a valid block must contain signatures from a minimum number of members (i.e. 10 out of 15). This framework would allow different healthcare companies to participate in the system while still maintaining a measure of decentralized management.

Additionally, by using only pre-authorized verification (mining) nodes, it will ensure that no rogue nodes could collude to insert false transactions into the chain, as well as eliminating the need to pay currency for proof-of-work. Instead, protocols such as Practical Byzantine Fault Tolerance (PBFT) can be utilized to achieve consensus since the participating nodes are known and vetted [5]. The smart contracts themselves will be modular and customizable for each patient and their devices. The structure will be tiered, with all master devices calling the same initial smart contract, which will in turn call the relevant sub-contract for the specific patient's device and pass it the input data and custom threshold values. This individual contract will analyze the data according to the threshold values, and then issue any necessary alerts or treatment commands based on its findings. A contract cannot be edited after deployment, but rather must be "killed" and a new contract issued, so this modular structure makes it easy to replace a device's contract without affecting the operation of others.

5.1.2 Security Analysis

For the sake of simplicity, it is assumed that all cloud and IP protocols are secure using encryption, and no more is added. Within the smart device, authentication must be present for the parties that could possibly be using the data (i.e. patients have the right to view but not edit their own data, while healthcare professionals have the right to edit the thresholds of their patients for the smart contracts). The proposed consortium blockchain makes it necessary to reach a majority of signatures from consortium members to make a block valid, preventing one party from manipulating the ledger. Viewing privileges of the blockchain itself are restricted to only authorized parties (patients, caregivers, etc). Second, no sensitive patient data is stored directly on the blockchain. The blockchain ledger storing the transactions also serves as a separate form of security for both the patient and the healthcare professional, as its detailed record could be useful for settling disputes and tracking procedures.

The electronic transmission of data falls under HIPAA. The most obvious aspect of the law that pertains to this system is the fact that data is not covered under HIPAA if it cannot be identified as belonging to a specific patient. As proposed, the data on the blockchain contains only information about transactions, and not sensitive health data. Furthermore, the patients are anonymized by the account addresses, so information is not easily linked to a specific person, thus making it permissible under HIPAA [9]. The Privacy Rule states that disclosure of personal data can only be to individuals on request or to the Department of Health and Human Services (HHS) in cases of investigation or enforcement action [9]. Another benefit of their system is that it provides authenticated and immutable records of a patient's monitoring for

HHS to use for settling disputes or investigating. Their system is HIPAA compliant because it takes reasonable safeguards to secure and provide tiered access to PHI.

5.2   Privacy-Preserving Blockchain Based IoT Ecosystem

In [27], Rahulamathavan et al. propose a new privacy-preserving blockchain architecture for IoT applications based on attribute-based encryption (ABE) techniques. They present security, privacy, and numerical analyses for validation of the proposed model. As an example of their model they present a healthcare case study tying their paper to Healthcare IoT through this as given in Fig. 7.

5.2.1   System Model

They describe the IoT network model considered as similar to the work in [7], they also consider a hierarchical approach where there will be a cluster head for a given set of IoT sensors. The cluster head is assumed to be more powerful than IoT devices and performs computationally intensive operations such as data processing and encryption. The data recorded by IoT devices are transmitted to the cluster head for processing and transmission. In their system, there are a number of blockchain miners who verify transactions and contribute to the blockchain. These miners could be service providers or even cluster heads. In order to provide ABE there will be

Fig. 7 System model [27]

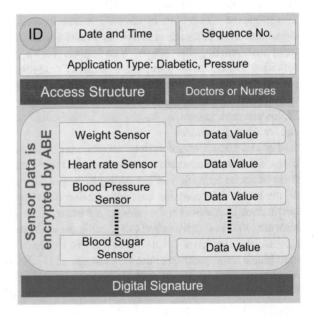

a number of attribute authorities (AAs) part of this network. They briefly define the concept of ABE and how it will be used for blockchain in the next subsection followed by the blockchain transaction architecture.

ABE supports both confidentiality and access control via single encryption [21]. There are four parties involved in ABE, namely cluster head (data owners), blockchain miners, attribute authorities (AA) and distributed ledger (or blockchain with blocks of transactions). The cluster head aggregates or processes the data from sensors and encrypts them before the transaction. The cluster head encrypts the data in such a way that the transactions can be seen and verified by particular miners who have the right attributes. In healthcare scenarios, for example, the cluster head may define a miner policy such as DOCTORS or NURSES to its encryption. Hence the miner who has DOCTORS attribute or NURSES attribute can decrypt and verify the transactions. Moreover, once these transactions are appended in the blockchain (i.e., distributed ledger system), only users who have these DOCTOR or NURSES attributes can be able to use the data. This will allow the data owner to control the data privacy through fine- grained access control.

5.2.2 Security Analysis

Since the proposed solution enforces ABE, the number of miners who qualify for verification is less than the traditional blockchain network. If the cluster head chooses too many at- tributes or very specific attributes then the number of qualified miners will be reduced. If there are too little miners who can verify the transaction then that may jeopardize the security of the blockchain technology. For example a malicious cluster head may collude with malicious miners to approve falsified transactions by assigning very specific attributes. To avoid this problem, the blockchain protocol will specify the minimum number of miners for verification. To avoid the case where only few miners are qualified for specific attributes, the AA will be forced to wait until the number of miners for an attribute surpasses the minimum number requirement set by the blockchain protocol. As discussed in the introduction, the related works either keep the transaction data in the plain domain or use symmetric encryption like the AES for encryption. If the transaction data is encrypted using AES then the encrypted key will need to be shared with the transaction to enable verification. This means anyone in the blockchain network can see the data and there is no advantage of encryption. In the proposed work, the number of miners who can view the data is limited. Only miners who have the right attributes can see the data. The AAs will scrutinize the miners for their claimed attributes before issuing the credentials. For example, miners associated with hospitals may get the credentials for DOCTORS and NURSES. However, once the verification is performed, any miners in the block chain network can contribute to mining a new block regardless of their attributes. Hence, the blockchain's concept of proof-of-work (PoW) is still preserved in the proposed model. Traditional IoT systems are known for sybil attacks. How- ever, in the proposed blockchain-powered IoT system, the transaction data is verified by a large number of miners before it is accepted. Unless the transaction data are added to the new block, sybil attacks have limited impact. Since the proposed model is built on top of the well researched decentralized ABE and blockchain technology, we can assume that there is no security vulnerability in the rest of the model.

5.3 A Decentralized Privacy-Preserving Healthcare Blockchain for IoT

In [9], Dwivedi et al. propose a novel framework of modified blockchain models suitable for IoT devices that rely on their distributed nature and other additional privacy and security properties of the network. These additional privacy and security properties in their model are based on advanced cryptographic primitives. The solutions given here make IoT application data and transactions more secure and anonymous over a blockchain-based network.

5.3.1 System Overview

Their system consists of five parts: Overlay network, Cloud storage, Healthcare providers, Smart contracts and Patient equipped with healthcare wearable IoT devices. An overview of the system given in Fig. 9.

Cloud Storage Instead of saving the IoT healthcare data over blockchain, we use cloud storage servers to save the patient data. The cloud storage groups user's data in identical blocks associated with a unique block number. These clouds are connected to overlay networks, once the data stored in a block, the cloud server sends the hash of the data blocks to the overlay network. The hash of the data in the single block is calculated using Merkle Tree. If the overlay network accepts the root hash of the new block, it adds the new hash with the previous has value and generates the new hash of the chain. In such cases, we do not need any third-party trust, because any changes in data could be easily traceable.

Overlay Network An overlay is a peer-to-peer network that is based on distributed architecture. The nodes connected to the network could be a computer, smartphone, tablet or any other IoT device as well (Fig. 8). (Please note that, in the description of overlay networks we assume that readers have sufficient knowledge of standard cryptographic protocols and use of the hash function in bitcoin mining.) In their model, a network consists of specific nodes and they need to prove that they are certified with a valid certificate. Such a certificate can be uploaded or verified before making an account on the network. Once authorized, he/she will be able to sign data/transaction over the network digitally. To increase network scalability and avoid network delay, we group the nodes in the form of many clusters. Each cluster has one Cluster Head that takes care of public keys of the nodes. Any node

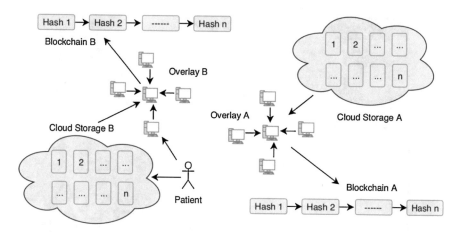

Fig. 8 Overlay network [9]

attached with any cluster can change the cluster at any time in case of delay. Also, the nodes attached to a cluster can change the cluster head. Cluster head maintains the public keys of requesters (healthcare providers), who can access the data of a particular patient, and the public key of requestees (patient) that are allowed to be accessed. Consider the case where a patient wants to share his/her data with a particular doctor, then the node digitally signs the transaction and sends it to the network with a public address of the doctors' node. The cluster head verifies the patient digital signature and patient public key, and if it is verified correctly, cluster head searches the public key of the doctor node in his own cluster. If the public key is available, then it will broadcast the transaction to its own cluster, and if doctor nodes public key is not available then cluster head will broadcast the transaction to other clusters. In the case where the digital signature or public key of any node is not verified then the cluster will not broadcast data in its cluster but transfer transaction to other cluster heads. Cluster heads are also responsible for storing the hash of the data block stored in the cloud. Each new block in the cluster contains the hash of the previous block also (Please note that each hash block says hash n is combined hash of all previous hashes such as hash 1. A cluster head can independently decide whether to keep hash of new data block or not. Once a cluster head adds new hash it will broadcast this to all clusters. Other clusters also verify the new block using the hash value of the previous chain. To follow the distributed trust in the network, each cluster head maintains a trust rating for other cluster head based on Beta Reputation System [14]. For more details of overlay networks we suggest readers to reference the following papers [1, 32].

Healthcare Providers Healthcare providers are appointed by insurance companies or by patients to perform medical tests or to provide medical treatments. Healthcare service providers deal with treatment of patients once they receive an alert from the

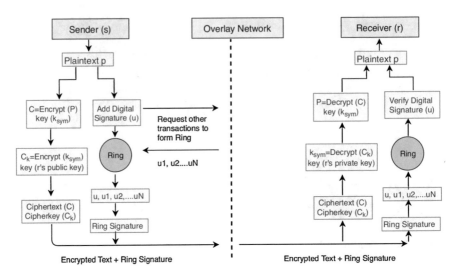

Fig. 9 System overview [9]

network. They are also treated as a node in the network and authorized to receive particular patient data from the cloud (Fig. 9).

Smart Contracts Smart contracts allow the creation of agreements in any IoT devices which is executed when given conditions are met. Consider we set the condition for the highest and lowest level of patient blood pressure. Once readings are received from the wearable device that do not follow the indicated range, the smart contract will send an alert message to the authorized person or healthcare provider and also store the abnormal data into the cloud so that healthcare providers can receive the patient blood pressure readings as well later on if needed. Patient with wearable IoT devices: The IoT device will collect all health data from the patient. Such data could be heartbeats, sleeping conditions, or walking distance to name a few. Patients themselves are the owners of their personal data and responsible for granting, denying or revoking data access from any other parties, such as insurance companies or healthcare providers. If the patient needs medical treatment, he/she will share personal health data with the desired doctor. Once the treatment is finished the patient can deny further access to the doctor, healthcare provider or health insurance company. We can see a logical flow of the entire system given in Fig. 10.

5.3.2 Security

In any model, there are three main security requirements that need to be addressed by model designers: Confidentiality, Integrity, and Availability. Confidentiality makes sure that only authorized users can access the system. Integrity is responsible for messages sent to the destination without any change, and Availability means data

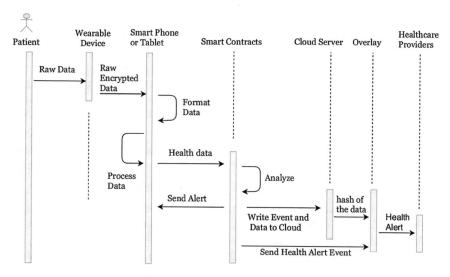

Fig. 10 Logical flow of system [9]

is always available to the users when needed. We evaluate the security margin of the model under various threats. In this model, the adversary can be a home device, the cluster head, or any other node in the network or part of the cloud storage. These adversaries can discard transactions, sniff communications, create false transactions, or change or delete information from the storage. However, their models' basic aim is to save the network from the adversary, and we focus on this rather than individual nodes. If a node is connected to the network and he verifies proof of authority and registered by the network, then we assume that he is an honest node. In the case where the network detects some malicious activity by the given node, we can block the malicious node from the network.

5.3.3 Limitations

As with all complex distributed system, all three proposed systems suffer from the largest challenge which is maintaining security at every individual node. As currently proposed, all three systems transmission between the patient's smart device and the blockchain nodes is over a possibly open channel (a patient's local WiFi, for instance), and relies on standard channel encryption. On a large scale, however, key management becomes an issue when there are many smart devices broadcasting their transactions to multiple nodes waiting to verify the next block. This could be resolved with a key management system designed to manage large numbers of keys. An important aspect of any healthcare system is the necessity for real-time data to be accumulated and acted upon. Block verification times can be manipulated, but will still introduce some minor delay. As proposed in all systems, the smart device collects and aggregates data from the sensor at small intervals, but sends the aggregated data in larger time intervals. The limitation here rests in perfecting the timing of the transmissions. Decisions must be made on a patient-by-patient basis, depending on the severity of the condition as well as the type of sensor they are using. It is important that this system, with current constraints, not be used for emergency response, as the delay might increase response time. In a consortium-style blockchain that uses a consensus method such as PBFT, some human-based verification must occur before a new node is added to the system in order to prevent the presence of rogue miners. Furthermore, there must be a sufficient number of nodes online at any time in order to meet the requirements for providing the minimum number of validation signatures and maintaining the integrity of the consensus algorithm. In PBFT, this typically means at most $\dfrac{N-1}{3}$ of the total nodes can be down at once, with N nodes overall [5]. As far as limitations, it is also important to note that this is an open research topic, and some of these limitations may be overcome with future development.

Overall, the three systems and healthcare IoT using blockchain suffers from a lack of experimental results and test networks to run simulations on. We would like to see the work done in [9, 12, 27] be properly tested and deployed in environments where there limitations can clearly be shown. There is some time complexity testing given in [27], but otherwise all three papers are theoretical in nature, thus providing a starting point for blockchain in healthcare IoT.

6 Conclusion

This chapter takes an in depth look at blockchain technology in the healthcare IoT realm and analyzes some of the security limitation of IoT that blockchain may be able to address in the future. A systematic study of the needs of a secure IoT and how current implementations are addressing those needs, provided a glimpse into the future of IoT. From a blockchain perspective, certain limitations will need to be corrected for it to be influential in a healthcare IoT setting. The three current proposed healthcare IoT frameworks using blockchain were presented and the security mechanisms as well as their limitations were discussed. As healthcare IoT develops, so will the opportunity to test and simulate usable schemes to help identify the vest way to address security in Healthcare Internet of Things.

References

1. D. Andersen, H. Balakrishnan, F. Kaashoek, R. Morris, *Resilient Overlay Networks*, vol. 35 (ACM, New York, 2001)
2. M. Antonakakis, T. April, M. Bailey, M. Bernhard, E. Bursztein, J. Cochran, Z. Durumeric, J.A. Halderman, L. Invernizzi, M. Kallitsis et al., Understanding the Mirai Botnet, in *26th* {USENIX} *Security Symposium* ({USENIX} *Security 17*), pp. 1093–1110 (2017)

3. A. Azaria, A. Ekblaw, T. Vieira, A. Lippman, MedRec: Using blockchain for medical data access and permission management, in *2016 2nd International Conference on Open and Big Data (OBD)* (IEEE, New York, 2016), pp. 25–30
4. M. Bartoletti, L. Pompianu, An empirical analysis of smart contracts: platforms, applications, and design patterns, in *International Conference on Financial Cryptography and Data Security* (Springer, Cham, 2017), pp. 494–509
5. C. Cachin, Architecture of the hyperledger blockchain fabric, in *Workshop on Distributed Cryptocurrencies and Consensus Ledgers*, vol. 310, p. 4 (2016)
6. T. Dimitriou, K. Ioannis, Security issues in biomedical wireless sensor networks, in *2008 First International Symposium on Applied Sciences on Biomedical and Communication Technologies* (IEEE, New York, 2008), pp. 1–5
7. A. Dorri, S.S. Kanhere, R. Jurdak, Towards an optimized blockchain for IoT, in *Proceedings of the Second International Conference on Internet-of-Things Design and Implementation* (ACM, New York, 2017), pp. 173–178
8. A.D. Dwivedi, L. Malina, P. Dzurenda, G. Srivastava, Optimized blockchain model for internet of things based healthcare applications. arXiv preprint. arXiv:1906.06517 (2019)
9. A.D. Dwivedi, G. Srivastava, S. Dhar, R. Singh, A decentralized privacy-preserving healthcare blockchain for IoT.Sensors **19**(2), 326 (2019)
10. S. Edwards, I. Profetis, Hajime: Analysis of a decentralized internet worm for IoT devices, in *Rapidity Networks*, Oct 16, 2016
11. J.P. Farwell, R. Rohozinski, Stuxnet and the future of cyber war. Survival **53**(1), 23–40 (2011)
12. K.N. Griggs, O. Ossipova, C.P. Kohlios, A.N. Baccarini, E.A. Howson, T. Hayajneh, Health-care blockchain system using smart contracts for secure automated remote patient monitoring. J. Med. Syst. **42**(7), 130 (2018)
13. D. Johnson, A. Menezes, S. Vanstone, The elliptic curve digital signature algorithm (ECDSA). Int. J. Inf. Secur. **1**(1), 36–63 (2001)
14. A. Josang, R. Ismail, The beta reputation system, in *Proceedings of the 15th Bled Electronic Commerce Conference*, vol. 5, pp. 2502–2511 (2002)
15. M.A. Khan, K. Salah, IoT security: Review, blockchain solutions, and open challenges. Futur. Gener. Comput. Syst. **82**, 395–411 (2018, May 1)
16. M. Kim, W. Jo, J. Kim, T. Shon, Visualization for internet of things: power system and financial network cases. Multimed. Tools Appl. **78**(3), 3241–3265 (2019)
17. P. Kumar, H.-J. Lee, Security issues in healthcare applications using wireless medical sensor networks: a survey. Sensors **12**(1), 55–91 (2012)
18. P. Kumar, S.-G. Lee, H.-J. Lee, E-SAP: efficient-strong authentication protocol for healthcare applications using wireless medical sensor networks. Sensors **12**(2), 1625–1647 (2012)
19. C. Lamb, Future potential attack patterns against nuclear power I&C systems. Technical report, Sandia National Lab. (SNL-NM), Albuquerque, NM (United States), 2018
20. X. Lin, R. Lu, X. Shen, Y. Nemoto, N. Kato, Sage: a strong privacy-preserving scheme against global eavesdropping for ehealth systems. IEEE J. Sel. Areas Commun. **27**(4), 365–378 (2009)
21. L. Malina, G. Srivastava, P. Dzurenda, J. Hajny, and R. Fujdiak. A secure publish/subscribe protocol for internet of things.
22. D. McGinn, D. Birch, D. Akroyd, M. Molina-Solana, Y. Guo, W.J. Knottenbelt, Visualizing dynamic bitcoin transaction patterns. Big Data **4**(2), 109–119 (2016)
23. H. Ng, M. Sim, C. Tan, Security issues of wireless sensor networks in healthcare applications. BT Technol. J. **24**(2), 138–144 (2006)
24. J.-T.C. Ngo, J.T. Webb, Managing the status of documents in a distributed storage system, US Patent 9,020,887, 28 Apr 2015
25. R.M. Parizi, A. Dehghantanha, K.-K.R. Choo, A. Singh, Empirical vulnerability analysis of automated smart contracts security testing on blockchains, in *Proceedings of the 28th Annual International Conference on Computer Science and Software Engineering*, pp. 103–113. IBM Corp. (2018)

26. R.M. Parizi, A. Dehghantanha et al., Smart contract programming languages on blockchains: an empirical evaluation of usability and security, in *International Conference on Blockchain* (Springer, Cham, 2018), pp. 75–91
27. Y. Rahulamathavan, R.C.-W. Phan, M. Rajarajan, S. Misra, A. Kondoz, Privacy-preserving blockchain based IoT ecosystem using attribute-based encryption, in *2017 IEEE International Conference on Advanced Networks and Telecommunications Systems (ANTS)* (IEEE, New York, 2017), pp. 1–6
28. L.G.A. Rodriguez, J.S. Trazzi, V. Fossaluza, R. Campiolo, D.M. Batista, Analysis of vulnerability disclosure delays from the national vulnerability database, in *Anais do Workshop de Segurança Cibernética em Dispositivos Conectados (WSCDC-SBRC 2018)*, vol. 1. SBC (2018)
29. G. Srivastava, A.D. Dwivedi, R. Singh, Automated remote patient monitoring: data sharing and privacy using blockchain. arXiv preprint. arXiv:1811.03417 (2018)
30. G. Srivastava, A.D. Dwivedi, R. Singh, Crypto-democracy: a decentralized voting scheme using blockchain technology, in *ICETE (2)*, pp. 674–679 (2018)
31. G. Srivastava, A.D. Dwivedi, R. Singh, Phantom protocol as the new crypto-democracy, in *IFIP International Conference on Computer Information Systems and Industrial Management* (Springer, Cham, 2018), pp. 499–509
32. M. Stemm, R.H. Katz, Vertical handoffs in wireless overlay networks. Mobile Netw. Appl. **3**(4), 335–350 (1998)
33. P.J. Taylor, T. Dargahi, A. Dehghantanha, R.M. Parizi, K.-K.R. Choo, A systematic literature review of blockchain cyber security, in *Digital Communications and Networks* (2019)
34. K.K. Venkatasubramanian, S.K. Gupta, Security for pervasive health monitoring sensor applications, in *2006 Fourth International Conference on Intelligent Sensing and Information Processing* (IEEE, New York, 2006), pp. 197–202
35. F. Wu, L. Xu, S. Kumari, X. Li, An improved and anonymous two-factor authentication protocol for health-care applications with wireless medical sensor networks. Multimedia Syst. **23**(2) ,195–205 (2017)
36. Y. Xiao, X. Shen, B. Sun, L. Cai, Security and privacy in RFID and applications in telemedicine. IEEE Commun. Mag. **44**(4), 64–72 (2006)
37. J. Yoo, J.H. Yi, Code-based authentication scheme for lightweight integrity checking of smart vehicles. IEEE Access **6**, 46731–46741 (2018)
38. Q. Zhang, R.M. Parizi, K.K.R. Choo, A pentagon of considerations towards more secure blockchains, in *IEEE Blockchain Technical Briefs* (2018)
39. Z. Zheng, S. Xie, H. Dai, X. Chen, H. Wang, An overview of blockchain technology: architecture, consensus, and future trends, in *2017 IEEE International Congress on Big Data (BigData Congress)*, pp. 557–564, June 2017
40. Z. Zheng, S. Xie, H.-N. Dai, X. Chen, H. Wang, Blockchain challenges and opportunities: a survey. Int. J. Web Grid Serv. **14**(4), 352–375 (2018)

Secure Healthcare Framework Using Blockchain and Public Key Cryptography

Randhir Kumar and Rakesh Tripathi

Abstract In the current scenario, healthcare organizations are facing a serious problem in sharing medical information among different stakeholders without sacrificing the privacy and integrity of information. To store and share such a large volume of healthcare information securely is an important research issue. Blockchain has been used successfully in the bitcoin for the decentralized exchange of cryptocurrency without the involvement of the third party. The new structure of blockchain has been designed to accommodate the need of another field such as healthcare. Blockchain technology has the potential of immutability, integrity and decentralized architecture to manage the health records of the patient. This paper aims to address the issues of data security and authentication in healthcare. We have proposed a blockchain based secure framework using public key cryptography.

1 Introduction

Healthcare organizations are managing large amounts of medical records pertaining to patient health data (PHD), doctor and pharmaceutical details to provide better health solutions. Securing this data from unauthorized users is a challenge for any healthcare organization [4]. Healthcare data are more sensitive as its disclosure might lead to revealing the identity of the patient and their ailments. Effective security mechanisms are required for the healthcare organizations that are growing exponentially in terms of medical data storage. These organizations are legally bound to provide security and protection of data from various malicious attackers [12]. To share and store the information of a healthcare organization securely, The blockchain is the way in which every data event is time-stamped and can't be tampered with [2, 17].

R. Kumar (✉) · R. Tripathi
Department of Information Technology, National Institute of Technology Raipur, Raipur, Chhattisgarh, India
e-mail: rkumar.phd2018.it@nitrr.ac.in; rtripathi.it@nitrr.ac.in

© Springer Nature Switzerland AG 2020
K.-K. R. Choo et al. (eds.), *Blockchain Cybersecurity, Trust and Privacy*, Advances in Information Security 79, https://doi.org/10.1007/978-3-030-38181-3_10

The transaction of blocks in blockchain are disseminated and shared by each participant. These blocks consist of important healthcare data and are necessary to encrypt the data from unauthorized access [20]. The current blockchain based Healthcare Information Exchange (HIE) is highly dependent on their private keys, due to symmetric cryptography, for data security [5, 13, 14]. The symmetric cryptography contains a similar key for encryption as well as decryption and the key must be shared using a secret communication channel. If the key is disclosed, then the encrypted message can be easily decrypted by the attacker.

The symmetric cryptography is used in blockchain for data security because it provides faster execution than asymmetric cryptography [18]. However, it has an overhead of sending secret key (private key) every time using a secure channel and there is a chance of security breach while sharing the secret key [1, 16]. These security breaches can lead to a big loss for healthcare organization owing to the disclosure of sensitive healthcare information. Moreover, symmetric cryptography does not provide the digital signature authentication, and the recipient can never identify that the information is coming from the authorized source which leads to non-repudiation. Hence, the symmetric key approach is not the proper solution for healthcare data security and authentication in the blockchain.

In order to solve these problems, we propose public key cryptography (PKC) infrastructure that uses a digital signature as an authentication mechanism. A digital signature has a built-in mechanism to manage signature and their associated keys. Further, it is a way to reliably identify the user claiming to be the owner of a specific public key. In public key cryptography such as ECC [7], the public-private key pair is unique for each and every individual. Anyone can verify the authenticity of a message using the public key and at the same time security of data is also not compromised owing to encryption of data by private key.

Organization This paper is organized as follows: Sect. 2 presents the related work on blockchain in healthcare, Sect. 3 describes the public key cryptography, Sect. 4 illustrates the proposed framework for HIE and also introduces data security in healthcare, Sect. 5 describes performance and security analysis in HIE, and Sect. 6 concludes the paper.

2 Related Work

There are a number of literatures addressing the symmetric key approach for data security in blockchain based HIE, where the same key is used for encryption and decryption of healthcare information. However, these techniques are not efficient for data security due to the share of the private key by the participants. This section discusses the literature only related to data security in blockchain based HIE.

The authors in [15], have proposed PDC (patient data contract) which is world state architecture where each registered user data will be stored. However, blockchain will store only the encrypted URL data such as names, usernames, and emails. To access the data of a patient with other entities the permission contract (PC) was created and notification will be sent to the patient for accepting and rejecting the permission of entities. Once the notification is accepted then the entity can see the information of the patient. Otherwise, the PC (permission contract) will be discarded automatically. This process takes more time in verification for sharing the HIE information.

The work in [9, 19], addressed how interoperability of healthcare data should be maintained. Here, patient Id is used for the information sharing between participants, and the same Patient id is used for cryptography. The work is similar to symmetric cryptography.

The authors in [8], have used merkele root for integrity and privacy while sharing the information between two authorized participants. In this paper, authors have only considered the immutability of data but the security of data has not been discussed. The authors in [10], have introduced the data sharing between the participant using Personal identification number (PIN) and medical identification no (MIN) which is provided by the hospital. To share the information between two parties such as patient and doctor both identification should be verified by the contract. This paper is using hyperledger fabric solo which works using centralized and private blockchain technique. The objective was to share the information with valid parties. This approach is not suitable for security, integrity, and transparency of information. The authors of [20], have proposed framework that maintains two different chains namely Chain-A and Chain-B where chain-A is used for storage of individual patient record and chain-B is used for individual patient and hospital record and the patient information sharing has been done by the symmetric key approach. However, digital signature verification was not considered. The authors of [6] have discussed various application based on digital identities such as voting system, healthcare system, where each individual identified by their private key and token number. The token number was used for the verification number by the regulatory body and private key for the individual user identification. To share the information between two participants, both the private key and the token number is required. While the study of literature, mostly addressed the symmetric key for data security in the healthcare system, till now work on public key cryptography in HIE is not focused. We have used a framework which ensures data security by asymmetric cryptography.

Motivation The work in this paper is motivated from various Literature where data security work has been done in HIE (Healthcare Information Exchange) with a symmetric key approach where everyone has to send their private key [6] while data sharing. There is no work has been mentioned with PKC based authentication, integrity and security in HIE [3, 15].

3   Public Key Cryptography

The PKC is a technique that facilitate pair of keys: public keys that are distributed widely, and private keys that are only known to the designated owner. This provides two functions: authentication, where the public key confirms that an owner of the private key has sent the message, and encryption, where only the paired private key owner can only decrypt the message [11].In this section, ECC has been used for PKC (public key cryptography). Elliptical curve cryptography (ECC) provides high security with low computation time (Sect. 5) than DSA and RSA. We have used ECDSA to verify the signatures in our proposed framework (Sect. 4).

The objective of Algorithm 1 is to generate Public and Private key pair for the authentic participant while sharing the data.The computation time for key generation is similar to symmetric cryptography but it provides both data security and authentication.

Algorithm 1: ECC Key Generation Algorithm

Input : $E_q(a, b)$, G, q
Output: private key, public key generation
1. $E_q(a, b)$: The parameter of Elliptic curve which includes a,b,q where q is a prime number and form of 2^m
   G: specific point on curve whose order is large value 'n'.
2. $sender_A$ key generation and private key selection n_A ; $n_A < n$, where n is limit of curve point. calculate public key p_A; $p_A = n_A * G$
3. $receiver_B$ key generation and private key selection n_B; $n_B < n$, where n is limit of curve point. public key calculation p_B; $p_B = n_B * G$
4. $sender_A$ secret key calculation $K_A = n_A * p_B$
5. $receiver_B$ secret key calculation $K_B = n_B * p_A$

As shown in Algorithm 2, the sender encrypt message 'M' by the receiver public key p_B, so that only authorized receiver can decrypt the message.

Algorithm 2: ECC Encryption

Following steps performed by the sender:-
1. Let the message be 'M'
2. First encode the message 'M' into a point on the elliptic curve
3. Let the point be P_m (Message must be represented to the point on curve)
4. To encrypt the point choose a random positive integer 'K'
5. $C_m = K*G*P_m + K\, p_B$ where G is the base point.

Similarly in Algorithm 3 private key K_B has been used for decryption of the message by the receiver. The originality of message can not be tempered owing to the secret key technique of PKC.

Algorithm 3: ECC Decryption

The recipient does following steps:-
1. Multiply first point in the pair with receiver$_B$ secret key
2. Compute K_B*G*n_B
3. subtract it from second point in the pair
   $P_m + K * p_B - (K*G*n_B)$
   $P_m + K * p_B - (K * p_B) = P_m$, where$[n_B * G = p_B]$

In Algorithm 4 digital signature is created by the sender for authentication of the valid or invalid sender so that receiver can easily identify whether the message has been changed by middle-man or not.

Algorithm 4: Creation of Digital Signature

The sender does following steps :-
1. Select a statistically unique and unpredictable integer k in the interval [1,n-1].
2. Find kP = (a, b) , r = a mod n.
   computer r ,if it become equal to zero then go to step 1
3. Evaluate k^-1 mod n.
4. Evaluate s = k^-1 (h(m) + K_Ar) mod n. where h denotes Hash Algorithm (SHA-1).
5. compute s and if it is equal to zero, then go to step 1.
6. the pair of integers (r, s) denotes signature for the message m

---

Similarly in Algorithm 5 digital signature verification is done at the receiver end to verify the authentication of the sender by matching the message digest.

Algorithm 5: Verification of Digital Signature

The Recipient does following steps :-
1. Obtain A's public key and check for authentication
2. Compute the r and s such that the interval [1, n - 1].
3. Evaluate $w = s^-1$ mod n and h(m).
4. Evaluate t_1 = h(m) w mod n , t_2 = rw mod n
5. Evaluate $t_1 P + t_2 p_A = (a_0, b_0)$ and v = a_0 mod n.
6. if v = r then accept the signature.

---

4 Proposed Framework for Secure Healthcare

In this section, we have applied various Algorithm of Sect. 3 for the proposed HIE framework to provide data security and authentication which is mentioned in Related work. There are three key points that has been discussed in the proposed framework such as Smart Contract Algorithm for Healthcare Framework (participants validation, digital signature verification, encryption, and decryption), Transparent data sharing between multi-participants (only authorized participants can access the data and valid transaction gets distributed to each participant), and Healthcare Ecosystem using blockchain. The smart contract algorithms are proposed for participants validation, digital signature verification, and data encryption/decryption.

4.1 Smart Contract Algorithm for Healthcare Framework

As shown in Algorithm 6, a public key pair of asymmetric cryptography is verified for the valid participant and access of smart contract function is provided for the authentic user. The public key pair generation has been mentioned in Sect. 3. All registered participants have their valid public key for authentication while getting access to smart contract functions.

Algorithm 6: *Participant$_i$* Validation

Input   : query($participant_i$)
Output: valid/invalid
if *query ($participant_i$) exist query ($participant_i$) is valid* **then**
  check *$participant_i$* is valid / invalid
  if *$participant_i$ is registered in the valid list* **then**
    check *$participant_i$* is valid / invalid
    if *$participant_i$.pbkey is valid* **then**
     | return valid
    end
    else
     | return invalid
    end
  end
  else
   | return invalid
  end
end
else
 | return invalid
end

As shown in Algorithm 7, receiver public key verification is done for encryption of message so that only valid receiver can decrypt the message by their private key.

Algorithm 7: Encryption by $participant_i$.pbkey

Input : query($participant_i$)
Output: Invalid pbkey
calling of Algorithm 6 for $participant_i$.pbkey verification $validation\_access$ ← valid /invalid
if $validation\_access$ is valid **then**
| encryption is done by $participant_i$.pbkey
end
else
| return Invalid pbkey
end

As shown in Algorithm 8 digital signature is verified for the authentic sender so that the receiver can easily identify the modification in the message. The digital signature verification is used by smart contract as sender cryptographic signature (ScS) for non-repudiation (message is sent by the authentic sender or not).

Algorithm 8: Validation of Digital Signature

Input : query($participant_i$)
Output: valid/invalid
ScS - Sender cryptographic signature **if** $query(participant_i)$ exist $query(participant_i)$ is valid **then**
| check $participant_i$ is valid / invalid
| **if** $participant_i$ is registered in the valid list **then**
| | check $participant_i$ is valid / invalid
| | **if** $participant_i$.ScS is valid **then**
| | | return valid
| | **end**
| | **else**
| | | return invalid
| | **end**
| **end**
| **else**
| | return invalid
| **end**
end
else
| return invalid
end

As shown in Algorithm 9, digital signature verification is done for the authentic sender and once it is verified then receiver decrypts the message by their private key. The purpose of verification for the digital signature is to check the integrity of data so that any modification can be clearly identified at receiver end.

Algorithm 9: Decryption by $participant_i$.prkey

Input : query($participant_i$)
Output: invalid ScS (private key)
prkey - private key
ScS- Sender cryptographic Signature
calling of Algorithm 8 for $participant_i$.ScS verification
digital_verification $\leftarrow$ valid /invalid
if *digital_verification is valid* **then**
| decryption is done by $participant_i$.prkey
end
else
| return Invalid ScS
end

4.2 Secure Data Sharing Between Multi-Participants

The security fundamental consist of confidentiality and integrity between a different participant of the blockchain. The decentralize characteristics of the blockchain are combined with the digitally signed transactions which assure that an opponent cannot pose as the user and corrupt the information. As shown in Fig. 1, all the signed transaction is updated with a ledger of existing participants which ensures the integrity of information. In the case of multi-participant sharing, each participant has their own ledger which gets updated by every successful transaction between the participants. Once the transaction gets updated to the ledger of all participants then no forgery can be made.

For example, $Doctor_i$ and $Patient_j$ have finished information sharing and then transaction gets updated with a ledger of all the valid participant. This kind of information sharing can be easily verifiable by the pbkey (public key) of receiver and ScS (sender cryptographic signature) of the sender.

The following steps are involved for Integrity

1. As shown in Fig. 1, if two participants $Doctor_i$ desire to know the medicine of various disease from $pharma_k$, then $Doctor_i$ will share the public key to $pharma_k$.
2. $pharma_k$ encrypt the details of medicine by $Doctor_i$ public key.
3. $Doctor_i$ decrypt the data by their private key.
4. $pharma_k$ also digitally sign the transaction for ScS (sender cryptographic signature) verification so that $Doctor_i$ can easily identify the valid $pharma_k$.
5. The verified transaction get updated to all the participant that ensure integrity.

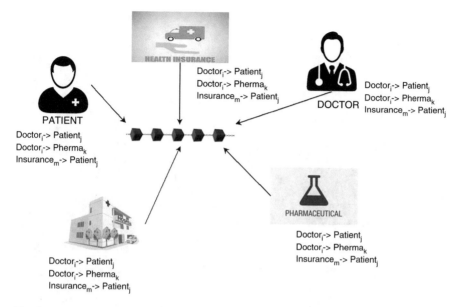

Fig. 1 Architecture of data sharing and transparency

4.3   Healthcare Ecosystem Using Blockchain

To understand the importance of the security and different level of privacy in healthcare framework we have proposed the secure healthcare ecosystem which contains a smart contract for the different participant validation-mentioned in (Algorithms 6, 7, 8, and 9). Figure 2 describes how the data will be encrypted initially by healthcare providers and stored in blockchain architecture for further communication of consolidated data among different participants. This current structure is proposed for patient health record (PHR) validation and accessed by the healthcare provider and participant of the healthcare framework. The following structure is divided in four different parts as listed below:

4.3.1   Healthcare Provider Organization

In the beginning, the healthcare providers give the clinical data to the individual patient, who is a valid participant of the following framework and also validate the public key of the patient before the submission of the patient transaction.

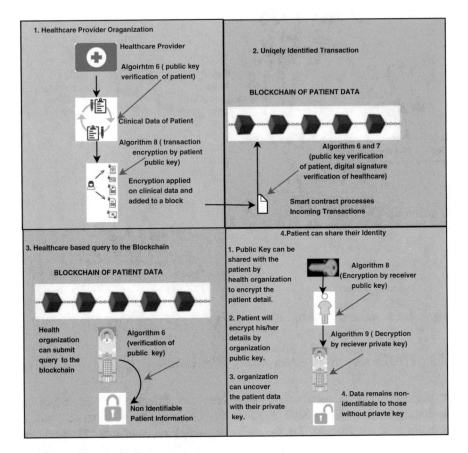

Fig. 2 Healthcare blockchain ecosystem

4.3.2 Uniquely Identified Transaction

The transaction (information) of the patient provided by the healthcare providers is checked against the smart contract verification such as valid provider, patient, medicationlist, visithistory. Once all the verification is done then the successful transaction will be added to the distributed ledger.

4.3.3 Healthcare Based Query to the Blockchain

The valid participant of the blockchain can query to the healthcare framework to get access to the individual patient record. The valid participant can be doctor, insurance organization, other healthcare organization (hospital). To get access of an individual patient record, the valid participant has to share their public key, Otherwise they cannot get the complete details of the patient.

4.3.4 Patient Can Share Their Identity to Health Organization

To get the complete transaction of the patient, the valid participant shares their public key to the individual patient, to encrypt the details and share with the same participant so that valid participant can decrypt the detail of individual patient by their own private key.

5 Performance and Security Analysis

In this section, we evaluate the proposed Algorithm (abbreviated as ECC) and present the results obtained. We compare the ECC with symmetric algorithms (AES, DES) and obtained the marginal execution time difference with respect to symmetric algorithms. We have also compared ECC with the Asymmetric algorithm (RSA) and obtained better performance in terms of execution time.

5.1 Experimental Analysis of Symmetric and Asymmetric Cryptography Techniques

The proposed algorithm is implemented using Hyperledger Composer business network archive (.bna) file deployment on Hyperledger Fabric v1.1 chaincode (smart contract). The Intel(R)Core (TM) i5-4590 CPU 3.30 GHz, 4GB of memory. We present the results obtained, implementing the proposed public key cryptography (ECC) by varying the different file size of healthcare. In every scenario, we execute the ECC and other algorithms ten times and average execution time has been taken.

Encryption Time Comparison In this experiment we compare the encryption time of ECC with symmetric algorithms. We increase the file size of healthcare from 32 to 280 KB and it can be seen that encryption time by ECC is closely approximate to the symmetric algorithms. It is also observed from Table 1, that encryption time decreases with smaller file size (32 KB).

Decryption Time Comparison Similarly, we compare the decryption time of ECC with symmetric algorithms using five different file size and concludes that decryption time is marginal with respect to symmetric algorithms. We also observed that the decryption time of ECC is similar to AES as we are using smaller file size (32 KB).

Table 1 Encryption and decryption time analysis of DES, AES, ECC, and RSA

Cryptographic algorithm	File size (KB)	Encryption time (s)	Decryption time (s)
DES	32	0.28	0.45
	126	0.83	0.65
	200	1.19	0.85
	246	1.44	1.23
	280	1.67	1.45
AES	32	0.15	0.15
	126	0.46	0.44
	200	0.72	0.63
	246	0.95	0.83
	280	1.12	1.10
ECC	32	0.13	0.15
	126	0.52	0.43
	200	0.74	0.66
	246	1.11	0.93
	280	1.39	1.23
RSA	32	0.45	0.43
	126	1.03	0.85
	200	1.41	1.13
	246	1.75	1.30
	280	1.83	1.64

5.2 Security Analysis Through Blockchain over Non-blockchain System

5.2.1 Denial of Service (DoS) Attacks

In the scenario of non blockchain based system which follow centralized and peer-to-peer network structure there can be two types of nodes namely honest and malicious nodes. The malicious nodes distribute the messages to increase traffic in network and this types of behavior makes obstacle for the honest nodes while making any transaction in the network. However, to mitigate the Dos attack we have used permissioned blockchain based system which only includes the registered peers (participants) in the network and all the states of transaction performed by the peers (participants) are recorded in the distributed ledger (shown in Fig. 7.), so it can be concluded that DoS attacks performed by any participants can be easily identified from the ledger and thus DoS attacks are very difficult to be performed over a peer-to-peer network in order to compromise the security of the entire network and the blockchain.

5.2.2 Sybil Attacks

The major issue in the non blockchain based peer-to-peer network is Sybil attack, where attackers pretends to be so many peers at the same time. Let's understand by an example, you are working in an insurance company which sells the insurance policy to the various customer over the phone. The company has given you a list of phone numbers of the customers. However,different phone numbers are pertaining to the one customer but you believe that these numbers belong to different customers. Hence, relate to the peer-to-peer network which is centralized and follows non blockchain architecture. The one peer can have different identity in the network and can performed malicious activity. The Sybil attack target whole network at a time not the single peer. Thus, Sybil attacks are very hard to trace in non blockchain based systems. In contrast to non blockchain, our permissioned blockchain systems doesn't allow different identity to one peer owing to the certificate verification in Hyperledger Fabric V1.1. peer-to-peer structure. Thus it becomes very hard to perform Sybil attack on permissioned blockchain based system owing to the identity verification while joining the network.

5.2.3 Eclipse Attacks

In contrast to Sybil attacks, Eclipse attacks monopolized a single peer from the whole network. This attack is again performed by malicious nodes over the honest nodes in the network. In Eclipse attack malicious nodes sends new identity of existing node in the network which they want to make target. In non blockchain system it becomes very easy to change the existing network identity with some set of existing node informations where as in permissioned blockchain all the identity and behavoiur of the peers are recorded in distributed ledger with timestamp such as when this peers has joined the network and what type of transaction has been performed by the peers shown in (Figs. 5, 6, and 7). Thus, permissioned blockchain provides the security to mitigate the Sybil attack over the peer-to-peer networks.

5.3 *Implementation of Healthcare Framework Using Permissioned Blockchain*

The implementation of our proposed Healthcare Framework (HIE) is carried out in the Hyperledger composer by the Linux Foundation. The experimental setup consists of Hyperledger composer playground v0.20.7 (permissioned BC), we have included 3 peers (Administrator, Doctor, Patient) which are hosted on the single server machine, each participant peer node is Intel(R) Core(TM) i5-4590 CPU @ 3.30GHZ running Window x64- based processor with 4 GB of RAM and 1 TB of local storage. The composer playground is interconnected through 1Gbps LAN

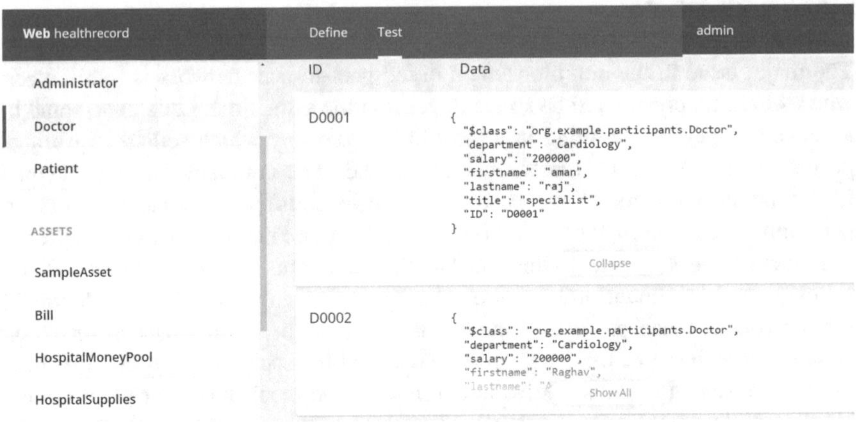

Fig. 3 List of doctor with their specialty in distributed ledger

cards. The source code of the healthcare framework is shared on github (*https://github.com/rkumarnit/healthcare_composer_code*).

5.3.1 List of Doctor

As shown in Fig. 3, the list of doctors with their specialty is recorded in the healthcare framework. In this distributed ledger, we have recorded the details of doctors with their department and specialty title. The patient can get the details of the doctor by this distributed ledger.

5.3.2 List of Patient

As shown in Fig. 4, The list of patient details is recorded in the distributed ledger. These patient are validated by the Administrator (Healthcare provider or Regulator) of the HIE framework. The valid patient can share their information with the doctor. We have also provided an Appointment facility for a patient to consult with the specialist.

5.3.3 Shared Information by Patient in Healthcare Framework

As shown in Fig. 5, the information is shared by the patient to a doctor, we have included four attributes i.e., patientId, name, medicationArray and pastvisitArray. The medicationArray attribute describe the details of medicine which patient is taking currently and pastVisitArray provides details about the last visit by a patient to a doctor. medicationArray is just like prescription details of a patient with all

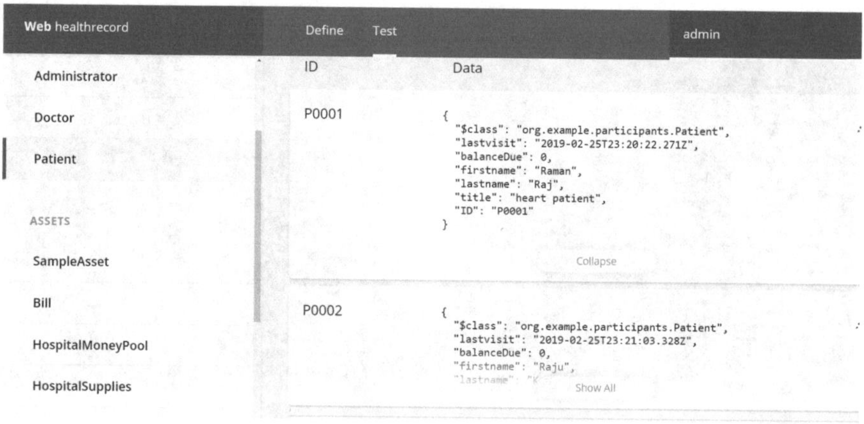

Fig. 4 List of patient in distributed ledger

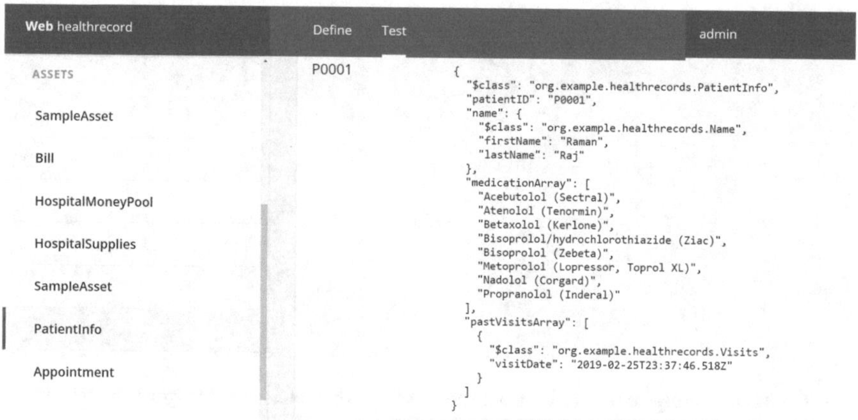

Fig. 5 Shared information by patient to a doctor with medication details

details like patient id, and name. The medicationArray can be updated by a doctor with new prescription given to a particular patient. similarly the pastVisitArray gets updated with every visit by the patient to a doctor.

5.3.4 Types of Transaction in Healthcare Framework

As shown in Fig. 6, We have provided different types of transactions which can be shared in the healthcare framework such as PayBill, SendBill, addAppointment, updateMedication,and UpdatePastVisit. The valid participants can perform these transactions in our healthcare framework.

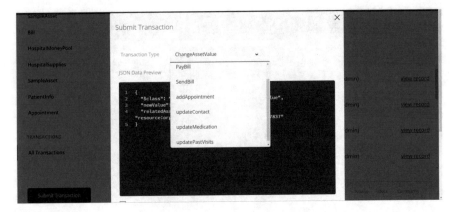

Fig. 6 Types of transaction in healthcare framework

Date, Time	Entry Type	Participant	
2019-02-25, 15:40:19	AddAsset	admin (NetworkAdmin)	view record
2019-02-25, 15:24:36	AddAsset	admin (NetworkAdmin)	view record
2019-02-25, 15:21:27	AddParticipant	admin (NetworkAdmin)	view record
2019-02-25, 15:20:59	AddParticipant	admin (NetworkAdmin)	view record

Fig. 7 List of transaction history for healthcare framework in blockchain ledger

5.3.5 History of Transactions in Healthcare Framework

As shown in Fig. 7, a list of all committed transactions in healthcare framework. The timestamp is recorded in blockchain ledger for each transaction with their hash value, and verified by smart contracts.

6 Conclusion

The proposed framework has been used with Blockchain and PKC (public key cryptography) for data security in Healthcare. This paper presented the healthcare framework for information sharing using blockchain to access the information with all the valid participants. The Current Healthcare Frameworks is working on symmetric cryptography techniques which is not very secure with the aspect of valuable medical data. The proposed framework is able to provide a distinction between valid and invalid participants and provides the facility to an authorized one. The proposed Framework has been implemented using cryptography techniques which provide better data security as well as authentication. In future work, we will consider different access control rules for the participants rather than cryptography techniques for our healthcare framework to share the information.

References

1. S. Chandra, S. Paira, Sk.S. Alam, G. Sanyal, A comparative survey of symmetric and asymmetric key cryptography, in *2014 International Conference on Electronics, Communication and Computational Engineering (ICECCE)* (IEEE, New York, 2014), pp. 83–93
2. M. Conti, S. Kumar, C. Lal, S. Ruj, A survey on security and privacy issues of bitcoin, in *IEEE Communications Surveys and Tutorials* (2018)
3. Deloitte, Blockchain–A New Model for Health Information Exchanges, August 2016
4. B.E. Dixon, C.M. Cusack, *Measuring the Value of Health Information Exchange* (Elsevier, New York, 2016)
5. C. Esposito, A. De Santis, G. Tortora, H. Chang, K.K.R. Choo, Blockchain: a panacea for healthcare cloud-based data security and privacy? IEEE Cloud Comput. **5**(1), 31–37 (2018)
6. S. Jiang, J. Cao, H. Wu, Y. Yang, M. Ma, J. He, Blochie: a blockchain-based platform for healthcare information exchange, in *Proceedings of IEEE International Conference on Smart Computing, SMARTCOMP 2018*, pp. 49–56 (2018)
7. A. Khalique, K. Singh, S. Sood, Implementation of elliptic curve digital signature algorithm. Int. J. Comput. Appl. **2**(2), 21–27 (2010)
8. X. Liang, J. Zhao, S. Shetty, J. Liu, D. Li, Integrating blockchain for data sharing and collaboration in mobile healthcare applications, in *2017 IEEE 28th Annual International Symposium on Personal, Indoor, and Mobile Radio Communications (PIMRC)* (IEEE, 2017, October), pp. 1–5
9. W. Liu, U. Krieger, Advanced block-chain architecture for e-Health systems. No. Etpha (2017), pp. 37–42
10. T. Mikula, R.H. Jacobsen, Identity and access management with blockchain in electronic healthcare records, in *2018 21st Euromicro Conference on Digital System Design*, pp. 699–706 (2018)
11. R. Rivest, A. Shamir, L. Adleman, A method for obtaining digital signatures and public key cryptosystems. Commun. ACM **21**(2), 120–126 (1978)
12. A.K. Saxena, S. Sinha, P. Shukla, A new way to enhance efficiency & security by using symmetric cryptography, in *2017 International Conference on Recent Innovations in Signal processing and Embedded Systems (RISE)* (IEEE, New York, 2017), pp. 157–162
13. Z. Shae, J.J.P. Tsai, On the design of a blockchain platform for clinical trial and precision medicine, in *Proceedings of International Conference Distributed Computing Systems*, pp. 1972–1980 (2017)
14. Y. Sun, R. Zhang, X. Wang, K. Gao, L. Liu, A decentralizing attribute-based signature for healthcare blockchain, in *2018 27th International Conference on Computer Communications and Networks*, pp. 1–9 (2018)
15. A. Theodouli, S. Arakliotis, K. Moschou, K. Votis, D. Tzovaras, On the design of a blockchain-based system to facilitate healthcare data sharing, in *Proceedings of - 17th IEEE International Conference on Trust, Security and Privacy in Computing and Communications. 12th IEEE International Conference on Big Data Science and Engineering (TrustCom/BigDataSE) 2018*, pp. 1374–1379 (2018)
16. C. Transaction, P. Blockchain: Opportunities for Health Care (CP Transaction, 2016)

17. M. Turkanovic, M. Holbl, K. Kosic, M. Heričko, A. Kamisalic, EduCTX: a blockchain-based higher education credit platform. IEEE Access **6**, 5112–5127 (2018)
18. X. Zhang, S. Poslad, Blockchain support for flexible queries with granular access control to electronic medical records (EMR), in *IEEE International Conference on Communications*, vol. 2018, pp. 1–6 (2018)
19. P. Zhang, M.A. Walker, J. White, D.C. Schmidt, G. Lenz, Metrics for assessing blockchain-based healthcare decentralized apps, in *IEEE International Conference on e-Health Networking, Application and Services*, pp. 17–20 (2017)
20. H. Zhao, P. Bai, Y. Peng, R. Xu, Efficient key management scheme for health blockchain. CAAI Trans. Intell. Technol. **3**(2), 114–118 (2018)

Public Blockchains Scalability: An Examination of Sharding and Segregated Witness

Amritraj Singh, Reza M. Parizi ⓘ, Meng Han, Ali Dehghantanha, Hadis Karimipour, and Kim-Kwang Raymond Choo ⓘ

Abstract Recently, public and permissionless blockchains such as Bitcoin and Ethereum have been facing a formidable challenge in the form of scalability which has hindered their expected growth. Both Bitcoin and Ethereum can process fewer than 20 transactions per second, which is significantly lower than their centralized counterpart such as VISA which can process approximately 1700 transactions per second. In realizing this hindrance for wide range adoption of blockchains for building advanced and large scalable systems, the blockchain community has proposed several solutions including *Sharding* and *Segregated Witness* (SegWit). Although these proposals are innovative, they still suffer from the blockchain trilemma of scalability, security, and decentralization. Moreover, at this time, little is known or discussed regarding factors related to design choices, feasibility, limitations, and other issues in adopting these solutions in public and permissionless

A. Singh
Department of Software Engineering and Game Development, Kennesaw State University, Marietta, GA, USA
e-mail: amritra@students.kennesaw.edu

R. M. Parizi (✉)
College of Computing and Software Engineering, Kennesaw State University, Marietta, GA, USA
e-mail: rparizi1@kennesaw.edu

M. Han
Department of Information Technology, Kennesaw State University, Marietta, GA, USA
e-mail: mhan9@kennesaw.edu

A. Dehghantanha
Cyber Science Lab, School of Computer Science, University of Guelph, Guelph, ON, Canada
e-mail: adehghan@uoguelph.ca

H. Karimipour
School of Engineering, University of Guelph, Guelph, ON, Canada
e-mail: hkarimi@uoguelph.ca

K.-K. R. Choo
Department of Information Systems and Cyber Security, University of Texas at San Antonio, San Antonio, TX, USA
e-mail: raymond.choo@fulbrightmail.org

© Springer Nature Switzerland AG 2020
K.-K. R. Choo et al. (eds.), *Blockchain Cybersecurity, Trust and Privacy*, Advances in Information Security 79, https://doi.org/10.1007/978-3-030-38181-3_11

blockchains. Hence, this paper provides the first comprehensive state-of-the-art review of sharding and segregated witness in public and permissionless blockchains, identifying current advancements, highlighting their limitations and discussing possible remedies for the overall improvement of the blockchain domain.

1 Introduction

Ever since the blockchain technology was brought under the limelight with the initial proposal of Bitcoin [1] in 2008, both the industrial and enterprise communities have been exploring its capabilities for various use cases by attempting to solve a diverse range of challenges. This has resulted in innovative new technologies including Ethereum [2], Hyperledger Fabric [3], etc. which are designed to be architecturally and politically decentralized [4] which allow trusted transactions between disparate parties. Blockchains are also being experimented in various computing and business domains such as cloud computing, supply-chains, Internet of Things (IoT), finance, and many others [5–8]. In recent years, academic research has also picked up the pace, especially in applying blockchain technology for developing decentralized applications [4, 9–11]. Additionally, research in recognizing technical challenges in the blockchain domain [12–16] has also been growing steadily along with studies that provide possible solutions to these challenges including, formal verification of smart contracts [17–19], scalability improvement of blockchains [20] and defining atomic cross-chain swap protocols [21]. This growth in interest from both the enterprise and research communities in blockchain related technologies has seen a major stumbling block in recent years in the form of scalability, which has quickly become the core problem surrounding blockchains. Scalability of a system or network is defined as its capacity to grow in size and manage increased demand from its user-base [22]. In other words, scalable systems can be efficiently enlarged to accommodate increased usage and activity from their user-base.

State-of-the-art blockchains are hindered by scalability due to the following two reasons: (1) There are limits on the number of transactions that a blockchain network can process and (2) blockchains are designed to provide solutions to a specific problem, they often tend to be vanilla in nature and hence, generally lack many features that traditional state-of-the-art centralized systems offer out of the box. For instance, a centralized database system can be built to provide several functionalities at once such as supply chain tracking, financial payments, and remote shopping, whereas on the other hand, a blockchain such as Bitcoin is built to provide only one functionality, i.e. to facilitate trustless peer-to-peer financial transactions within its network. Hence, it cannot store supply-chain information or provide the comforts of remote shopping to a user on its network by itself. In fact, it is extremely difficult if not impossible to implement a universal blockchain that could solve all problems with the current technology.

State-of-the-art blockchains face a trilemma of scalability, security, and decentralization [23] (Fig. 1). Blockchains can only have two of these three attributes:

Fig. 1 The blockchain
trilemma

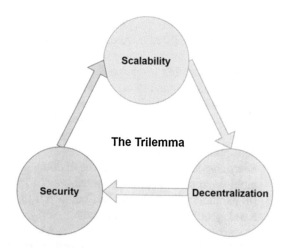

- *Scalability* concerns with the ability of a blockchain to process transactions in bulk. If public blockchains are to become mainstream, then they need to be able to handle the scenario in which there are millions of users on the network.
- *Security* is concerned with the immutability of the blockchain and its robustness to attacks such as Sybil [24], Distributed Denial of Service (DDoS) [25] and 51% attacks.[1]
- *Decentralization* is the core tenant upon which the blockchain community is built upon which provides censorship resistance and allows any user to participate in a decentralized environment without prejudice.

Public and permissionless blockchains such as Bitcoin and Ethereum were designed around decentralization and security as core features. However, this came at the expense of scalability as both Bitcoin and Ethereum have extremely low throughput when it comes to transaction processing rates. For instance, Bitcoin can only process approximately 7 transactions per second[2] and Ethereum can process approximately 15 transactions per second.[3] When compared to their centralized counterparts such as VISA which can process approximately 1700 transactions per second,[4] these public blockchains do not post impressive numbers.

Realizing this hindrance in the growth and further adoption of blockchains for building advanced and complicated software systems, both the research and enterprise communities have proposed the following solutions for blockchain scalability.

---

[1] https://medium.com/chainrift-research/bitcoins-attack-vectors-51-attacks-a96deac43774.

[2] https://blockexplorer.com/blocks.

[3] https://etherscan.io/.

[4] https://altcointoday.com/bitcoin-ethereum-vs-visa-paypal-transactions-per-second/.

- *Segregated witness (SegWit)*: Segregated Witness [26] is a proposed scaling solution for the Bitcoin protocol that changes the way data is stored on the Bitcoin blockchain. The proposal is to remove the signature data from each transaction of a block to free up space for more transactions to be included in Bitcoin's current 1 megabyte block size. In its current implementation, the signature data in Bitcoin takes up almost 70% of the block space which leaves behind little space for transactions. Hence, removing signature information from a Bitcoin block would save tremendous space which would allow for more transactions to be included in each block.
- *Sharding*: Sharding [26] proposes dividing or breaking down a blockchain into multiple smaller blockchains called *shards*. These shards operate simultaneously (in parallel) with each another. In, such a multi-blockchain environment, each shard processes transactions within its group, which in turn increases the processing output overall. Fragmenting a blockchain network (such as Ethereum) in this manner into smaller manageable parts allows the blockchain to function as the sum of its parts, rather than being limited by the speed of each node.

Although promising, sharding and segregated witness are still in the state of infancy and to this date, little is known or discussed regarding factors related to design choices, feasibility, limitations and other issues in adopting these scaling solutions. Moreover, there is a lack of comparative and empirical studies both in academic and industrial environments to analyze such protocols comprehensively. Hence, the motivation of this research is to provide the first comprehensive analysis of sharding and segregated witness for public and permissionless blockchains to understand the design choices, advancements, and limitations of such solutions. The specific contributions of this research are as follows:

- Provide a thorough analysis of sharding and segregated witness for Ethereum and Bitcoin.
- Analyze the most common design choices for these scaling solutions by highlighting their advantages and disadvantages
- Identify open issues and discuss possible solutions to mitigate those issues with state-of-the-art blockchain scaling solutions

The rest of this paper is structured as follows: Section 2 provides a background of sharding and segregated witness. Section 3 describes our research methodology and highlights the Research Questions (RQs). Section 4 answers the research questions raised by discussing the design choices of sharding and segregated witness, their limitations and hinderance in implementation. Section 5 sheds light on open issues and limitations while proposing future directions and possible solutions to mitigate these issues and limitations. Finally, Sect. 6 provides the conclusion of this work.

2 Background

In this section, we provide a brief overview of segregated witness and sharding which have been proposed for the Bitcoin and Ethereum protocols respectively.

2.1 Sharding

At the time of writing this paper, Ethereum, the most prominent smart contract platform in the world, can only process approximately 15 transactions per second. This severe limitation, coupled with the popularity of the platform, leads to high gas prices (the cost of executing a transaction on the network) and long confirmation times. Although a new block is added every 10–20 s on Ethereum blockchain, the average time for a transaction to be added on to the blockchain is over 1 min, according to ETH Gas Station.[5] Thus, low throughput, high gas prices, and high latency have rendered Ethereum unsuitable for building scalable services and applications.

Ethereum's low throughput is based on the fact that each node on the network has to process each transaction that occurs on the platform. To address this limitation, the blockchain community has proposed a few solutions which target the Ethereum protocol. Most of these solutions introduce central entities to process transactions at a high frequency. This is usually done by delegating all the computation to a small subset of powerful nodes. For instance, Thunder[6] runs a single node to process all transactions and claims to achieve approximately 1200 transaction per second, which is 100 times faster than current Ethereum capabilities. Other examples of such solutions are Algorand,[7] SpaceMesh,[8] and Solana[9] who are all attempting to improve the consensus protocols and design of blockchains to process high volumes of transactions each second. In addition to decentralization, another limitation of these solutions is that they are all bounded by the processing capabilities of a single node and hence, are vulnerable to a complete shutdown in case of power failures, natural disasters, etc.

In contrast, the other proposed solution, Blockchain sharding, delegates work such that, each node on the network only performs a subset of the total amount of work in processing a transaction on the blockchain. Sharding is the solution being used by the Ethereum foundation for improving the scalability of the Ethereum platform.

---

[5]https://ethgasstation.info/.

[6]https://www.thundercore.com/.

[7]https://www.algorand.com/.

[8]https://spacemesh.io/.

[9]https://solana.com/.

The concept of sharding in the domain blockchains comes from the world of databases where it is used to make servers and databases more efficient. This is done by storing each shard which a horizontal chunk of a database on a separate server instance consequently, spreading the load on the server.

In blockchains, the idea is to have each node store only a part of the blockchain (called a shard in this context), instead of the entire blockchain itself. This means that a node that stores a shard only maintains information on that shard in a shared manner, thus, maintain decentralization. However, each node doesn't load the information on the entire blockchain, thus helping in scalability.

Proof of Work (PoW)[10] consensus algorithm cannot be used in conjunction with sharding this is because all participant nodes cannot be involved in transaction validation as each node only has information regarding a particular shard, i.e. the shard it belongs to. Thus, the ideas that have been proposed for blockchain sharding are based on consensus mechanisms like Proof of Stake (PoS).[11]

In Proof of Stake consensus mechanism transaction validation responsibilities are undertaken by specifically designated nodes called "stakers". Stakers are required to stake their digital assets such as tokens to participate in transaction validation. A staker earns a part or the entirety of the transaction fees upon transaction validation. The number of transaction validations allowed for a staker is directly proportional to the amount and duration of their assets on stake. Additionally, the Proof of Stake consensus mechanism provides the following advantages over the Proof of Work:

- A subset of all nodes validates each transaction instead of the entire network nodes.
- Absence of mining eliminates the requirement for expensive special-purpose, high-performance hardware including CPUs, GPUs, and SSDs. This consequently decreases energy costs.
- It is easy to identify loyal and honest validators based on the amount and duration of the digital assets staked.

Each shard in a sharded blockchain identifies stakers who assume the transaction validation responsibilities for that shard. Since transaction validation is done by honest and loyal stakers, it is easy to presume that the security of the blockchain is still well preserved when compared to blockchains with Proof of Work mechanisms.

2.2 Segregated Witness

The Bitcoin blockchain comprises of several systems called *nodes*, which are distributed across a peer-to-peer network. These nodes validate the authenticity of Bitcoin transactions. Each validated transaction is broadcasted across the Bitcoin

---

[10]https://cointelegraph.com/explained/proof-of-work-explained.

[11]https://blockgeeks.com/guides/proof-of-work-vs-proof-of-stake/.

network in order to update the copies of the blockchain stored on other nodes. This makes it virtually impossible to corrupt or tamper with an already validated and stored transaction.

Each transaction on the Bitcoin blockchain consists of (1) *inputs* and (2) *outputs*. Input is the public address of the sender whereas, an output is the public address of a recipient. A transaction can have multiple inputs and outputs. A sender requires a recipient's public address in order to make payments to them. A large portion of the space involved in a transaction comprises of a digital signature (a part of each input) which verifies that the sender has the necessary funds to make the payment to the recipient. So, in effect, a Bitcoin moves from inputs to outputs for each transaction transmitted. As soon as each node has verified the validity of a transaction, it is included in a new block which is then added to Bitcoin blockchain.

The challenge that the Bitcoin blockchain faces today is that the shear volume of the transactions on the platform is increasing at a rapid pace, which requires more blocks to be added on to the network to satisfy this increased demand. Currently, a new block is generated every 10 min and is constrained by the block size of 1 megabyte (MB). This constraint limits the number of transactions that can be added in each block, which results in a backlog of transactions, waiting to be validated and added onto the blockchain. In some cases, transactions take several hours to be validated; this has quickly become one of the core problems surrounding the Bitcoin network.

One of the ways to solve this problem is with the segregated witness, which proposes the segregation of digital signature from transaction information. Currently, a Bitcoin transaction comprises approximately 65–70% of the total space available in each transaction. With a segregated witness, the signature data attached to a transaction input is ignored by removing and moving it to a separate structure at the end of a transaction. Such a design would result in an increase in block size from 1 MB to approximately 4 MB. Additionally, the segregated witness can also solve the problem where a recipient could intercept and modify a sender's transaction ID in order to steal more coins from the sender. Since the digital signature would be segregated from the transaction input, a malicious entity would have no way of manipulating the transaction ID without also nullifying the digital signature.

3   Research Methodology

In this work, we analyze proposed sharding and segregated witness solutions for improving the scalability of public and permissionless blockchains including Bitcoin and Ethereum. For this work, we adopted a Systematic Literature Review (SLR) based information and data gathering approach which helped us in identification, evaluation, and interpretation of all available research, solutions or platforms relevant to one or more research questions which are mentioned below [27, 28]. Based on the formulated research questions (RQs) (see Sect. 3.2), we designed a custom data gathering protocol for the identification of relevant resources and platforms for this research.

3.1 Research Protocol

An important characteristic of every research work is the identification of a problem and a protocol to solve that problem. Figure 2 outlines the protocol for this work.

It can be seen from the figure that our work started with the identification of a problem (in this case, scalability of public and permissionless blockchains), which led us into raising research questions regarding the state-of-the-art solutions. We then collected, filtered and expanded our inclusion criteria to include all relevant research resources and proceeded to answer the raised research questions which allowed us to identify open issues and ultimately, propose initial steps to solve or mitigate these issues. In the following sub-section, we will enlist the research question raised and our data gathering strategy to answer these questions.

3.2 Research Questions (RQs)

The most compelling motivation behind this research is to answer the following research questions (RQs) based on the proposed sharding and segregated witness solutions.

- *RQ1*: What are the Design Choices available for sharding and segregated witness?
- *RQ2*: What are the limitations of sharding and segregated witness?
- *RQ3*: What is the major hindrance in implementing sharding and segregated witness?

To answer these questions, we designed a custom protocol to search and identify all relevant resources such as journal articles, conference papers, workshop articles, etc. in the realms of blockchain scalability. In the subsequent sections, we describe the various steps that we performed for filtering the relevant resources to accurately answer the research questions in this section.

3.3 Search Strategy

Once we determined the digital libraries and search engines to be used for gathering relevant resources, we constructed several search terms to be used on these libraries and search engines based on our research questions. Some examples of our search terms are mentioned in Table 1.

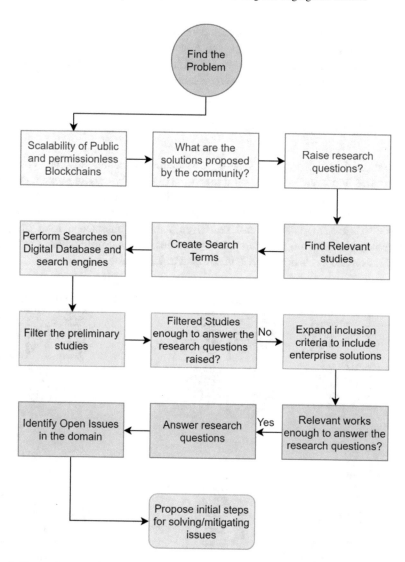

Fig. 2 Research protocol

Table 1 Search string and terms

Terms	Blockchain, scalability, sharding, segregated witness, smart contracts, bitcoin, interoperability, ethereum, etc.
Search terms used	Ethereum sharding, bitcoin scalability, blockchain scalability, smart contracts scalability, blockchain interoperability, etc.

Next, we performed manual searches with several combinations of search terms on digital libraries and search engines such as Google, Duck-Duck Go and Yahoo which yielded the results as shown in Fig. 3. This provided us with the unfiltered preliminary set of works on blockchain scalability.

3.4 Preliminary Set of Works

As mentioned in the previous section, we conducted manual searches based on search terms and keywords on several identified digital libraries and search engines to identify and collect the preliminary set of works. The results from these searches are summarized in Fig. 3, which shows the total number of preliminary studies acquired from each database and search engine. We obtained a total of 2136 preliminary studies from our search. These studies were carefully chosen based on the inclusion and exclusion criteria mentioned in Table 2.

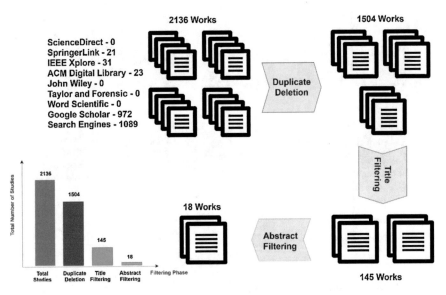

Fig. 3 Initial filtering of the relevant works

Table 2 Inclusion and exclusion criteria for relevant works

Inclusion criteria	Exclusion criteria
Be published online digital databases such as IEEE, ACM Digital Library, SpringerLink, etc.	Resources not published in English
Studies are in the domain of blockchain scalability	Resources from unreliable online sources
Studies offer technical quality in the presentation of ideas and reviews	Studies with poor presentation quality
Studies used current technical quality aspects	Grey literature, studies with incomplete ideas and poor explanation of concepts

Out of these 2136 studies, only 1047 were from online digital databases, namely ScienceDirect, IEEE Xplore, ACM Digital Library, SpringerLink, John Wiley, Taylor and Forensic, Word Scientific, and Google Scholar. The remaining 1089 resources were from search engine results such as Google, Yahoo, and Duck-Duck Go. It is important to mention at this time the results obtained in the search engines were considerably larger than just 1089 studies, but, most of these results covered repetitive topics or were not from trustworthy sources. Hence, after we collected the 2136 preliminary set of works, we started the initial filtering phase where, the collected studies were carefully removed based on duplicate removal, title filtering, and abstract filtering. The studies remaining after each filtering stage is shown in Fig. 3.

The initial filtering stages reduced the relevant works to just 18 studies. These studies are shown in Table 3. The next step in the filtering process was content filtering, where we removed studies with irrelevant content regarding this research by carefully and thoroughly reading each of the 18 studies. This process further reduced the relevant studies into single digits. This research focuses on public and permissionless blockchain such as Ethereum and Bitcoin's scalability and most of the 18 preliminary studies fell out of the scope of this study as they focus on the scalability of private or permissioned blockchains.

At this stage, we were forced to turn our attention towards the enterprise blockchain community and other online resources published by credible sources and individuals such as CoinDesk, Vitalik Buterin, and other well-established platforms such as the Lightening Network[12] for Bitcoin. Hence, we have answered our research questions based on the results of our thorough investigation and analysis of both resources from online digital databases and other credible technical sources including but not limited to white papers, conference presentations, technical talks, etc.

4   Results

In this section, we answer the research questions (RQs) raised in Sect. 3.2 to discuss the design choices for sharding and segregated witness, the limitations of sharding and segregated witness and the major hinderance in implementing sharding and segregated witness in the Ethereum and Bitcoin protocol respectively.

---

[12]https://lbtc.io/.

Table 3 Search results from digital databases

Digital database	Year	Article name	References
IEEE	2018	The blockchain for domain based static sharding	[29]
IEEE	2018	A scale-out blockchain for value transfer with spontaneous sharding	[30]
IEEE	2018	OmniLedger: a secure, scale-out, decentralized ledger via sharding	[31]
IEEE	2018	A scalable and extensible blockchain architecture	[32]
IEEE	2018	Challenges and pitfalls of partitioning blockchains	[33]
IEEE	2018	A game-theoretic analysis of shard-based permissionless blockchains	[34]
IEEE	2017	A prototype evaluation of a tamper-resistant high performance blockchain-based transaction log for a distributed database	[35]
IEEE	2018	Chameleon: a scalable and adaptive permissioned blockchain architecture	[36]
IEEE	2018	Blockchain and scalability	[37]
IEEE	2018	ProductChain: scalable blockchain framework to support provenance in supply chains	[38]
ACM Digital Library	2016	A secure sharding protocol for open blockchains	[39]
ACM Digital Library	2018	RapidChain: scaling blockchain via full sharding	[40]
ACM Digital Library	2018	Towards solving the data availability problem for sharded ethereum	[41]
ACM Digital Library	2016	Bringing secure bitcoin transactions to your smartphone	[42]
SpringerLink	2018	Pruneable sharding-based blockchain protocol	[43]
SpringerLink	2017	Short paper: service-oriented sharding for blockchains	[44]
SpringerLink	2018	A decentralized sharding service network framework with scalability	[45]
SpringerLink	2016	On scaling decentralized blockchains	[46]

4.1 What Are the Design Choices Available for Sharding and Segregated Witness?

In this sub-section, we will discuss the design choices available for sharding and segregated witness to answer our first research question (Sect. 3.2)

4.1.1 Sharding Design Choices

Now, we will discuss the various design choices for implementing sharding that shas been proposed by the blockchain community:

Scaling by Thousand Altcoins

The co-founder of the Ethereum platform, Vitalik Buterin, introduced the concept of "Scaling by a thousand Altcoins" in his presentation [47]. This design proposes the use of multiple blockchains instead of a single blockchain. Each blockchain in this multi-blockchain environment consists of its own set of validators and is known as a shard. For the rest of this discussion, we use a generic term "validator" to refer to participants or entities that validate transactions and produce new blocks, with the help of a suitable consensus mechanism such as mining with Proof of Work, or via a voting-based mechanism. For now, let's assume that the shards never communicate with each other. Although this design is simple, it is sufficient to highlight some of the major challenges in sharding.

The first challenge is the weakening of security of each shard as having their validator makes them several magnitudes insecure than the entire chain. So, if a non-sharded chain with 'x' validators decides to hard-fork into a sharded blockchain, and splits 'x' validators across 10 shards, each shard now only has x/10 validators, and corrupting one shard only requires corrupting (51/10)% or 5.1% of the total number of validators as can be seen from Fig. 4.

This paves the way for the second challenge: Who selects the validators for each shard? Controlling 5.1% of validators is only damaging if all 5.1% of the validators are in the same shard. If validators can't choose which shard they get to validate in, a participant controlling 5.1% of the validators is highly unlikely to get all their validators in the same shard, heavily reducing their ability to compromise the system [48].

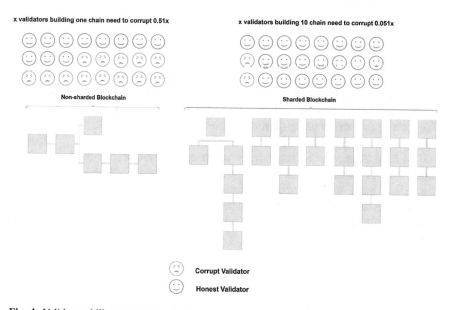

Fig. 4 Validator ability to corrupt a shard

Almost all sharding designs today rely on some source of randomness to assign validators to shards. Randomness on the blockchain is a challenging topic in itself and requires more research in the future, but for now, let's assume there's some source of randomness we can use.

Both the randomness and the validators assignment require computation that is not specific to any particular shard. For that computation, practically all existing designs have a separate blockchain that is tasked with performing operations necessary for the maintenance of the entire network. Besides generating random numbers and assigning validators to the shards, these operations often also include receiving updates from shards and taking snapshots of them, processing stakes and slashing in Proof-of-Stake systems, and rebalancing shards when that feature is supported. Such a chain is called a Beacon chain [48] in Ethereum.

Quadratic Sharding

Sharding is often advertised as a solution that scales infinitely with the number of nodes participating in the network operation. While it is in theory possible to design such a sharding solution, any solution that has the concept of a Beacon chain doesn't have infinite scalability. To understand why, note that the Beacon chain has to do some bookkeeping computation, such as assigning validators to shards, or snapshotting shard chain blocks, that is proportional to the number of shards in the system. Since the Beacon chain is itself a single blockchain, with computation bounded by the computational capabilities of nodes operating it, the number of shards is naturally limited.

However, the structure of a sharded network does bestow a multiplicative effect on any improvements to its nodes. Consider the case in which an arbitrary improvement is made to the efficiency of nodes in the network which will allow them faster transaction processing times.

If the nodes operating the network, including the nodes in the Beacon chain, become four times faster, then each shard will be able to process four times more transactions, and the Beacon chain will be able to maintain 4 times more shards. The throughput across the system will increase by the factor of $4 \times 4 = 16$; thus, the name *quadratic sharding* [48].

It is hard to provide an accurate measurement for how many shards are viable today, but it is unlikely that in any foreseeable future, the throughput needs of blockchain users will outgrow the limitations of quadratic sharding. The sheer number of nodes necessary to operate such a volume of shards securely is orders of magnitude higher than the number of nodes operating all the blockchains combined today.

State Sharding

Up until now, we haven't defined very well what exactly is and is not separated when a network is divided into shards. Specifically, nodes in the blockchain perform three important tasks: not only do they (1) process transactions, but they also (2) relay validated transactions and completed blocks to other nodes, and (3) store the state and the history of the entire network ledger. Each of these three tasks imposes a growing requirement on the nodes operating the network:

- The necessity to process transactions requires more compute power with the increased number of transactions being processed;
- The necessity to relay transactions and blocks requires more network bandwidth with the increased number of transactions being relayed;
- The necessity to store data requires more storage as the state grows. Importantly, unlike the processing power and network, the storage requirement grows even if the transaction rate (number of transactions processed per second) remains constant.

From the above list, it might appear that the storage requirement would be the most pressing since it is the only one that is being increased over time even if the number of transactions per second doesn't change, but in practice, the most pressing requirement today is the computational power. The entire state of Ethereum as of this writing is 100 GB, easily manageable by most of the nodes. But the number of transactions Ethereum can process is around 20, orders of magnitude less than what is needed for many practical use cases.

Practically, under State sharding [48], the nodes in each shard build their blockchain that contains transactions that affect only the local part of the global state that is assigned to that shard. Therefore, the validators in the shard only need to store their local part of the global state and only execute, and as such only relay, transactions that affect their part of the state. This partition linearly reduces the requirement on all compute power, storage, and network bandwidth, but introduces new problems.

4.1.2 Segregated Witness (SegWit)

To analyze the idea behind segregated witness, we need first to explain how a current transaction takes place on the Bitcoin network. This would allow us to demonstrate the potential impact of a segregated witness on scalability, in particular, Bitcoin's transaction throughput.

As shown in Fig. 5, with non-segregated witness transactions, the signatures needed to unlock the inputs are included along with the rest of the transaction data in the hash to get the transaction ID (TXID) [49]. Non-segregated witness transactions include the signatures in the hash to get the TXID. These transactions are then included in each block up to the 1 MB limit in structures called Merkle Trees.

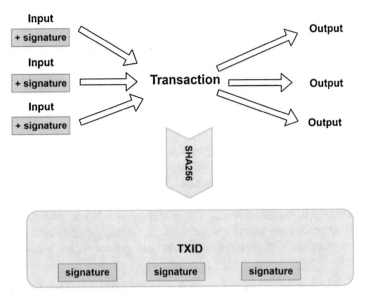

Fig. 5 Non-segregated witness transaction

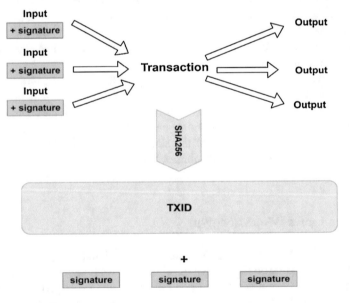

Fig. 6 Segregated witness transaction

On the other hand, as can be seen in Fig. 6, with segregated witness transactions, we have two fundamental changes. Segregated witness transactions do not hash the signature data. Signature data is stored as "witness" data in the block.

- The signature data is not included in the hash to form the TXID. Signatures are still stored in the block with the transactions as part of "witness" data, but they are longer included in the TXID hash.
- The block size limit is changed from 1 MB (1,000,000 bytes) to a 4,000,000 "weight" limit, an arbitrary new metric. A normal byte in a transaction weights 4 while a witness byte weights 1.

Hence, there are two significant benefits of segregated witness transactions, which we will discuss now.

Transaction Malleability

With Bitcoin transactions before segregated witness, there was a bug in the software called "transaction malleability" [48]. As we know by now, the TXID pre-segregated witness is the result of hashing the transaction data, including the signatures. Although there were checks and balances to ensure that the inputs and outputs couldn't be changed (i.e. the parties in a transaction and the amounts of Bitcoin being sent), the signature used to unlock the inputs could be modified slightly (such that it was still a valid signature) but would completely change the TXID when hashed. With the signature no longer a part of the TXID in segregated witness, transaction malleability is no longer a problem.

Increased Block Capacity

By changing the block size limit from a byte's limit to a new 4,000,000 weight limit, the number of transactions allowed in each block can be increased while maintaining backward compatibility with the existing cap of 1 MB per block. The equation for segregated witness nodes is as follows [48]:

$$4 * \text{normal bytes} + (1 * \text{witness byte}) = 4,000,000$$

Non-segregated witness nodes in the network will not be able to see the witness data, making the equation:

$$4 * \text{normal bytes} = 4,000,000$$

$$\text{normal bytes} = 1,000,000$$

So, with segregated witness, we will never exceed the 1 MB block size limit on older nodes, which would make it backward compatible although it would mean that only segregated witness nodes will be able to see the signature data. But, existing nodes will still have access to all the transactions. Segregated Witness will not result in nodes with a block size of 4 MB, as blocks aren't comprised 100% of witness bytes. The actual size of the blocks will depend on the adoption rate of segregated witness. By estimation, the expected average block size could be around 1.7–2 MB based on tests showing around 60% of a transaction to be witness data.

4.2 What Are the Limitations of Sharding and Segregated Witness?

We will now discuss some of the limitations of sharding and segregated witness to answer this research question.

4.2.1 Sharding Limitations

There are three main issues that arise with the proposed sharding solutions. We will assess these limitations in detail in this section:

Cross-Shard Transactions

"Scaling by a thousand Altcoin" as a model is not a very useful approach to sharding, because if individual shards cannot communicate with each other, they are no better than multiple independent blockchains. Even today, when sharding is not available, there's a huge demand for interoperability between various blockchains.

Let's for now only consider simple payment transactions, where each participant has an account on exactly one shard. If one wishes to transfer money from one account to another within the same shard, the transaction can be processed entirely by the validators in that shard. If, however, Alice that resides on shard 1 wants to send money to Bob who resides on shard 2, neither validators on shard 1(they won't be able to credit Bob's account) nor the validators on shard 2 (they won't be able to debit Alice's account) can process the entire transaction. There are two families of approaches to cross-shard transactions:

- *Synchronous*: whenever a cross-shard transaction needs to be executed, the blocks in multiple shards that contain state transition related to the transaction get all produced at the same time, and the validators of multiple shards collaborate on executing such transactions.
- *Asynchronous*: a cross-shard transaction that affects multiple shards is executed in those shards asynchronously, the "Credit" shard executing its half once it has sufficient evidence that the "Debit" shard has executed its portion. This system is

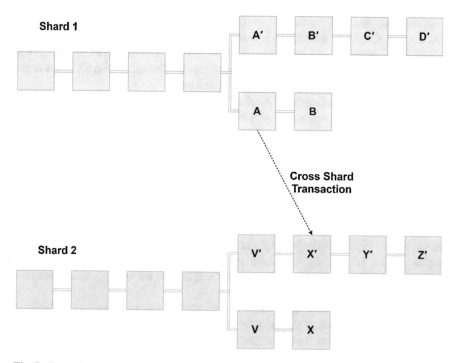

Fig. 7 Cross-shard transactions

today proposed in Cosmos,[13] Ethereum Serenity,[14] Near,[15] Kadena,[16] and others. A problem with this approach lies in that if blocks are produced independently, there's a non-zero chance that one of the multiple blocks will be orphaned, thus making the transaction only partially applied. Consider Fig. 7 above that depicts two shards, both of which encountered a fork, and a cross-shard transaction that was recorded in blocks A and X' correspondingly. If the chains A–B and V'–X' – Y'–Z' end up being canonical in the corresponding shards, the transaction is fully finalized. If A'–B'–C'–D' and V–X become canonical, then the transaction is fully abandoned, which is acceptable. But if, for example, A–B and V–X become canonical, then one part of the transaction is finalized, and one is abandoned, creating an atomicity failure.

Note that communication between chains is useful outside of sharded blockchains as well. Interoperability between chains is a complex problem that many projects are trying to solve [23, 50–53]. In sharded blockchains, the problem

---

[13]https://cosmos.network/.

[14]https://medium.com/utopiapress/what-is-ethereum-serenity-f433d824c974.

[15]https://nearprotocol.com/.

[16]https://kadena.io/en/.

is somewhat easier since the block structure and consensus are the same across shards, and there's a Beacon chain that can be used for coordination. In a sharded blockchain, however, all the shard chains are the same, while in the global blockchains ecosystem, there are lots of different blockchains, with different target use cases, decentralization, and privacy guarantees.

Building a system in which a set of chains have different properties but use sufficiently similar consensus and block structure and have a common beacon chain could enable an ecosystem of heterogeneous blockchains that have a working interoperability subsystem. Such a system is unlikely to feature validator rotation, so some extra measures need to be taken to ensure security.

Malicious Forks

A set of malicious validators might attempt to create a fork. Note that it doesn't matter if the underlying consensus is Byzantine Fault Tolerant (BFT) or not, corrupting a sufficient number of validators will always make it possible to create a fork.

It is significantly more likely for more than 50% of a single shard to be corrupted than for more than 50% of the entire network to be corrupted. As discussed above, cross-shard transactions involve certain state changes in multiple shards, and the corresponding blocks in such shards that apply such state changes must either be all finalized (i.e. appear in the selected chains on their corresponding shards), or all be orphaned (i.e. not appear in the selected chains on their corresponding shards). Since generally the probability of shards being corrupted is not negligible, we can't assume that the forks won't happen even if a Byzantine consensus was reached among the shard validators, or many blocks were produced on top of the block with the state change.

This problem has multiple solutions, the most common one being occasional cross-linking of the latest shard chain block to the beacon chain. The fork choice rule in the shard chains is then changed always to prefer the chain that is cross-linked and only applies the shard-specific fork-choice rule for blocks that were published since the last cross-link.

Approving Invalid Blocks

A set of validators might attempt to create a block that applies the state transition function incorrectly. For example, starting with a state in which Alice has 10 tokens and Bob has 0 tokens (see Fig. 8 [48]), the block might contain a transaction that sends 10 tokens from Alice to Bob but ends up with a state in which Alice has 0 tokens and Bob has 1000 tokens.

In a classic non-sharded blockchain such an attack is not possible since all the participant in the network validates all the blocks, and the block with such an invalid state transition will be rejected by both other block producers and the participants

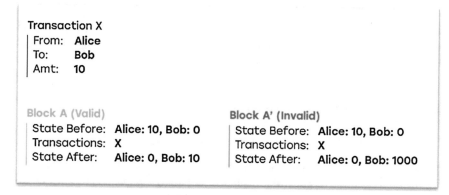

Fig. 8 Approving invalid blocks

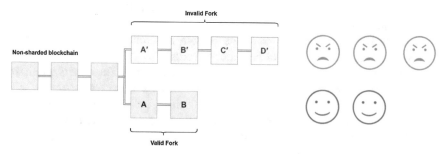

Fig. 9 Malicious and honest validator behavior

of the network that do not create blocks. Even if the malicious validators continue creating blocks on top of such an invalid block faster than honest validators build the correct chain (the chain with the invalid block being longer), it wouldn't matter, since every participant that is using the blockchain for any purpose validates all the blocks and discards all the blocks built on top of the invalid block.

Figure 9 shows five validators, three of whom are malicious. They created an invalid block A', and then continued building new blocks on top of it. Two honest validators discarded A' as invalid and were building on top of the last valid block known to them, creating a fork. Since there are fewer validators in the honest fork, their chain is shorter. However, in the classic non-sharded blockchain, every participant that uses blockchain for any purpose is responsible for validating all the blocks they receive and recomputing the state. Thus, any person who has any interest in the blockchain would observe that A' is invalid, and thus also immediately discard B', C', and D', as such taking the chain A–B as the current longest valid chain.

In a sharded blockchain, however, no participant can validate all the transactions on all the shards, so they need to have some way to confirm that at no point in the history of any shard of the blockchain no invalid block was included.

Note that unlike with forks, cross-linking to the Beacon chain is not a sufficient solution, since the Beacon chain doesn't have the capacity to validate the blocks. It can only validate that a sufficient number of validators in that shard signed the block (and as such attested to its correctness).

4.2.2 Segregated Witness Limitations

Some of the risks associated with segregated witness are as follows:

- Miners would get lower transaction fees for each transaction on the blockchain.
- The implementation segregated witness is extremely complex, and it requires all the wallets to implement segregated witness as well.
- segregated witness would significantly increase the number of resources required to maintain the network since, the network capacity, transactions, bandwidth would increase.
- It might result in a hard fork of the Bitcoin network which may ultimately, decrease the financial value of both the networks.
- Finally, segregated witness would be difficult to maintain. The miners will have to maintain the sidechain containing the signature data. However, the miners will receive no incentives for maintaining this sidechain, unlike the main blockchain. Hence, some sort of reward protocol needs to be implemented to incentivize the miners to maintain the signatures on the sidechain.

4.3 What Is the Major Hindrance in Implementing Sharding and Segregated Witness?

Since both sharding and segregated witness require a change in the codebase of an existing blockchain, these changes are incredibly difficult to implement in public permissionless blockchains such as Ethereum and Bitcoin. This problem arises because of the political decentralization nature of these blockchains. In order for such protocol changes, all the nodes on the blockchain network must agree on the change in protocol otherwise, this change may create a hard-fork of the network which ultimately decreases its financial value. For instance, both Ethereum and Bitcoin suffered from hard-forks of their mainchain which led to the creation of Bitcoin Cash and Ethereum Classic. On the bright side, this difficulty in protocol change implementation on a public blockchain has given birth to in other innovative approaches of targeting blockchain scalability without changing the original codebase of such blockchains, but by implementing a second layer of blockchain on top of the mainchain. These solutions are known as second-layer scalability solutions and the most prominent of such proposals are the concept of sidechains [4].

5   Open Issues and Future Directions

Both sharding and segregated witness face multiple implementation threats and challenges such as threats of a hard fork, miner incentivization, extreme physical resource requirement, etc. In this section, we will discuss some of the issues that the blockchain community faces when it comes to implementing sharding and segregated witness.

5.1   Data Validation in Sharding

Consider Fig. 10, which shows a corrupted *Shard 1*, where a malicious entity produces an invalid *block B*. Let us consider a scenario where 1000 tokens where minted onto Alice's account out of thin air in *block B*. A valid *block C* is then produced by the malicious entity on top of *block B*, which obfuscates *block B* (as it is invalid). The malicious entity then attempts to transfer the 1000 tokens to Bob's account by initiating a cross-shard transaction to *Shard 2*. This creates an issue because, from this point on, the maliciously generated 1000 tokens reside on *Shard 2* which is completely valid. This issue could be tacked in the following manner:

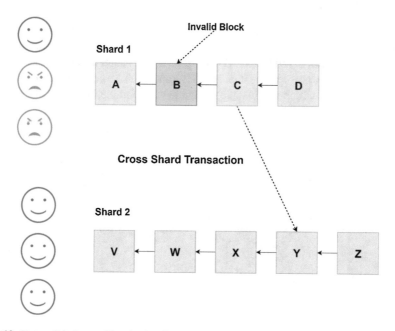

Fig. 10 Data validation problem in sharding

- *Shard 2* validators can validate the block from where the cross-shard transaction is initiated on Shard 1. But, such a solution would not work in all scenarios, for example, the scenario discussed above and depicted in Fig. 10, as *block C* is valid when seen from *Shard 2*.
- *Shard 2* validators can validate 'n' (where, n ∈ Z^+) blocks preceding the block from where the cross-shard transaction was attempted on *Shard 1*. But again, this solution has its own caveats, for instance, if the validators decide to validate 'n' blocks on Shard 1, the malicious validators could have created 'n + m' (where, m ∈ Z^+) blocks which are perfectly valid in themselves, on top of the already existing invalid block [54].

One possible way to solve this issue would be to use an undirected graph-based approach. Multiple shards could be arranged as an undirected graph in a way such that: (1) each shard is connected to more than one distinct shard, and (2) a cross-shard transaction is only allowed amongst neighboring shards [54]. A cross shard transaction between non-neighboring shards could take place by routing such transaction through multiple shards [55, 56]. With such a design, each validator in a shard would be required to validate (1) all the block in their shard and (2) all the blocks in each neighboring shard. Let's consider the example depicted in Fig. 11 where we have 10 shards with all shard having four neighbors each. With this architecture, cross-shard communication can be established within two links between any two given shards.

As explained earlier, *Shard 2* will validate both (1) all its own blocks, and (2) all the blocks of its neighboring shards, which includes *Shard 1*. Hence, if a corrupt entity from *Shard 1* attempts a cross-shard transaction by creating an invalid *block B* and then building a valid *block C* on top of it, then such an invalid cross-shard transaction would easily be detected, as the validators on *Shard 2* will validate all the blocks of *Shard 1*, which would enable them to pin point the invalidity of *block B*.

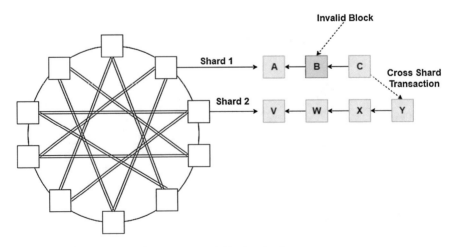

Fig. 11 Cross-shard transactions amongst neighboring shards

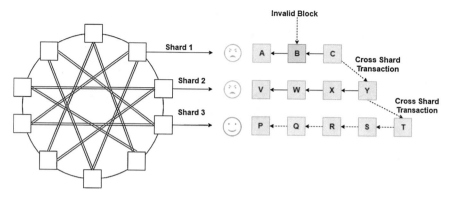

Fig. 12 An adversary executing cross-shard transaction

With this approach, corrupting a single shard won't be a viable attack on the system. But, corrupting multiple shards remains a challenge that needs to be solved. Consider Fig. 12 which shows an adversary that has successfully corrupted both *Shard 1* and 2. If such an adversary attempts to transfer funds to *Shard 3* with a cross-shard transaction from an invalid *block B*, then this invalid cross-shard transaction would not be detected, as although the validators on *Shard 3* validate each block of *Shard 2*, they don't do the same for *Shard 1*. Hence, the validators on *Shard 3* have no way of detecting the invalid *block B* on *Shard 1*.

The idea behind solving the data validation problem in blockchain sharding is shown in Fig. 13. After a cross chain communication such as cross-shard transaction or cross-linking to the Beacon chain, there could be a fixed period where an honest validator could submit proof of invalidity for the invalid block. Hence, with such an approach, the system would be secure as long as the shard consists of at least one honest validator.

5.2 A Threat of Hard Forks

We have emphasized a major problem with the implementation of sharding and segregated witness on public and permissionless blockchains (Sect. 4.3), i.e. the agreement within the miners regrading a specific change in the protocol of the blockchain. There will often be times when a proposed change in protocol for a blockchain will not be agreed upon by the majority of the miners of the blockchain network. This leads to a difficult situation in which forcing a change in the protocol of the blockchain is likely to cause a hard fork of the network as can be seen in the case of Bitcoin forking into Bitcoin Cash. Thus, this makes public and permissionless blockchains such as Bitcoin and Ethereum extremely stringent and deterrent to change, even when the change is for the overall improvement of the blockchain network. This aspect of a public blockchain is a major limitation and a huge stumbling block in the implementation of sharding and segregated witness.

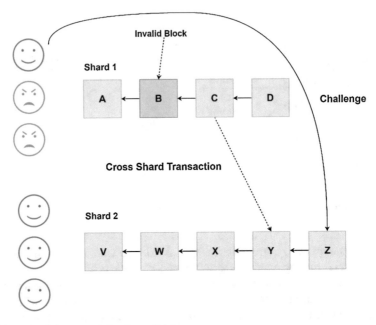

Fig. 13 A possible approach for data validation

Often times lack proper communication amongst the miners of a blockchain regarding a proposed change in protocol might also result in change resistance. Although there are protocols available for proposing changes to the Ethereum and Bitcoin protocol such as Ethereum Improvement Proposals (EIP) [57] and Bitcoin Improvement Proposals (BIP) [58], these proposals are hardly ever advertised to the blockchain community especially the miners of these networks [59]. Hence, we suggest a lightweight broadcasting and voting system for clearly describing and advertising the proposed changes, their advantages and limitations to the miners of a blockchain network. The system can then be used for conducting polls within the miners on whether a change in the protocol should be implemented or not. This would be an effective way of conveying or advertising a change in protocol for a public blockchain amongst its miners instead of directly forcing a change which may result in a hard-fork or just waiting and hoping that the miners will reach an agreement regarding the change at some point in the future.

6 Conclusions

In the last decade, blockchain technology has grown exponentially with seemingly new use cases being discovered almost every day [60–64]. Consequently, research in the domain has picked up pace in recent years both to discover issues and vulnerabilities in blockchains and to provide solutions to these problems and challenges. Scalability and limited functionality have shackled blockchains ever since its proposal and implementation in 2008. In response to this, the community has proposed scaling several scaling solutions including sharding and segregated witness.

In this paper, we have discussed these two solutions, i.e., segregated witness and sharding. Although these solutions are promising, a comprehensive study is still lacking in the literature to study the impact of such solutions on the scalability of public blockchains such as Bitcoin and Ethereum. Hence, the motivation of our study was to take the first step and provide a comprehensive review of the available design choices for sharding and segregated witness in Ethereum and Bitcoin, respectively. Moreover, we have discussed general open issues that need well-deserved attention from the community for the advancement of the overall blockchain domain.

References

1. S. Nakamoto, Bitcoin: a peer-to-peer electronic cash system. www.Bitcoin.Org (2008) (Online). https://bitcoin.org/bitcoin.pdf. Accessed 30 Jan 2019
2. G. Wood, Ethereum: a secure decentralised generalised transaction ledger. Ethereum Proj. Yellow Pap. **151**, 1–32 (2014)
3. E. Androulaki et al., Hyperledger fabric: a distributed operating system for permissioned blockchains, in *Proceedings of the Thirteenth EuroSys Conference*, pp. 30:1–30:15 (2018)
4. P. Robinson, Requirements for Ethereum private sidechains. CoRR (2018). arXiv:1906.06517
5. D. Miller, Blockchain and the Internet of Things in the Industrial Sector. IT Prof. **20**(3), 15–18 (2018)
6. J. Fiaidhi, S. Mohammed, S. Mohammed, EDI with blockchain as an enabler for extreme automation. IT Prof. **20**(4), 66–72 (2018)
7. L. Zhou, L. Wang, Y. Sun, P. Lv, BeeKeeper: a blockchain-based IoT system with secure storage and homomorphic computation. IEEE Access **6**, 43472 (2018)
8. M. Mylrea, S.N.G. Gourisetti, Blockchain for supply chain cybersecurity, optimization and compliance, in *2018 Resilience Week (RWS)*, pp. 70–76 (2018)
9. S. Yu, K. Lv, Z. Shao, Y. Guo, J. Zou, B. Zhang, A high performance blockchain platform for intelligent devices, in *2018 1st IEEE International Conference on Hot Information-Centric Networking (HotICN)*, pp. 260–261 (2018)
10. J. Lou, Q. Zhang, Z. Qi, K. Lei, A blockchain-based key management scheme for named data networking, in *2018 1st IEEE International Conference on Hot Information-Centric Networking (HotICN)*, pp. 141–146 (2018)
11. L. Kan, Y. Wei, A. Hafiz Muhammad, W. Siyuan, G. Linchao, H. Kai, A multiple blockchains architecture on inter-blockchain communication, in *2018 IEEE International Conference on Software Quality, Reliability and Security Companion (QRS-C)*, pp. 139–145 (2018)
12. R.M. Parizi, Amritraj, A. Dehghantanha, Smart contract programming languages on blockchains: an empirical evaluation of usability and security, in *Blockchain—ICBC 2018*, pp. 75–91 (2018)
13. N. Atzei, M. Bartoletti, T. Cimoli, A survey of attacks on ethereum smart contracts (SoK), in *International Conference on Principles of Security and Trust*, pp. 1–24 (2017)
14. G. Giaglis et al., Under-optimized smart contracts devour your money, in *2017 26th International Conference on Computer Communication and Networks (ICCCN)*, vol. 55, no. 9, pp. 1–5 (2017)

15. R.M. Parizi, A. Dehghantanha, K.K.R. Choo, A. Singh, Empirical vulnerability analysis of automated smart contracts security testing on blockchains, in *28th Annual International Conference on Computer Science and Software Engineering (CASCON'18)* (2018)

16. P.J. Taylor, T. Dargahi, A. Dehghantanha, R.M. Parizi, K.-K.R. Choo, A systematic literature review of blockchain cyber security, in *Digital Communications and Networks* (2019). https://doi.org/10.1016/j.dcan.2019.01.005

17. K. Bhargavan et al., Formal verification of smart contracts: short paper, in *Proceedings of the 2016 ACM Workshop on Programming Languages and Analysis for Security*, pp. 91–96 (2016)

18. S. Amani, M. Bégel, M. Bortin, M. Staples, Towards verifying ethereum smart contract bytecode in Isabelle/HOL, in *Proceedings of the 7th ACM SIGPLAN International Conference on Certified Programs and Proofs*, pp. 66–77 (2018)

19. T. Abdellatif, K.-L. Brousmiche, Formal verification of smart contracts based on users and blockchain behaviors models, in *2018 9th IFIP International Conference on New Technologies, Mobility and Security (NTMS)*, pp. 1–5 (2018)

20. R. Dennis, G. Owenson, B. Aziz, A temporal blockchain: a formal analysis, in *Proceedings of the 2016 International Conference on Collaboration Technologies and Systems (CTS)*, pp. 430–437 (2016)

21. M. Herlihy, Atomic cross-chain swaps, in *Proceedings of the 2018 ACM Symposium on Principles of Distributed Computing*, pp. 245–254 (2018)

22. L. Duboc, D.S. Rosenblum, T. Wicks, A framework for modelling and analysis of software systems scalability, in *Proceedings of the 28th International Conference on Software Engineering*, pp. 949–952 (2006)

23. European Union Blockchain Observatory & Forum, Scalability interoperability and sustainability of blockchains (2019), Thematic Report, https://www.eublockchainforum.eu/sites/default/files/reports/report_scalaibility_06_03_2019.pdf

24. J.R. Douceur, The sybil attack, in *International Workshop on Peer-to-Peer Systems*, (Springer, Berlin, 2002), pp. 251–260

25. L. Feinstein, D. Schnackenberg, R. Balupari, D. Kindred, Statistical approaches to DDoS attack detection and response, in *Proceedings DARPA Information Survivability Conference and Exposition*, vol. 1, pp. 303–314 (2003)

26. A. Dolce, Blockchain scalability solutions: overview of crypto scaling solutions (2018) (Online). https://masterthecrypto.com/blockchain-scalability-solutions-crypto-scaling-solutions/. Accessed 04 Jan 2019

27. B. Kitchenham, Procedures for performing systematic reviews, Keele, UK, Keele University, vol. 33, no. TR/SE-0401, p. 28 (2004)

28. B. Kitchenham, S. Charters, Guidelines for performing Systematic Literature Reviews in Software Engineering. Engineering **2**, 1051 (2007)

29. H. Yoo, J. Yim, S. Kim, The blockchain for domain based static sharding, in *2018 17th IEEE International Conference On Trust, Security And Privacy In Computing And Communications/12th IEEE International Conference On Big Data Science And Engineering (TrustCom/BigDataSE)*, pp. 1689–1692 (2018)

30. Z. Ren, K. Cong, T. Aerts, B. de Jonge, A. Morais, Z. Erkin, A scale-out blockchain for value transfer with spontaneous sharding, in *2018 Crypto Valley Conference on Blockchain Technology (CVCBT)*, pp. 1–10 (2018)

31. E. Kokoris-Kogias, P. Jovanovic, L. Gasser, N. Gailly, E. Syta, B. Ford, OmniLedger: a secure, scale-out, decentralized ledger via sharding, in *2018 IEEE Symposium on Security and Privacy (SP)*, pp. 583–598 (2018)

32. Y. Yu, R. Liang, J. Xu, A scalable and extensible blockchain architecture, in *2018 IEEE International Conference on Data Mining Workshops (ICDMW)*, pp. 161–163 (2018)

33. E. Fynn, F. Pedone, Challenges and Pitfalls of Partitioning Blockchains, in *2018 48th Annual IEEE/IFIP International Conference on Dependable Systems and Networks Workshops (DSN-W)*, pp. 128–133 (2018)

34. M.H. Manshaei, M. Jadliwala, A. Maiti, M. Fooladgar, A game-theoretic analysis of shard-based permissionless blockchains. IEEE Access **6**, 78100–78112 (2018)

35. L. Aniello, R. Baldoni, E. Gaetani, F. Lombardi, A. Margheri, V. Sassone, A prototype evaluation of a tamper-resistant high performance blockchain-based transaction log for a distributed database, in *2017 13th European Dependable Computing Conference (EDCC)*, pp. 151–154s (2017)
36. G. He, W. Su, S. Gao, Chameleon: a scalable and adaptive permissioned blockchain architecture, in *2018 1st IEEE International Conference on Hot Information-Centric Networking (HotICN)*, pp. 87–93 (2018)
37. A. Chauhan, O.P. Malviya, M. Verma, T. S. Mor, Blockchain and scalability, in *2018 IEEE International Conference on Software Quality, Reliability and Security Companion (QRS-C)*, pp. 122–128 (2018)
38. S. Malik, S.S. Kanhere, R. Jurdak, ProductChain: scalable blockchain framework to support provenance in supply chains, in *2018 IEEE 17th International Symposium on Network Computing and Applications (NCA)*, pp. 1–10 (2018)
39. L. Luu, V. Narayanan, C. Zheng, K. Baweja, S. Gilbert, P. Saxena, A secure sharding protocol for open blockchains, in *Proceedings of the 2016 ACM SIGSAC Conference on Computer and Communications Security*, pp. 17–30 (2016)
40. M. Zamani, M. Movahedi, M. Raykova, RapidChain: scaling blockchain via full sharding, in *Proceedings of the 2018 ACM SIGSAC Conference on Computer and Communications Security*, pp. 931–948 (2018)
41. D. Sel, K. Zhang, H.-A. Jacobsen, Towards solving the data availability problem for sharded ethereum, in *Proceedings of the 2Nd Workshop on Scalable and Resilient Infrastructures for Distributed Ledgers*, pp. 25–30.
42. D. Frey, M. X. Makkes, P.-L. Roman, F. Taïani, and S. Voulgaris, Bringing secure bitcoin transactions to your smartphone, in *Proceedings of the 15th International Workshop on Adaptive and Reflective Middleware*, pp. 3:1–3:6 (2016)
43. X. Feng et al., Pruneable sharding-based blockchain protocol, *Peer-to-Peer Netw. Appl.* (2018)
44. A.E. Gencer, R. van Renesse, E.G. Sirer, Short paper: service-oriented sharding for blockchains," in *Financial Cryptography and Data Security*, pp. 393–401 (2017)
45. S. Cai, N. Yang, Z. Ming, A decentralized sharding service network framework with scalability, in *Web Services—ICWS 2018*, pp. 151–165 (2018)
46. K. Croman et al., On scaling decentralized blockchains, in *International Conference on Financial Cryptography and Data Security*, pp. 106–125 (2016)
47. L. Luu, V. Narayanan, C. Zheng, K. Baweja, S. Gilbert, R. Saxena, A secure Sharding protocol for open Blockchains, in *Proceedings of the 2016 ACM SIGSAC Conference on Computer and Communications Security (CCS '16). Association for Computing Machinery*, (USA, New York, NY, 2016), pp. 17–30
48. A. Skidanov, The authoritative guide to Blockchain Sharding, part 1 (2018) (Online). https://medium.com/nearprotocol/the-authoritative-guide-to-blockchain-sharding-part-1-1b53ed31e060. Accessed 01 Apr 2019
49. B. McManus, Understanding segwit and the bitcoin scaling debate, *Medium* (2017) (Online). https://medium.com/@brenmcma/understanding-segwit-and-the-bitcoin-scaling-debate-c9f7170e9e79
50. V. Arasev, POA network whitepaper (2018). (Online). https://github.com/poanetwork/wiki/wiki/POA-Network-Whitepaper. Accessed 30 Jan 2019
51. POA, Proof of authority: consensus model with identity at stake (2017 (Online). https://medium.com/poa-network/proof-of-authority-consensus-model-with-identity-at-stake-d5bd15463256. Accessed 18 Jan 2019
52. V. Buterin, Chain interoperability, *R3 reports*, 2016
53. H. Jin, X. Dai, J. Xiao, Towards a novel architecture for enabling interoperability amongst multiple blockchains, in *Proceedings of the International Conference on Distributed Computing Systems*, vol. 2018, pp. 1203–1211 (2018)
54. A. Skidanov, Unsolved problems in blockchain sharding (2018) (Online). https://medium.com/nearprotocol/unsolved-problems-in-blockchain-sharding-2327d6517f43. Accessed 04 Apr 2019

55. A. Skidanov, So what exactly is Vlad's Sharding PoC doing? (Online), https://medium.com/nearprotocol/so-what-exactly-is-vlads-sharding-poc-doing-37e538177ed9. Accessed 04 Mar 2019
56. Quaintance Martino and Popejoy, Chainweb, A proof-of-work parallel-chain architecture for massive throughput. (May 2018)
57. Ethereum, Ethereum improvement proposals (EIP) (Online). http://eips.ethereum.org/
58. Bitcoin, Bitcoin improvement proposals (BIP) (Online). https://github.com/bitcoin/bips. Accessed 04 Jul 2019
59. S. Khatwani, What is a BIP (Bitcoin Improvement Proposal)? Why do you need to know about it? (2017) (Online). https://coinsutra.com/bip-bitcoin-improvement-proposa/
60. S. Homayoun, A. Dehghantanha, R.M. Parizi, K.K.R. Choo, A blockchain-based framework for detecting malicious mobile applications in app stores, in *32nd IEEE Canadian Conference of Electrical and Computer Engineering (IEEE CCECE'19)*, Canada (2019)
61. R.M. Parizi, A. Dehghantanha, On the understanding of gamification in blockchain systems, in *6th IEEE International Conference on Future Internet of Things and Cloud (FiCloud'18)*, Barcelona, Spain (IEEE Computer Society, 2018)
62. A. Yazdinejad, R.M. Parizi, A. Dehghantanha, K.R. Choo, Blockchain-enabled authentication handover with efficient privacy protection in SDN-based 5G networks, in *IEEE Transactions on Network Science and Engineering*. https://doi.org/10.1109/TNSE.2019.2937481
63. R.M. Parizi, S. Homayoun, A. Yazdinejad, A. Dehghantanha, K.K.R. Choo, Integrating privacy enhancing techniques into blockchains using sidechains, in *32nd IEEE Canadian Conference of Electrical and Computer Engineering (IEEE CCECE'19)*, Canada (2019)
64. E. Nyaletey, R.M. Parizi, Q. Zhang, Kim-Kwang Raymond Choo, BlockIPFS - Blockchain-enabled Interplanetary File System for Forensic and Trusted Data Traceability, in *2nd IEEE International Conference on Blockchain (IEEE Blockchain-2019)* (2019)

Immutable and Secure IP Address Protection Using Blockchain

Kelly Click, Amritraj Singh, Reza M. Parizi (iD), **Gautam Srivastava, and Ali Dehghantanha**

Abstract IP addresses can be passed on to new recipients even with a damaged reputation score. It takes a lot of effort to defend a network against storing IP address data using current required practices. A blockchain network offers a decentralized, immutable ledger to record IP data which ensures that the data will not be tampered with and the data is trustworthy. Master nodes and digital IDs are two ways the blockchain can be used to preserve a digital identity. Master nodes can act as a mediator and store the entire blockchain to improve the validity of the blockchain. Digital IDs can make it easier to verify an identity on the blockchain. In this chapter, we explore how blockchain technology can preserve user's digital identity more effectively. This chapter also offers a sample program that can be used to store and retrieve information with the use of the Solidity language used on the Ethereum network. Data pertaining to IP addresses is added to a solidity contract with several methods offered for reading data. The IP address data ends up more secure than if it was simply stored in a central database.

K. Click · A. Singh
Department of Software Engineering and Game Development, Kennesaw State University, Marietta, GA, USA
e-mail: kclick@students.kennesaw.edu; amritra@students.kennesaw.edu

R. M. Parizi (✉)
College of Computing and Software Engineering, Kennesaw State University, Marietta, GA, USA
e-mail: rparizi1@kennesaw.edu

G. Srivastava
Department of Mathematics and Computer Science, Brandon University, Brandon, MB, Canada
e-mail: srivastavag@brandonu.ca

A. Dehghantanha
Cyber Science Lab, School of Computer Science, University of Guelph, Guelph, ON, Canada
e-mail: adehghan@uoguelph.ca

© Springer Nature Switzerland AG 2020
K.-K. R. Choo et al. (eds.), *Blockchain Cybersecurity, Trust and Privacy*, Advances in Information Security 79, https://doi.org/10.1007/978-3-030-38181-3_12

1 Introduction

On a centralized network, IP addresses are vulnerable to being used by a malicious entity, and that IP address may be assigned to a new user who is innocent of the activity of the previous user. This can damage the reputation of the new owner of that IP address. Blockchain networks can help defend against these risks by offering a tamper proof record of IP address data [1–9]. The blockchain network provides timestamps of every transaction [10]. Consensus or agreement between all nodes on the blockchain would hold preserve data reliability related to IP addresses and not the organizations themselves. The timestamp combined with the records of the IP address can be linked to owners of accounts on the blockchain.

Securing centralized databases presents an extremely difficult challenge to organizations [11]. Decentralized networks can take the burden off of organizations, by having a record of the IP assignments on the blockchain itself. This reduces the effort an organization needs to make in order to understand the history of IP Addresses.

There are many challenges in protecting enterprises on a centralized network which endangers organizations. On a centralized network, accounts need to be kept secure by protecting passwords [12], securing email [13], and using two-step authentication [14]. Spyware and anti-virus software need to be put in place along with keeping applications up to date [15, 16]. Domain registration records need to be kept up to date while protecting contact information from the public. E-mails have to be protected with SSL certificates and Domain Name System Security Extensions. Geographic diversity in workforces makes it difficult for organizations to keep track of the practices of its employees [17]. Distributed but decentralized applications allow for users to login from multiple devices making it difficult to manage user identities. Policies in organizations that allow for bringing your own devices to work make it difficult to keep track of which ones need to access sensitive information [18]. Furthermore, remembering passwords for many cloud-based services can become frustrating for employees [19]. Challenges to revoking access to central locations can also arise. Resources might need to be expended to devise single login systems. There are differing regulations at the local and state levels that organizations have to follow. Assuring identity being under proper control can have challenges including varying vetting processes among multiple organizations. Interoperable organizations also need to establish trust among themselves which requires multiple technical solutions [20]. Replication of data, such as replicating IP address records, needs to take place in order to create a fault tolerant system [21]. Identity Provider (*idP*) discovery where the destination of authentication requests need to be determined can be another challenging aspect of centralized systems including being very "labor intensive" [22, 23]. Ultimately, security, revocation of credentials, privacy and interoperability present challenges to centralized systems.

In this chapter, we propose a blockchain that stores IP Address data. This would decentralize the storage of IP Address details along with providing a fault tolerant database for the information. A contract will be used to store each data point about an IP Address. Each transaction can post a new IP Address to the blockchain.

1.1 Sender Reputation

IP addresses are rated by the emails that are sent from that address and other activities coming from the address. Known as "sender reputation", this measure can be obtained from multiple companies such as SenderScore.org being the most common one. The IP Address sender score measures the health of the email program and will give an idea of how mailboxes view emails coming from these IP addresses [24].

The factors that are taken into consideration when assigning a sender score are

- whether the IP address is found on a spam complaints blacklist
- whether the IP address sends mail to unknown users
- if the IP address is found on a whitelist
- the level of subscriber engagement
- the amount of mailing to spam traps.

IP reputation needs to be acquired over time. In other words, the address begins with high levels of suspicion and engaging in trusted communication over time will decrease that suspicion. The classification of the domain (e.g. industry, education, finance, dating, or gambling) on the web also has an impact on this IP reputation score. *CISCO*, a well-known American multinational technology company, has listed all these categories classified on the web [25]. What is required to clean IP addresses and a reputation score includes several things. First, cleaning mailing lists can be difficult, expensive, and may put your IP reputation in more jeopardy. All email bounce backs, emails that were not received but sent back, need to be removed. All spam complaints attached to an IP reputation also need to be removed. A solid stream of content needs to be sent to a new, safe list to help recover the IP reputation. There is a difference between email reputation and web reputation. Email reputation is based on the email server whereas web reputation is based on the entire domain. Sender Score can be queried by both email networks and ISPs to determine if an address needs to be blacklisted. There is also a difference between IP reputation and Domain reputation. With IP reputation, the reputation can be better controlled by maintaining a static address. When looking at domain reputation however, networks place more importance on the domain brand and not the IP address itself.

Blocks of IP addresses are assigned to Internet Service Providers (ISPs). From there, a specific ISP holds the full responsibility for allocated out distinct IP addresses. Static addresses remain constant over time whereas dynamic addresses change from minor changes including restarting the router. There are both benefits and drawbacks to both dynamic and static IP addresses as given in Table 1.

Table 1 Advantages and disadvantages of dynamic and static IP addresses

	Advantages	Disadvantages
Dynamic	Automated configuration, unlimited devices, no additional fees	More downtime, less accurate geolocation, limited remote access
Static	Simple server hosting, convenient remote access, reliable communication, easy file transfer	More expensive, complex setup, potential security weakness

The two types of Internet Protocols are *IPv4* and *IPv6*. IPv4 was deployed in 1983 and IPv6 began in 1999. An IP address is binary numbers but can be stored as text for human readers. For example, a 32-bit numeric address (IPv4) is written in decimal as four numbers separated by periods. Each number can be zero to 255. For example, 1.160.10.240 could be an IP address. IPv6 addresses are 128-bit IP address written in hexadecimal and separated by colons. An example IPv6 address could be written like this: 3ffe:1900:4545:3:200:f8ff:fe21:67cf.

2 Related Work

Fukushima et al. discuss about how IP addresses can be used successfully for identifying high risk malicious actors in [26]. In their work, the authors present a strong blacklist solution for identifying potential malicious actors. Fukushima did not discuss the effects that IP addresses marked as malicious could potentially have if assigned to new users.

Chalaemwongwan et al. discuss about how Thailand can use Digital IDs with the blockchain to provide a secure government identification system [10]. Their paper provides a security analysis of blockchain used in this capacity to show the potential blockchain has for securing a network. The authors do not discuss the uses of Digital IDs with putting IP data on the blockchain.

Bocu discuss the effects of spam emails sent from an IP address on the reputation of that IP address in [27]. The author presents both a need and a solution, through IP pools, for preserving the reputation of email servers. Bocu does not discuss a decentralized solution to this problem and also does not discuss the effects the reputation will have on future recipients of those IP addresses.

3 Proposed Solution

A blockchain network can protect the identity of an organization along with defending against intrusions of a central IT service. By having identifiable information put on the blockchain, an organization can have a reliable and immutable solution to keeping record of the organization's identifiable information [28, 29]. Lemieux determined

> through cryptographically securing records and distributing copies that can be compared, it is possible to protect and validate the integrity of records [30].

Public and private blockchains are two different potential types of blockchains that can be used. Public blockchains allow anyone who wants to join the network join. Private blockchains are closed to only authorized entities and are controlled by a single entity which could be a private company. An advantage of private blockchains include a limited number of nodes making transactions cheaper [31]. Blockchains can also be a hybrid of both public and private blockchains.

There are multiple benefits of blockchain for security. Blockchains are

- decentralized
- offer validation
- very difficult to hack
- can be both private and public

Each computer, or node, has a copy of the ledger and multiple nodes can go down without the network itself going down [32]. The data is backed up, remains unchanged and offers reliable, independent validation. The data on a blockchain is decentralized, encrypted, and cross-checked by the network. Blockchain has the potential to improve both data integrity, and digital identities [33]. Two additional ways that the blockchain can provide a way of securing data is through the use of master nodes and digital ids.

3.1 Blockchain's Protection from Identity Theft and Fraud

3.1.1 Masternodes Can Be Used to Verify User Identity

A *masternode* can act as a 'mediator as well as a guarantor', while requiring high cost in order to run a masternode [34]. Along with a large staking of currency, different cryptocurrencies have different guidelines for maintaining a masternode. A masternode can perform tasks that other miners in *Proof of Work* cannot that can help protect identity. One service that includes the use of masternodes is Dash and is one of the first services to do so.

Masternodes can quickly verify new transactions and mined blocks. The Dash service InstaSend can accommodate nearly instantaneous transactions. InstaSend transactions are confirmed in less than 1 s and are required to be approved by masternodes. The blocktime of Dash without InstaSend is about 2.5 min which is noticeably faster than Bitcoin. There are many benefits from masternodes including

- independent verification
- keep record of unspent transaction output

- allow for users to make and receive anonymous payments
- decentralized governance.

Masternodes can take full responsibility in approving transactions such as those in the service InstaSend used with the Dash network. Each masternode keeps a full record of the blockchain. Different political or technical decisions on the blockchain can be voted on. There is a requirement for masternodes to possess more than 1000 Dash so as to avoid a Sybil attack that includes a centralized force creating many fake accounts. Some examples of exchanges that use masternodes are Block Net and Exscudo. Block Net allows for second layer blockchain interoperability. Block Net uses the blockchain to guarantee the security of transactions and exchanges occurring on the network. Any transfer of funds using the network will not be controlled by any single entity and users will have self-sovereignty over their personal data. Exscudo combines centralization and decentralization to support the use of a blockchain for the security of funds. The access layer of the centralized exchange is a decentralized blockchain [35–38].

3.1.2 Use of Digital IDs

Digital IDs are affixed to every transaction. The use of Digital IDs can bring digital and legal certainty to transactions made on a blockchain network. Digital IDs can be assigned to an individual user across both a single blockchain and an interoperable system of multiple blockchains. They can be used to maintain an identity from one blockchain without updating the identity after transferring funds. Digital IDs also allow for private blockchains, even ones from large organizations such as Internet Service Providers, to open themselves up to public blockchains and still protect the identity of its users. Digital IDs provide another way to guarantee legal certainty of an identity on a network in situations such as those who would put their IP address data on the blockchain [28]. In our proposed model, someone's national identity is stored on their phone with the use of the blockchain with only high officials being able to view any information put on the blockchain. Due to the public nature of the blockchain, whenever the information is viewed the viewing transaction is also recorded on the distributed ledger [39].

4 Implementation

We shown an overview of the system in Fig. 1. An IP address can easily be looked up and information like location, Internet Service Provider, organization, and address type can be confirmed. The IP address, ISP, organization, country, state and city are recorded on the network. That information can easily be retrieved from a list of IP addresses added using Solidity. All the information is stored with an address associated with the contract. This Solidity code allows all the information to be

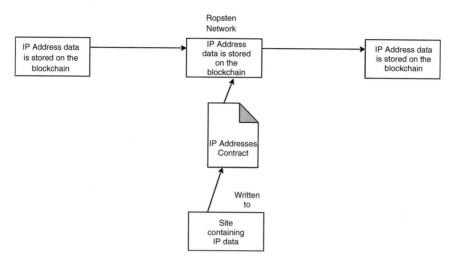

Fig. 1 Overview of system

retrieved at once or specifically by property with the use of an ID assigned in the order the IP address was added.

In order to get IP address information, the command *nslookup* was run in the command prompt of a Windows operating system for two different sites. There were 10 different sites that were looked up with this experiment.

A template Ownable contract was written so only the owner of the contract was permitted to write to the contract, as seen in Fig. 2. The ownership of the contract can be instantiated with the msg.sender which is the deployer of the contract. There are functions to transfer ownership, renounce ownership, checking an account for ownership, and a modifier named onlyOwner that can be attached to a function in a child contract restricting the use of that function to the owner.

In Fig. 2, the class IPAddresses inherits from the class Ownable so only the owner of the contract can post the IP data. A message event is added so that when IP address data is added a message is recorded saying that the data was successfully added. The IPData struct includes seven different strings containing the IP Address, the Internet Service Provider, the organization, the type of address, the country, state, and city. A public list of IPData structs named ips is declared. In the storeIPInfo function a new struct instance is added to the ips list. The getIPAddress function returns every string in the struct IPData after an index is entered so the 1st struct saved in the list would be returned from a 0 index whereas a 9 index would return the 10th struct saved. A potential continuation of this concept would be to return a struct based on the IP Address or any other string. One more idea for continuing this concept is to list every IPAddress with the id included. The rest of the functions retrieve an individual string based on the index of the struct in the list.

The rest of the functions retrieve an individual string based on the index of the struct in the list. The IP Address, Internet Service Provider, Organization, type of

```solidity
1    pragma solidity >= 0.4 .22 < 0.6 .0;
2
3    /**
4     * @title Ownable
5     * @dev The Ownable contract has an owner address, and provides basic authorization control
6     * functions, this simplifies the implementation of "user permissions".
7     */
8    contract Ownable {
9        address private _owner;
10       event OwnershipTransferred(
11           address indexed previousOwner,
12           address indexed newOwner
13       );
14       /**
15        * @dev The Ownable constructor sets the original `owner` of the contract to the sender
16        * account.
17        */
18       constructor() internal {
19           _owner = msg.sender;
20           emit OwnershipTransferred(address(0), _owner);
21       }
22       /**
23        * @return the address of the owner.
24        */
25       function owner() public view returns(address) {
26           return _owner;
27       }
28       /**
29        * @dev Throws if called by any account other than the owner.
30        */
31       modifier onlyOwner() {
32           require(isOwner());
33           _;
34       }
35       /**
36        * @return true if `msg.sender` is the owner of the contract.
37        */
38       function isOwner() public view returns(bool) {
39           return msg.sender == _owner;
40       }
41       /**
42        * @dev Allows the current owner to relinquish control of the contract.
43        * @notice Renouncing to ownership will leave the contract without an owner.
44        * It will not be possible to call the functions with the `onlyOwner`
45        * modifier anymore.
46        */
47       function renounceOwnership() public onlyOwner {
48           emit OwnershipTransferred(_owner, address(0));
49           _owner = address(0);
50       }
51       /**
52        * @dev Allows the current owner to transfer control of the contract to a newOwner.
53        * @param newOwner The address to transfer ownership to.
54        */
55       function transferOwnership(address newOwner) public onlyOwner {
56           _transferOwnership(newOwner);
57       }
58       /**
59        * @dev Transfers control of the contract to a newOwner.
60        * @param newOwner The address to transfer ownership to.
61        */
62       function _transferOwnership(address newOwner) internal {
63           require(newOwner != address(0));
64           emit OwnershipTransferred(_owner, newOwner);
65           _owner = newOwner;
66       }
67   }
```

Fig. 2 Ownable contract

```
1    contract IPAddresses is Ownable {
2        event MsgEvent(string msg);
3        uint ipCount;
4        struct IPData {
5            string ipAddress;
6            string intsp;
7            string organization;
8            string addressType;
9            string country;
10           string state;
11           string city;
12       }
13       IPData[] public ips;
14       function storeIPInfo(string memory ipAdd, string memory isp, string memory org, string memory at,
15       string memory cou, string memory st, string memory cty) public onlyOwner {
16           ips.push(IPData(ipAdd, isp, org, at, cou, st, cty));
17           emit MsgEvent("IP Data recorded.");
18       }
19       function getIPData(uint index) external view returns(string memory, string memory, string memory,
20       string memory, string memory, string memory, string memory) {
21           return (ips[index].ipAddress, ips[index].intsp, ips[index].organization, ips[index].addressTyp
22            ips[index].country, ips[index].state, ips[index].city);
23       }
24       function getIPAddress(uint index) external view returns(string memory) {
25           return ips[index].ipAddress;
26       }
27       function getISP(uint index) external view returns(string memory) {
28           return ips[index].intsp;
29       }
30       function getOrganization(uint index) external view returns(string memory) {
31           return ips[index].organization;
32       }
33       function getIPAddressType(uint index) external view returns(string memory) {
34           return ips[index].addressType;
35       }
36       function getCountry(uint index) external view returns(string memory) {
37           return ips[index].country;
38       }
39       function getState(uint index) external view returns(string memory) {
40           return ips[index].state;
41       }
42       function getCity(uint index) external view returns(string memory) {
43           return ips[index].city;
44       }
45   }
```

Fig. 3 IP addresses

address, country, state, and city can all be accessed individually. All these functions grant read access to the public so anybody can retrieve data from these functions, as shown in Fig. 3.

5 Experimental Evidence and Analysis

Ten different random but common URLs were chosen. IP addresses for those ten different URLs were looked up using the nslookup command. Each IP address was looked up using whatismyipaddress.com and the data for that IP address collected. This included the IP Address, the Internet Service Provider, Organization, type of address, country, state, and city.

This data was added to the Ropsten network through 10 different transactions after the contract was deployed from Remix, an online IDE for Solidity. With the use of Metamask, a Google Chrome add on, the contract written using Remix could be deployed to the Ropsten network. After deployment using Remix, the contract needed to be verified on ropsten.etherscan.io. Once the contract was verified, the ropsten.etherscan.io site allowed for input fields for each IP address data point to be written to the contract.

Using the input fields for the storeIPInfo() function, the seven data points were successfully entered and written through a transaction on the blockchain. The website ropsten.etherscan.io offers a "write to" button that can interact with the Metamask plugin. Once the transaction is confirmed, Ropsten is spent and moments later the transaction is permanently added to the blockchain.

After the data is added to the blockchain through the storeIPInfo() function, all the data can be accessed through function calls and all at once through the GetIPData() function, as given in Fig. 3. Each IP address has its data accessed through an integer ID assigned in the order added to the list (Table 2).

The IP Address data put on the blockchain can be retrieved and saved quite easily. Solidity contracts can have write access restricted to a single owner and read access available to the public which is true in the case of this contract. Any of the seven data points can be accessed one at a time with the use of one of the functions in the contract. All of this data is protected by the security features of Ethereum.

The data was successfully put on the Ropsten network and accessible to the owner of the contract. This is a demonstration of how the blockchain can store information about an IP address and be accessed through a Solidity contract. The information that was placed on the network is permanently secured and accessible through the contract. Sets of seven data points for ten different IP addresses were placed using this method. In the future, this process could be automated and multiple individuals and business could save data from online resources and access this data with confidence that the data was not tampered with. Automation of this method would also allow more IP addresses to be recorded on the blockchain. Any updates to sites such as whatismyipaddress.com would be noticed and the correct information could be retrieved. Also, the data could be directly added to the Ethereum or Ropsten blockchain. Another future development of this concept could be the use of web Graphical User Interfaces to display the information in a table like the one above or in a more organized manner.

6 Conclusion

When IP addresses are reassigned to new users the reputation formed by the former user is still relevant to that IP Address. Centralized databases and centralized control over data leads to many challenges in providing security for that data. There are numerous steps to take in providing the necessary protection for customer's data. For this reason, the blockchain is a strong solution to storing IP Address information

Table 2 Table of retrieved IP address data

	Test 1	2	3	4	5	6	7	8	9	10
ipAdd: string	34.216.127.34	161.170.230.170	2600:1403:15:49f::eaf	23.54.149.103	2a03:2880:f12c:83:face:b00c:0:25de	23.37.81.208	184.26.75.244	69.187.23.20	104.244.42.193	72.21.92.201
intsp: String	Amazon.com	Wal-Mart Stores	Akamai Technologies	Akamai Technologies	Facebook	Akamai Technologies	Akamai Technologies	Bloomberg financial market	Twitter	Verizon business
Organization: String	Amazon.com	Wal-Mart stores	Akamai Technologies	Akamai Technologies	Facebook	Akamai Technologies	Akamai Technologies	Bloomberg LP	Twitter	Verizon business
addressType: string	Likely static IP	Likely static IP	Likely static IP	Likely static IP	Likely static IP	Likely static IP	Likely static IP	Likely static IP	Likely static IP	Likely static IP
Country: String	United States	United States	United States	United States	Ireland	United States	United States	United States	United States	United States
State: String	Oregon	N/A	N/A	N/A	N/A	N/A	N/A	N/A	West Virginia	N/A
City: string	Boardman	N/A	N/A	N/A	N/A	N/A	N/A	N/A	Lost Creek	N/A

and protecting against fraudulent uses of IP addresses and past uses of IP addresses. Through the use of master nodes and digital IDs, reputation on the internet can be even more secure and immutable. As demonstrated, solidity contracts provide a method to store this data in a way that is tamper proof and accessible. This paper presented the ways the blockchain can provide for a more secure storage of IP address information while also presenting a practical method of storing this information.

References

1. S. Homayoun, A. Dehghantanha, R.M. Parizi, K.K.R. Choo, A blockchain-based framework for detecting malicious mobile applications in app stores, in *32nd IEEE Canadian Conference of Electrical and Computer Engineering (IEEE CCECE'19)*, Canada (2019)
2. A. Yazdinejad, R.M. Parizi, A. Dehghantanha, K.R. Choo, Blockchain-enabled authentication handover with efficient privacy protection in SDN-based 5G networks, in *IEEE Transactions on Network Science and Engineering*. https://doi.org/10.1109/TNSE.2019.2937481
3. R.M. Parizi, S. Homayoun, A. Yazdinejad, A. Dehghantanha, K.K.R. Choo, Integrating privacy enhancing techniques into blockchains using sidechains, in *32nd IEEE Canadian Conference of Electrical and Computer Engineering (IEEE CCECE'19)*, Canada (2019)
4. P.J. Taylor, T. Dargahi, A. Dehghantanha, R.M. Parizi, K.K.R. Choo, A systematic literature review of blockchain cyber security. Digit. Commun. Netw. https://doi.org/10.1016/j.dcan.2019.01.005
5. E. Nyaletey, R.M. Parizi, Q. Zhang, K.-K.R. Choo, BlockIPFS - blockchain-enabled interplanetary file system for forensic and trusted data traceability, in *2nd IEEE International Conference on Blockchain (IEEE Blockchain-2019)* (2019)
6. R. M. Parizi, A. Dehghantanha, K. K. R. Choo, A. Singh, Empirical vulnerability analysis of automated smart contracts security testing on blockchains, in *28th ACM Annual International Conference on Computer Science and Software Engineering (CASCON'18)*, Ontario, Canada (IBM, 2018)
7. Q. Zhang, R.M. Parizi, K.-R. Choo, A pentagon of considerations towards more secure blockchains, in *IEEE Blockchain Technical Briefs* (2018)
8. R. M. Parizi, Amritraj, A. Dehghantanha, Smart contract programming languages on blockchains: an empirical evaluation of usability and security, in *1st International Conference on Blockchain (ICBC'18)*, Seattle, USA, LNCS (Springer, 2018), pp. 75–91
9. R.M. Parizi, A. Dehghantanha, On the understanding of gamification in blockchain systems, in *6th IEEE International Conference on Future Internet of Things and Cloud (FiCloud'18)*, Barcelona, Spain (IEEE Computer Society, 2018)
10. N. Chalaemwongwan, W. Kurutach, A practical national digital ID framework on blockchain (NIDBC), in *15th International Conference on Electrical Engineering/Electronics, Computer, Telecommunications and Information Technology*, pp. 497–500 (2019)
11. L. Wilbanks, What's your IT risk approach? IT Prof. **20**(4), 13–17 (2018)
12. V.R. Pagar, R.G. Pise, Strengthening password security through honeyword and honeyencryption technique, in *International Conference on Trends in Electronics and Informatics, ICEI 2017*, vol. 2018, pp. 827–831 (2018)
13. T. Li, A. Mehta, P. Yang, Security analysis of email systems, in *4th IEEE International Conference on Cyber Security and Cloud Computing, CSCloud 2017 and 3rd IEEE International Conference of Scalable and Smart Cloud*, pp. 91–96 (2017)
14. B.S. Archana, A. Chandrashekar, A.G. Bangi, B.M. Sanjana, S. Akram, Survey on usable and secure two-factor authentication, in *2nd IEEE International Conference on Recent Trends in Electronics Information & Communication Technology*, pp. 842–846 (2018)

15. M. Wazid et al., A framework for detection and prevention of novel keylogger spyware attacks, in *7th International Conference on Intelligent Systems and Control*, pp. 433–438 (2013)
16. N.B. Vasilyevna, S.S. Yeo, E.S. Cho, J.A. Kim, Malware and antivirus deployment for enterprise IT security, in *2008 International Symposium on Ubiquitous Multimedia Computing*, pp. 252–255 (2008)
17. A. Tiwari, A. Tiwary, Y. Bhatt, A distributed web conferencing architecture to meet inorganic training needs of an enterprise, in *2010 International Conference on Education and Management Technology, Proceedings* (IEEE), pp. 636–640
18. K. Madzima, M. Moyo, H. Abdullah, Is bring your own device an institutional information security risk for small-scale business organisations? in *2014 Information Security*, (South Africa, Johannesburg, 2014), pp. 1–8
19. A.M. Eljetlawi, U. Teknologi, Graphical password: prototype usability survey, in *2008 International Conference on Advanced Computer Theory and Engineering*, pp. 351–355 (2008)
20. M. Chen, Reputation-based recommendation trust model in the interoperable environment, in *2011 International Conference on Electronics, Communications and Control*, pp. 2226–2228 (2011)
21. A. Stiemer, Analyzing the performance of data replication and data partitioning in the cloud: the BEOWULF approach, in *2016 IEEE International Conference on Big Data*, pp. 2837–2846 (2016)
22. B. Carrara, C. Adams, On achieving a digital identity management system with support for non-transferability, in *2010 Eighth Annual International Conference on Privacy, Security and Trust*, pp. 150–159 (2010)
23. T.H. Tran, Proactive multicast-based IPSEC discovery protocol and multicast extension, ed. by H. Trung, in *Tran SPAWAR Systems Center*, San Diego, pp. 1–7
24. Sender Score. www.senderscore.org. Accessed 11 Aug 2019
25. Cisco. www.cisco.com/c/en/us/solutions/industries.html. Accessed 11 Aug 2019
26. Y. Fukushima, Y. Hori, K. Sakurai, Proactive blacklisting for malicious web sites by reputation evaluation based on domain and IP address registration, in *2011 International Joint Conference of IEEE TrustCom*, pp. 352–361 (2011)
27. R. Bocu, IP pooling-based email systems reputation assurance, in *2011 RoEduNet International Conference 10th Edition: Networking in Education and Research*, (Iasi, 2011), pp. 1–6
28. K. Mudliar, H. Parekh, P. Bhavathankar, A comprehensive integration of national identity with blockchain technology, in *2018 International Conference on Communication, Information & Computing Technology*, pp. 1–6 (2018)
29. Z. Jia, L. Jiqiang, H. Zhen, S. Changxiang, Identity based digital signature algorithm of XTR system, in *2008 9th International Conference on Signal Processing*, (Beijing, 2008), pp. 2816–2819
30. V.L. Lemieux, A typology of blockchain recordkeeping solutions and some reflections on their implications for the future of archival preservation, in *2017 IEEE International Conference on Big Data (Big Data)*, (Boston, MA, 2017), pp. 2271–2278
31. J. Chen, Y. Xue, Bootstrapping a Blockchain based ecosystem for big data exchange, in *2017 IEEE International Congress on Big Data (BigData Congress)*, (Honolulu, HI, 2017), pp. 460–463
32. I. Zikratov, A. Kuzmin, V. Akimenko, V. Niculichev, L. Yalansky, Ensuring data integrity using blockchain technology, in *2017 20th Conference of Open Innovations Association (FRUCT)*, (St. Petersburg, 2017), pp. 534–539
33. T. Moura, A. Gomes, Blockchain voting and its effects on election transparency and voter confidence, in *Proceedings of the 18th Annual International Conference on Digital Government Research (Dg.O '17). Association for Computing Machinery*, (New York, NY, USA, 2017), pp. 574–575
34. H. Lee, M. Shin, K.S. Kim, Y. Kang, J. Kim, Recipient-oriented transaction for preventing double spending attacks in private blockchain, in *2018 15th Annual IEEE International Conference on Sensing, Communication, and Networking*, pp. 1–2 (2018)

35. A. Culwick, D. Metcalf, The Blocknet design specification. Blocknet. www.blocknet.co/wp-content/uploads/whitepaper/Blocknet_Whitepaper.pdf. Accessed 11 Aug 2019
36. C. Harper, What are masternodes? An introduction and guide. Coin Central. www.coincentral.com/what-are-masternodes-an-introduction-and-guide/. Accessed 11 Aug 2019
37. PIVX. www.ivx.org. Accessed 11 Aug 2019
38. Exscudo. www.exscudo.com/exchange.html. Accessed 11 Aug 2019
39. Digital IDs on the Blockchain. InsureBlocks. www.insureblocks.com/ep-30-digital-ids-on-the-blockchain/. Accessed 11 Aug 2019

On the Application of Financial Security Standards in Blockchain Platforms

Gabriel Bello and Alfredo J. Perez

Abstract Security standards such as the Payment Application Data Security Standard (PA-DSS) have been developed to keep transaction data secured in traditional payment systems. However, blockchain systems are not in the scope of these security standards. In this work, we highlight the differences between traditional and decentralized payment platforms and we present an adaptation of the PA-DSS standards to apply them in transaction-supported, decentralized blockchain platforms. We evaluate the QTUM and Ethereum blockchain platforms by using our adapted standards and we report security gaps on each platform. We conclude that neither platform is suitable for business adoption based on the adapted PA-DSS standard's evaluation results.

1 Introduction

Legal liability in the digital age is increasingly dynamic, both in theory and practice. Paper and pen have morphed to lines of code, and with it, legal contracts have transformed as industries grow more adjusted to technology. The definition of a contract remains the same: an agreement between two parties outlined by the terms and conditions, wherein value is exchanged [1]. The conditions set by this definition allow both parties to protect their interests through a document that binds them to a set of rules. As the world transitions to a more digitized era, smart contracts have been introduced as a replacement for the arduous, tedious legal agreements of the past.

Smart contracts were first devised by Nick Szabo, who documented the idea of a contract automation in 1997 [2]. To present his idea, Szabo provided an example between a human and a vending machine: The vending machine, depending on the human's input (in coins) would allow or disallow candy to be dispensed from

G. Bello (✉) · A. J. Perez
Columbus State University, Columbus, GA, USA
e-mail: bello_gabriel@columbusstate.edu; perez_alfredo@columbusstate.edu

© Springer Nature Switzerland AG 2020
K.-K. R. Choo et al. (eds.), *Blockchain Cybersecurity, Trust and Privacy*, Advances in Information Security 79, https://doi.org/10.1007/978-3-030-38181-3_13

247

the machine. At the base-level, this is precisely what a smart contract does: assure an exchange of data with anybody who satisfies the constraints set forth by the contract. His rationale envisioned the smart contracts' adoption across the industry, spanning over multitudes of applications. His focus, however, revolved around the profitability and feasibility of implementing this technology on a large scale. In his vision, any smart contract that is created should have safeguards whose robustness depends on the process performed.

According to Szabo [2], the security concerns for each smart contract should exist within the bounds of the business transaction. Essentially, as in any security system, the controls in place should not outstrip nor fall short of the functionality of the process. For example, the vending machine that Szabo described also featured security controls, such as a lock to open the machine. These mechanisms should not inhibit profitability. In 2002, Szabo developed a second work [3] that defined a set of guidelines to follow when designing smart contracts. Overall, this second work serves as a reference to create contracts, especially in the scope of auditing.

Current smart contracts are built on blockchain technology: all instances of cryptocurrency, beginning with Satoshi Nakamoto and Bitcoin, are built on blockchain technology [4]. Blockchain provides a decentralization of information on a given network. In contrast, typical networks often have one central point where all the information is stored. The decentralized design of blockchain serves both as a failsafe and a protection against malicious data alteration as the information is distributed and spread over multiple hosts (called nodes). Consequently, there is a copy of all data on each device that cannot be altered. Additionally, account management on blockchain platforms are often rooted in privacy measures to ensure anonymity on this decentralized network. From the perspective of cybersecurity, the challenge in smart contracts lies within the authentication, communication, and execution of the technology. The difference in implementation between centralized and decentralized networks results in a difference in security approach. Decentralized platforms may necessitate additional measures in place to verify a legally binding agreement, ensure privacy on a distributed network, and conduct a secure transaction of goods.

Smart contracts, along with blockchain as a whole, have grown in popularity over the past years. From business optimization to disaster recovery, smart contracts and blockchain offer alternative methods to common business practices. However, with the industry adoption, especially within the realms of the Payment Card Industry (PCI), healthcare, and other industries who handle private user data, user privacy protection is mandatory. As such, smart contract platforms that wish to be adapted to enterprise environments must comply or exceed certain security standards, often modeled after industry best practices. Whatever standard an organization chooses to use matters in the case of smart contracts, as often times the immutability of blocks on a blockchain result in tedious efforts to prevent disastrous vulnerabilities. That is, a smart contract with a security flaw must be disabled and replaced, which is a much greater task than rolling out a patch for centralized systems.

As the roles of smart contracts and blockchain platforms grow as payment systems, so too does the necessity for proper auditing and compliance to ensure proper data protection. In this work we provide a method to analyze the security of a smart contract's platform. We categorize and analyze the controls and mechanisms that the platform enforces for security to determine their compliance by using an application security framework paired with a risk assessment framework.

The needs for security standards on blockchain and smart contract platforms are increasing with the growth and popularity of these systems. We adapt the Payment Application Data Security Standard (PA-DSS) to meet the needs of blockchain payment systems. We then analyze two smart contract platforms as case studies: QTUM and Ethereum. QTUM [5] is a smart contracts system that works across multiple devices. Claiming functionality on mobile, QTUM seeks to bridge the gap between blockchain systems and the business world by managing the spatial complexity (storage size) required for blockchains. QTUM offers solutions for the adoption of smart contract systems into enterprise environments. Ethereum [6] is a popular smart contract platform that supports blockchain with a large user base. Its structured smart contract language makes it ideal for business adoption. Both platforms have strengths that make them more adaptable to business functions than other platforms.

2 Smart Contracts, Blockchain Transaction Models and the Payment Application Data Security Standard

2.1 Smart Contract Anatomy

Smart contracts operate on blockchain technology, which acts as a distributed ledger for all present information. Blockchain, in essence, is a decentralized platform on which transactions are executed, recorded, and maintained. The blockchain itself is not stored on a central location; rather, it is stored on every participating node (computer) in a given network. This quality is what differentiates blockchain from other centralized platforms. There is no single point of failure, nor is there any single target for attack. The blockchain is immutable, and it provides a platform in which permanent items can be stored. One such item is a smart contract.

If blockchain is the platform where transactions are executed, recorded, and maintained, then smart contracts can be described as the mechanisms to automate these transactions. Figure 1 depicts two individuals agreeing on a smart contract to sell an asset (a house). Upon agreement of the sale, the system automates the transfer of the house's deed and the funds for the purchase based on the smart contract. In the figure, the contract is stored on the blockchain, ensuring its immutability and authenticity for both parties regardless of party trust. Within smart contracts, there are multiple avenues for their implementation, each offering varying levels of privacy and security.

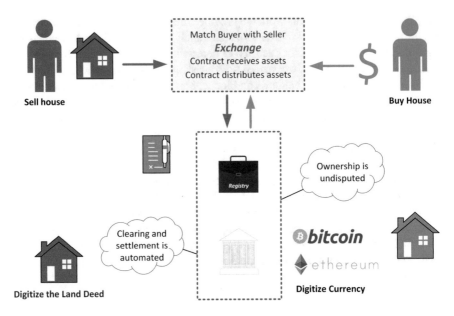

Fig. 1 Anatomy of a smart contract

2.2 Blockchain Transaction Models

Above all, smart contracts offer automated transactions with reduced administrative overhead when compared to traditional contracts. These transactions can be carried out through two models: the unspent transaction output model and account-based model. Both models have seen widespread use in blockchain technologies, and both have benefits and disadvantages regarding decentralization and privacy.

The Unspent Transaction Output model (hereafter referred to as UTXO) was developed by Satoshi Nakamoto, first seen in the publication for Bitcoin [4] in 2008. In this work, Satoshi covered a range of topics to implement blockchain technology, including the UTXO model, proof of work, and cryptocurrency mining. UTXO works by assigning a unique identifier for each transaction. It should also be noted that this is true for the initial mining of the bitcoin, which returns a determined value. These unique identifiers are the backbone of UTXO, as they are used as inputs and outputs for each transaction that occurs on the blockchain. The users in the transaction are somewhat anonymized, for the accounts used in transactions are not directly linked to personal information. Therefore, UTXO is, by default, primitively anonymous for users on the blockchain. The steps for UTXO (as shown in Fig. 2) are as follows:

- User 1 (a3fa29ce) sends currency. This step is depicted as one arrow and may be interpreted as a single currency or coin sent, but the reality may be multiple transactions of smaller amounts that comprise the required transaction amount.

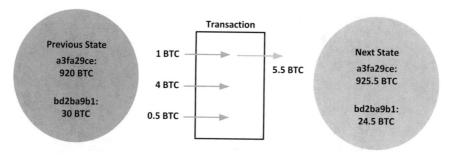

Fig. 2 UTXO transaction example. Adapted from [7]

For example, User 1 may need to send 5.5 coins for the transaction. Then user may send coins of values 1, 4, and 0.5 to sum 5.5. Alternatively, a single transaction of value 5.5 can be sent.

- The required transaction amount is sent to User 2 (bd2ba9b1) and a unique output value that is different from the input value sent in step 1. This is a critical step in the UTXO model. These are referred to as *states*, where the previous state is the inputted currency, and the next state is the outputted currency. These states are identified uniquely from each other, making each transaction distinct.
- If applicable, User 1 is sent *change* from the inputted values. This only applies if User 1 sent more currency than required by the transaction. This output is different from the input value(s) (e.g., if User 1 sends 7 currency on a 5.5-currency transaction, the user will be refunded 1.5 currency during this step).

The account-based model resembles what one might see in a traditional banking system. Two users are given accounts, and they are able to conduct transactions, given there is enough money to be sent. This model differs greatly from UTXO, as it seemingly eliminates a portion of the decentralization by forcing a trusted party to maintain accounts on the blockchain. Essentially, there is an established account system that mirrors a digital bank, which limits the privacy of this transaction model. Figure 3 depicts the transaction. The steps can be seen below:

- Account 1 (a3fa29ce) sends currency (10 eth)
- Account 2 (bd2ba9b1) receives currency (10 eth)
- Previous state is the state of the accounts before the transaction occurs. Next state is the state of the accounts after the transaction is complete.

Each transaction model has benefits and detriments to its design, but each is popular within its own niche. UTXO was the first transaction model, introduced when blockchain was initially proposed, and the goal lies in anonymity. UTXO surpasses the account-based model in this sense, for UTXO offers a transaction without basis in accounts. It simply takes the currency much like a vending machine, computing the return value and forwarding the transaction to its intended destination. The downfall here is complexity. With UTXO, transactions rely on more computations to sum the inputs and return *change* if applicable. As a result, there

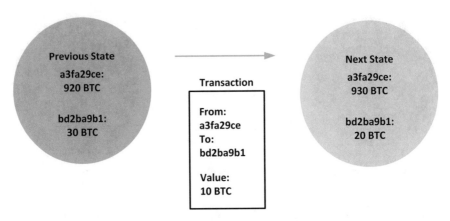

Fig. 3 Account-based model transaction example. Adapted from [7]

are multiple steps to the transaction that do not exist when using a simpler design. This is where the account-based model succeeds.

Account-based systems, which can be seen in many popular blockchains such as Ethereum, utilize a much more standardized method to execute transactions. Not unlike a bank, there exist two parties looking to conduct a transaction. These two parties, much like in modern banking, have accounts wherein their balance is stored. The account-based model utilizes these accounts to verify that there is enough currency to be sent for the transaction. The benefit here is the simplicity of the model streamlined by accounts: the transactions rely only on verification of valid funds to execute. However, the anonymity is called into question when accounts can be linked to one another through transactions. Both UTXO and account-based models have found homes in various blockchain technologies, often dependent on the goal of the blockchain.

2.3 The PA-DSS Standard

The Payment Application Data Security Standard (PA-DSS), was first published in 2008 as the Payment Application Best Practices (PABS) [8]. It is currently governed by five major global payment brands: American Express, Discover Financial Services, JCB International, MasterCard Worldwide, and Visa Inc. These organizations collaborate to determine the security requirements for third-party payment applications. It should be noted that this standard specifically targets third-party payment applications, for their systems are likely to be distributed to multiple vendors. As such, their system will not be tailored for a single organization; tailored solutions or applications built for a single company are not mandated by this standard.

Table 1 Summary of the PA-DSS standard version 3.0

Major requirement	Number of standards
1. Do not retain full track data, card verification code or value (CAV2, CID, CVC2, CVV2), or PIN block data	5
2. Protect stored cardholder data	7
3. Provide secure authentication features	3
4. Log payment application activity	2
5. Develop secure payment applications	4
6. Protect wireless transmissions	3
7. Test payment applications to address vulnerabilities and maintain payment application updates	2
8. Facilitate secure network implementation	3
9. Cardholder data must never be stored on a server connected to the Internet	1
10. Facilitate secure remote access to payment application	2
11. Encrypt sensitive traffic over public networks	2
12. Encrypt all non-console administrative access	2
13. Maintain a PA-DSS Implementation Guide for customers, resellers, and integrators	1
14. Assign PA-DSS responsibilities for personnel, and maintain training programs for personnel, customers, resellers, and integrators	3

The PA-DSS standards have existed since 2008 (version 1), but they have been through several iterations since then. In 2010, version 2.0 was released, and in 2013, version 3.0 was published [9]. As the current version (v3.2) provides minor changes to the version 3.0 of the standard, we chose to work with version 3.0. Each version of the standard is composed of requirements that belong to a requirement category. In addition, each requirement specify a testing procedure as well as an explanation (guidance) on the requirement. Table 1 summarizes the version 3.0 of the standard.

Any payment application is within the scope of the PA-DSS standard regardless of the specified technology. Thus, blockchain platforms, in most use cases, can be considered payment systems. Because they are also not typically developed by organizations that may use them, they can also be assumed, in general, to be third-party applications. By definition, they should follow the described standards of PA-DSS. We use these standards as a guideline for best security practices on payment applications, and blockchain platforms fall under the umbrella.

3 Security Issues in Blockchain

Blockchain, as with any other digital system, has vulnerabilities and gaps leading to exploitations. Still in its infancy, the technology is constantly evolving to create new and secure ways to operate. Moreover, each blockchain comes with its own set of challenges which depend on the mechanisms they use. For example, Ethereum may face different security concerns than Bitcoin simply because Ethereum makes use of an account-based transaction model. Many issues, whether severe flaws or privacy preferences have been documented to highlight the evident or perceived shortcomings of each blockchain. They can be separated into three major categories: anonymity of users, privacy of transactions, and software assurance of contracts. Each entails its own set of challenges and solutions, but all are relevant to the comprehensive security of a given blockchain system.

3.1 User Security

User security has been a point of discussion on more than blockchain systems for years, and the contention continues onto this technology. Countless debates (and blockchains) are dedicated to provide users with ample anonymity for transactions on a blockchain. It is important to differentiate user privacy from the other categories, as doing so will help to outline the type of works included in this field. The goal of blockchain, and especially the Unspent Output from Bitcoin Transactions (abbreviated as UTXO) transaction model, is to provide a mechanism for secure transactions between two untrusting parties. As such, user information is one of the most important types of data that can be disclosed. This has been a focal point for many in the blockchain community, and user privacy is a part of the reason so many different blockchains exist. Slight adaptations to a blockchain sometimes necessitate a new system altogether. Overall, the idea of user anonymity is not new, but with blockchain, it primarily concerns the user's preference rather than a severe security flaw (with exceptions).

Ferrante and Mercer [10] outline the privacy improvements that can be made to the existing Bitcoin platform. The focus of the paper centers on the UTXO model and its transaction sources and destinations. Since the basis of UTXO is untrusting, user anonymity is paramount. The researchers detail improvements to the model to prevent the source or destination from knowing who has sent or received the transaction. By doing so, there is no room for de-anonymization. Furthermore, this work overlaps heavily with transaction privacy, wherein multiple solutions are proposed to further increase privacy. Conti et al. [11] document blockchain vulnerabilities on its transaction system; however, this work does not mention security and privacy aspects of Bitcoin wallets and user identity. Koshy et al. [12] utilized network traffic analysis to heuristically determine the IP addresses that linked with the Bitcoin accounts. This is a severe vulnerability that compromises the anonymity supposed on Bitcoin's platform.

User privacy is essential in a decentralized platform. With the blockchain's intrinsic availability to users, anonymity it is necessary and cannot be overlooked as a luxury. Account privacy works hand-in-hand with transaction security, for each transaction generally links to a particular user or set of users. As smart contracts are more widely considered for adoption, the security and privacy of users and transactions cannot be of question. It must be at least as reliable as modern centralized platforms. Even though these works support progress in smart contract platforms, there is still more work to be done.

3.2 Transaction Security

Transaction security is undeniably important when considering overall security of an application or platform. Data in transit must be protected against both passive, active eavesdropping, and unintended alteration. When dealing with smart contracts, users still face similar issues of traditional transaction systems. However, blockchain technology has allowed certain growth from the perspective of absolute privacy during transactions. Such advancements are detailed, and their benefits and drawbacks are outlined.

Ferrante and Mercer describe in their research the benefits of using the UTXO transaction model to optimize transaction privacy, especially between distrusting parties [10]. The intrinsic security features of the UTXO model, which include supposedly unidentifiable accounts linked to unique transactions, by default outstrip the privacy capabilities of the standard account-based model. However, there have been studies that exploit certain aspects of the model to track users. Due to possible vulnerabilities of the UTXO base model, Koshy et al. [12] offer solutions to boost user privacy and anonymity. The two recommended controls are linkable ring signatures and stealth addresses. Linkable ring signatures allow users to verify that they are a part of a group without revealing exactly which user they are. This group may be a set of public keys, where a user may have to use his or her private key to authenticate. Stealth addresses ensure that a given user's identity (address) is indistinguishable from random, and they also guarantee that only a user can conduct transactions through that account. These modifications to the UTXO model raise the level of privacy for transactions on the blockchain, eliminating the possibility of transaction identification or spoofing. The work done by Sompolinsky and Zohar regarding a GHOST protocol for Bitcoin's transactions centers around mitigating double-spending attacks on the blockchain [13]. In standard environments, malicious users may have the opportunity to access and spend the same currency two or more times before the blockchain realizes the error; this defines a double-spending attack. With the GHOST protocol, the researchers theorize a system where lightweight processing allows the high-rate transactions to execute without this vulnerability. This protocol not only enhances the security features while also presenting interesting follow-up inquiries regarding the scalability of a blockchain platform. In essence, to process transactions on a large scale, the GHOST protocol or an equivalent is necessary to maintain security when scaling.

In the work done by the researchers Shunli et al, proposals for account-based transaction models are used to boost privacy [14]. By implementing homomorphic encryption, a method where encrypted data can be used to perform operations without decrypting the data, information can be altered by authorized users. This eliminates the need to decrypt information to utilize it, which is standard practice in most payment systems. Another feature mentioned was a zero-knowledge (ZK) approach, which relies on hiding information from users unless absolutely necessary to the transaction. These solutions are proposed on the account-based model, which may boost the intrinsic privacy to match that of the UTXO model.

The work done by Andrychowicz et al. [15] pertains to *honest participants* and transactional assurance. While not directly tied to privacy, assurance is still an integral component of security, and these researchers designed a trustless protocol to prevent fraud and exploitation. On a similar note, Zhang et al. [16] proposes an authenticated data feed for smart contracts. This work doesn't refer to smart contract security itself, but rather the data that would inevitably feed into a smart contract platform. The authenticity of this data is just as vital as the data generated on the blockchain itself, and it should be considered relevant to the overall maturity of smart contract security. Gray and Hadju have also contributed to the smart contract security realm with a practical implementation utilizing *Cryptlets* [17–19]. In their work, they contextualize the need for an optimized, trustless mode for transactions and analyze the Ethereum platform, wherein they describe the optimization woes that it has faced in the past. They offer a platform optimization using Cryptlets, a seemingly third-party-reminiscent repository which stores the logic of a smart contract to be executed by a node on the blockchain. Based on a semi-trust or fully-trust model, Cryptlets offer an optimized platform that does not rely on each node to execute the logic of a smart contract, providing a reduced computational overhead for the blockchain as a whole. This is known outside of blockchain technology as cyber-offloading.

Cyber-offloading, particularly on a blockchain, is dangerous to the integrity of decentralized systems, as it relies on a trusted third-party to maintain integrity parallel to the blockchain. However, in a more pragmatic sense, offloading is a reasonable risk for business implementations of smart contract technology. There is incentive for organizations to use a trust or semi-trust model, considering there is some liability and governance surrounding the execution of smart contracts. This may be seen as a transitional middle-ground between centralized and decentralized platforms. In 2016, Hawk was created as a smart contract platform, which boosted security measures for code design on that platform [20]. This adaptive platform automates cryptographic protocols, such as encryption, for smart contracts. Essentially, developers do not need to manually code the cryptography on the contracts as this process is handled by the compiler. This protocol remediates the traditional lack of privacy on most popular decentralized platforms, and it does so without burdensome interference for the users and developers. Since this platform was designed with transactional privacy in mind, it may be difficult to port this technology or protocol to other platforms without a complete redesign. Regardless, the success of this automated cryptographic protocol shows that security can be implemented intuitively and automatically, given the right design.

Transactional security is a focal point for many different works on smart contracts, and the progression towards optimal privacy is undeniable. Many of the researchers referenced, as well as many other smart contract developers, have designed unique, separate platforms for each protocol change. The challenge, at this time, is not solving the issue of transactional privacy on a decentralized network, but rather implementing the solutions already discovered, governing the maintenance of said solutions, and ensuring there are as few vulnerabilities as possible.

3.3 Software Assurance of Contracts

Many researchers have also chosen to target the smart contract code itself, finding various shortcomings with regards to software assurance. These issues are outside the scope of this paper, but the impact of software assurance is evident, and it is necessary to acknowledge its progress. Bartoletti and Pompianu, in their research, analyze the popular smart contract platforms, Ethereum and Bitcoin, for their security implementation [21]. Their focus is on the available code for smart contracts on each platform, analyzing it for patterns in design. The purpose of this paper is to find a recurring issue in the design of smart contracts such that it may be remediated. The empirical process the researchers follow is highly adoptable and may follow the structure of organizations that review smart contract code.

Delmolino et al. have also seen the value in software assurance for smart contracts, like any other piece of code [22]. By analyzing public-domain smart contracts, they noticed patterns and recurring issues in the programming practices. As a result, the researchers created open-source platforms to teach programming for smart contracts. This paper largely focuses on the education of safe programming practices, but the core aspects of smart contracts and their code are the programmers and their practices. Therefore, the training of such practices is necessary for proper progression in smart contract security.

Similar to the work of Delmolino et al, Luu et al. [23] documented their findings of smart contract bugs on the Ethereum platform. Their work is limited to a single platform, albeit the largest smart contract blockchain used at the moment. By describing the pitfalls of smart contracts on Ethereum, they both contextualize the impact of smart contracts' bugs and they find common threads between them. Smart contract bugs often result in lost or stolen cryptocurrencies, sometimes totaling the equivalent of millions of dollars, and this paper describes how each attack or bug executed. Furthermore, the common characteristics of the bugs allow a conclusion to be made around the specific programming practices that lead to each vulnerability.

Buterin's work describes Ethereum bugs that have the same principal practices that lead to bugs on the smart contract platform [24]. Bugs like Transaction Ordering Dependence, timestamp dependence, mishandled exceptions, and many others, are pervasive throughout smart contract code. Still in its infancy, smart contract software assurance's state can be seen through the lens of the bugs documented so far. Blockchain and smart contract bugs have stumbled into infamy with their costly mistakes, and each vulnerability seems to uncover more. In a blog post written on Ethereum's website, a list of the most popular bugs can be found with a description of their causes and effects [25]. This work serves as another indication that software assurance is at the forefront of most people's minds when discussing smart contract security.

From the research compiled on software assurance, it is clear that, while there has been significant progress to remediate and prevent bugs from existing, there is still much work to be done. Specifically, the shortcomings of non-Ethereum bug documentation, along with cross-platform bug documentation, limit the progress of new smart contract platforms from prospering. Without formal code review, it is difficult to determine the strength of smart contracts. Many platforms have not had the attention that Ethereum has; as a result, there may be undiscovered bugs present on their platforms. Furthermore, software assurance has received the bulk of focus from the community as a whole, leaving protocol-level security with fewer resources. The community of blockchain and smart contracts has developed a handful of useful protocols, practices, and platforms that boost security. Nevertheless, there is a clear ceiling on smart contracts that must be conquered before adoption in enterprise business environments.

3.4   Limitations of Current Blockchain Platforms

With major popularity in the community, blockchains and smart contracts have been subject to both praise and scrutiny. Even with its revolutionary design to eliminate many of the issues centralized systems face, there are still many shortcomings that must be addressed before the technology is deemed mature by security standards. Aside from the aforementioned security concerns and research, there are still some remaining limitations of smart contract platforms.

Some of the most popular platforms, namely Bitcoin and Ethereum, have succeeded both due to their first-to-market status and simplicity in execution. However, they both fall victim to an issue that serves as a substantial roadblock to large-scale adoption: space on disk. Ethereum, as of 2017, was documented at over 350GB, with Bitcoin being a very comparable size. Simply put, this spatial requirement is not sustainable for widespread adoption, which inevitably involves mobile devices. There is a balance to be struck between complete access to the blockchain and computational viability on mobile. So far, there are only a handful of platforms, none of them as popular as Ethereum or Bitcoin, that attempt to solve this issue.

Due to the communal nature of blockchain as a whole, smart contracts suffer from the same detriment: lack of standardization. With everyone's hand in the proverbial cookie jar, there is little room to prevent a myriad of unmanageable smart contracts and unsafe protocols. Only recently has there been more effort in the space of academic and professional research to expand on the security controls of smart contract platforms. More work is needed here to advance the viability of smart contracts in enterprise environments. Security and privacy concerns will always be forthcoming and newfound, but the baseline by which smart contracts are standardized must be developed to ensure the proper measures are in place to protect private information.

From the related work, it is clear that the community surrounding blockchain and smart contract technology is very focused on user and transaction privacy. Based on the research already conducted, we find a few proposed solutions to boost user security based on disallowing deanonymization of user addresses, using stealth addresses, and implementing linkable ring signatures. Furthermore, proposed solutions for transaction security show promise as well. The GHOST protocol, along with the ZK approach with homomorphic encryption, both show substantial results in boosting the overall security of transactions on a blockchain. Integrity maintenance on these platforms is paramount, so work done to boost transaction assurance through authenticated data feeds is undoubtedly valuable to a security-focused blockchain. We begin to notice room for concern when researchers drift away from a zero-trust approach for blockchain systems. With Cryptlet's cyber-offloading architecture, maintaining integrity for the centralized storage point is the weak link in the structure. Moving toward a semi-trust or full-trust model can only work with proper governance over the central unit.

With all of the work done with respect to blockchain security, especially the research that uncovered identity linking with supposedly-anonymous pseudonyms on Bitcoin [7], it is interesting to note that no researcher has acknowledged the security and privacy of the ledger itself. Bitcoin, and a number of other platforms, have no record of protecting the transaction data logged on the ledger from viewing. With the de-anonymization of user IDs and addresses, it is a point of concern to keep in mind when discussing the comprehensive security of blockchain platforms.

4 Adapting the PA-DSS Standard to Blockchain Systems

As previously described, the PA-DSS Standard [9] defines the set of guidelines for traditional transaction applications. To adapt these standards to blockchain systems, we analyzed each guideline and highlighted the shortcomings with respect to their applicability on decentralized systems. Based on its ability to be directly applicable to decentralized platforms, we categorized each guideline as either *Fully Applicable*, *Partially Applicable*, or *Not Applicable*. If a guideline is deemed *Fully Applicable*, it can be applied without alteration to a decentralized system [26]. If a guideline is deemed *Partially Applicable*, it can be applied to decentralized platforms with modifications. If a guideline is deemed *Not Applicable*, it cannot be applied to a decentralized system without major alteration (in these cases, alteration would essentially create a new standard).

Rationalizations for the categorization of guidelines are given in the full PA-DSS analysis table [26]. Each guideline was categorized for a specific reason, and the rationalization field dictates why each decision was made. This field may also contain supplemental considerations for *Fully Applicable* guidelines, wherein suggestions are proposed to incorporate decentralized platforms into the scope of the standard. That is, the *Fully Applicable* guidelines may be fully applicable to traditional payment systems, and they may also be applicable to decentralized payment systems, but supplemental information is necessary (and proposed) to cover the scope of decentralized systems. Upon analysis of the PA-DSS standards, we found that, of the forty (40) standards reviewed, thirty (30) were fully *Fully Applicable*, seven (7) were found to be *Partially Applicable* and three were found to be *Not Applicable*. Tables 2 and 3 present the *Partially Applicable* and the *Not Applicable* standards as described by our proposed adapted standard [26]. For the *Partially Applicable* standards, we provide an updated version of the standard. For the *Not Applicable* we provide an explanation as to why the standard cannot be adapted. Even though the majority of the standards are still applicable to Blockchain systems/platforms, still there are gaps in the scope of the PA-DSS standard.

A key area for revision is the classification of sensitive data and how to properly manage the data. Five of the standards marked *Partially Applicable* deal with the mandatory secure storage and transmission of sensitive information. With traditional payment systems, cardholder data is clearly defined, and the PA-DSS standards match the definitions. The current standards explicitly list fields that must be securely handled, such as credit-card number (CCN), primary account number (PAN), and PIN numbers. However, due to the anatomy of blockchain transactions, with user IDs as the main form of identification and direction for the transaction, user IDs have a much larger role than most cardholder data fields. User IDs are essentially used as source and destination placeholders for the transaction, and the same is true for the data stored on the ledger. As such, the standards must be revised to account for this difference in core architecture of the payment platform.

Data access and platform logging are two more categorical issues with the current standards. On traditional platforms, data access is, in most situations, restricted only to a select number of business employees; on traditional platforms, this is understandable considering this data is vulnerable to manipulation and/or destruction. Logging is typically implemented in the same scenario to ensure that the organization knows who is accessing the data at any time. However, there is a fundamental change in data access on blockchain platforms: the data is available for all participants to view. As a result, data access cannot be restricted, lest the integrity of the blockchain be compromised. If data access was limited on blockchain platforms, then the trust model that blockchain technology is built on would be destroyed altogether. Access logging is also difficult logistically (and arguably needless) on blockchain platforms. If all participating nodes have access to the ledger, then it is safe to assume every participant can or has viewed the data, secured or not. The three standards associated with data access and logging, consequently, are revised to match the information dynamic present on blockchains.

Vulnerability identification and remediation, including the process of patching, are specified in the PA-DSS standards, but they understandably lack the exceptions necessary for an immutable blockchain. For traditional payment systems, vulnerability scanning and remediation is an arduous and ongoing challenge. Patches to code and platforms are difficult on traditional payment systems, but blockchain platforms impose an entirely unique and complex roadblock to remediation. Blockchain

Table 2 Partially applicable PA-DSS standards in blockchain

Current standard	Adapted standard
2.1 Software vendor must provide guidance to customers regarding purging of cardholder data after expiration of customer-defined retention period	Software vendor must provide guidance to customers regarding purging of cardholder data after expiration of customer-defined retention period. Retention period of customer data is dependent on transactional method. Blockchain ledgers will securely store transactional data permanently regardless of transaction method
2.2 Mask PAN when displayed (the first six and last four digits are the maximum number of digits to be displayed)	Mask PAN when displayed (the first six and last four digits are the maximum number of digits to be displayed). On blockchain platforms, UTXO and Account-Based transaction models require user ID for transactions. User ID or any information determining a transaction's source or destination should be masked when displayed
2.3 Render PAN, at a minimum, unreadable anywhere it is stored	Render PAN, at a minimum, unreadable anywhere it is stored. If on a blockchain platform with blockchain-specific transaction models, render user ID unreadable by unauthorized users when stored
3.1 The "out of the box" installation of the payment application in place at the completion of the installation process, must facilitate use of unique usernames and secure authentication for all administrative access and for all access to cardholder data	The "out of the box" installation of the payment application in place at the completion of the installation process, must facilitate use of unique usernames and secure authentication for all privileged and administrative access and for all access to cardholder data
7.2 Software vendors must establish a process for timely development and deployment of security patches and upgrades, which includes delivery of updates and patches in a secure manner with a known chain-of-trust, and maintenance of the integrity of patch and update code during delivery and deployment	Software vendors must establish a process for timely development and deployment of security patches and upgrades, which includes delivery of updates and patches in a secure manner with a known chain-of-trust, and maintenance of the integrity of patch and update code during delivery and deployment. On blockchain platforms, proper steps must be taken to ensure the security of the system. The disabling of vulnerable smart contracts or the forking of the blockchain itself may be necessary
11.2 If the payment application facilitates sending of PANs by end-user messaging technologies, the payment application must provide a solution that renders the PAN unreadable or implements strong cryptography or specify the use of strong cryptography to encrypt the PANs	If the payment application facilitates sending of PANs by end-user messaging technologies, the payment application must provide a solution that renders the PAN unreadable or implements strong cryptography or specify the use of strong cryptography to encrypt the PANs. On blockchain platforms and transaction models, all sensitive transactional data will be protected through cryptography
12.2 The payment application must never send unencrypted PANs by end-user messaging technologies (for example, e-mail, instant messaging, chat)	The payment application must never send unencrypted PANs by end-user messaging technologies (for example, e-mail, instant messaging, chat). On blockchain platforms and transaction models, no sensitive transactional data should be unencrypted when sent over end-user messaging technology

Table 3 Non-applicable PA-DSS standards in blockchain

Standard	Rationale
4.1 At the completion of the installation process, the "out of the box" default installation of the payment application must log all user access	The nature of the blockchain ledger makes it unfeasible to logistically log individual events of access to the ledger
4.2 Payment application must implement an automated audit trail to track and monitor access	The nature of the blockchain ledger makes it unfeasible to logistically log or audit individual events of access to the ledger. On a blockchain platform, user access to the ledger will not be monitored or logged for auditing, as it is available to all blockchain nodes
10.1 If payment application updates are delivered via remote access into customers' systems, software vendors must tell customers to turn on modem only when needed for downloads from vendor, and to turn off immediately after download completes. Alternatively, if delivered via VPN or other high-speed connection, software vendors must advise customers to properly configure a firewall or a personal firewall product to secure "always-on" connections	Decentralized platforms and applications do not "update" in the same manner as centralized systems. Platforms "fork" and applications (smart contracts) are destroyed to prevent further use when "updated."

platforms, inherently unchangeable, do not allow the same process of vulnerability remediation. Smart contracts are stored on the blockchain, and the only solution to remediate a vulnerable smart contract is to disallow it from further use and create a new (remediated) code to store on the blockchain. Moreover, blockchain platforms as a whole have been known to have vulnerabilities; to remediate weaknesses to the entire platform, the blockchain must be forked to create a new, but related, platform to be used. The current PA-DSS standards do not account for such processes, and revisions are necessary to accommodate blockchain systems. Based on the above observations and revisions to the PA-DSS standards, we compile a list of controls to look for when analyzing the case-study blockchain platforms. Overall, the PA-DSS standards are excellent measures for protecting traditional payment platforms, but they fall short in several aspects concerning blockchain platforms.

There are many standards developed by the Payment Card Industry (PCI) to govern the way transaction information is stored, transmitted, and used, but the PA-DSS standard applies directly to the context of new payment systems, such as blockchain. By analyzing this standard, we reimagine transaction data protection in a context where current standards do not match current technology. By creating a structured approach to analyzing the blockchain platforms against the revised PA-DSS standards, we ensure that each platform is adequately analyzed for its implemented security mechanisms. Ultimately, we achieve a sound result in adapting traditional payment standards to a nontraditional technology that is gaining more popularity by the day.

5 Case Study: Applying the Revised Standards to QTUM and Ethereum

The two blockchain platforms in our case study, QTUM [5] and Ethereum [6], are popular and well-developed systems that have been considered for business adoption. These platforms signified advancements from the early stages of blockchain platforms, such as Bitcoin, for they offered supposed enhancements to the weaknesses of Bitcoin-like platforms. Based on the analysis of each platform, we found shortcomings for both platforms when considering business adoption in the US financial industry, based on the adapted PA-DSS standards. We identified key points of security weakness with respect the adapted standards.

The Ethereum platform is one of the most popular blockchains with a key advancement from early cryptocurrency platforms: smart contract support. With this advancement, Ethereum established its potential for financial technology adoption. Upon analysis, we found that Ethereum has a fundamental design, non-protected transaction information, that undermined the PA-DSS standards. We found that User IDs were publicly available on the blockchain ledger, along with currency transaction data. From this information, it was trivial to link all transactions to a single pseudonym, and Ethereum had a dedicated webpage that allowed anyone to see all transactions made by a given user. Furthermore, Ethereum did not adopt most of the privacy-boosting mechanisms that more recent blockchains have developed. As a result, there was little obfuscation between two users conducting a transaction.

The implications of Ethereum's security measures mattered most when considering real-world business adoption. A common use case for smart contracts in enterprise is as follows: two businesses automate a contractual subscription to goods or services. In this use case, businesses must know who they are sending money to, and vice versa. Without proper data security, namely on the transactional information, it is possible to make inferences towards inter-business transactions from the ledger alone. The reality is that complete anonymity is not feasible for business adoption; therefore, proper data security is necessary to obfuscate the representation of the transaction on the ledger. Proper data security can be achieved via the revised PA-DSS standards, but was not achievable on the Ethereum platform.

The PA-DSS standards, when used to analyze Ethereum's platform, showed a significant oversight regarding data security. While the oversight may be understandable considering business or enterprise adoption was not foreseen by Ethereum, it resulted in the platform's weakness towards large-scale financial adoption. To remediate, Ethereum would have to fundamentally alter the way data is stored on the blockchain, encrypting sensitive data before the ledger stores it. As it stands, Ethereum did not meet the revised PA-DSS standards.

QTUM was designed specifically to be a platform ready for lightweight, versatile business deployment, according to its white papers. Its main features, in addition to the blockchain itself, included a lite wallet for mobile use and a transaction-model abstraction layer to allow transactions between UTXO and Account-Based platforms (e.g. Bitcoin and Ethereum). The business viability seemed to be strong, but the PA-DSS standards show that the platform faced similar issues to Ethereum. Static user IDs and transaction data were stored on the ledger without encryption. QTUM, too, has a webpage that allowed users to search for specific transactions and list all of a specific user's transactions. However, with QTUM's added functionality of lite wallets, there was more to analyze against the standards. After review, the lite wallet featured a robust security system to protect the account and transaction data when it was on mobile devices. Furthermore, I found no weaknesses in the data transmission between lite wallets and the core wallet of the blockchain.

The implications of QTUM were almost identical to the ones of the Ethereum's platform given a real-world scenario. User data stored on the ledger was not private, and inferences can be made based on repeated transactions on the system. Moreover, peer-to-peer communications did not obfuscate the source or destination addresses, meaning anonymity was only partially achieved. No modern security measures of community-developed blockchains were adopted to ensure proper privacy between users or transactions. However, the lite wallets showed some attention to security, with standard security measures in place to protect local account information when stored.

The PA-DSS standards uncovered significant issues concerning both QTUM and Ethereum. From the table, the exact standards that each platform violated from the adapted PA-DSS standards are listed, along with a total count for the violations. Each platform had five violations, all directly related to data security and handling. Table 4 shows a summary of the violations for each platform. Data security is a vital portion of overall payment application security, and both platforms fell short in this regard. More work is needed to ensure that businesses are able to adopt blockchain platforms as payment systems. In their current state, actual usability and transactional functionality is not the challenge; instead, the platforms face the challenge of adhering to financial technology's security standards.

Table 4 Summary of violations of the adapted PA-DSS standards in Ethereum and QTUM

Technology	Total violations	Violations
Ethereum	5	2.1, 2.2, 2.3, 11.2, 12.2
QTUM	5	2.1, 2.2, 2.3, 11.2, 12.2

6 Conclusion and Future Work

Blockchain technology and smart contracts are peaking in popularity, and many businesses are considering the adoption of such technology. Smart contracts allow the automation of many tasks on a blockchain, including the automation of payments themselves. Smart contracts, consequently, have garnered attention from businesses for reducing the overhead of traditional contracts. However, this new technology has many shortcomings, some of which are not easily remediated.

The communal nature of blockchain development leads to a lack of accountability in the products. There is no governance or standardization of the platform development. With businesses seeking out blockchain platforms, there is a need for a structured methodology to fully analyze the capabilities and security of these new, decentralized payment systems. Considering the financial technology industry as a gold-standard for rigorous auditing, we adapted the Payment Application Data Security Standards (PA-DSS) to blockchain platforms. By revising the standards to meet the requirements of both parties, blockchain and financial technology organizations, we solidified the methodology used to critique modern smart contract platforms. Through two case studies, QTUM and Ethereum, we reported key weaknesses in the foundations of the blockchain platforms. Data security was the main issue, for neither system offered adequate user privacy concerning transaction information. Transaction data were openly available through the ledger, and privacy as a whole was compromised as a result. There were critical alterations, including proper data protection, to be made to each platform for PA-DSS compliance.

Fundamentally, smart contract platforms offer tremendous business potential, but the lack of security governance is overwhelming. With sensitive transaction information present on these immutable platforms, data security is essential and should not be overlooked. Even with the modern security-focused blockchains, there has been little effort to standardize the solutions and provide a template for a comprehensive blockchain security solution. This work sets the precedent for continuing security practices into decentralized payment systems.

From the results of the case studies and the adapted PA-DSS standards, there is a clear set of next steps for contributors of the Ethereum and QTUM platforms. Security changes can be made to the existing platforms, or a new platform can be developed to both implement a smart contract transaction platform and securely store data. Developing such a system would be time-consuming, but it would provide the necessary security measures to ensure proper data handling at the transaction level. Moreover, analyzing more smart contract platforms would prove useful in creating a survey of common security practice (or malpractice) in the blockchain community. The Payment Card Industry is a well-known, established field where security standards are heavily enforced, but there are many other technology industries that would benefit from the same type of standards adaptation. The Healthcare industry, for example, has several data privacy laws to follow with respect to health information. There have been discussions and research surrounding the adoption of blockchain models to healthcare, but the extent at which the security measures have been thought out is unclear. There is, at the least, room for consolidation of information.

Data privacy and security is the main focus of this work, but there are other aspects that lie outside the scope of this work. Blockchain solves one of data protection's most notable issues: data integrity. That is, data on the blockchain is immutable. There have been many experiments and new blockchains that propose new methods to enhance the blockchains speed or usability. However, a comprehensive analysis of such innovations may prove helpful in determining the best approach for designing payment systems for particular purposes or audiences.

References

1. Contract Law - How to Create a Legally Binding Contract. U.S. Small Business Administration (2016), https://www.sba.gov/blogs/contract-law-how-create-legally-binding-contract. Cited 31 July 2019
2. N. Szabo, The Idea of Smart Contracts (1997), http://www.fon.hum.uva.nl/rob/Courses/InformationInSpeech/CDROM/Literature/LOTwinterschool2006/szabo.best.vwh.net/idea.html. Cited 31 July 2019
3. N. Szabo, A Formal Language for Analyzing Contracts (2002), http://www.fon.hum.uva.nl/rob/Courses/InformationInSpeech/CDROM/Literature/LOTwinterschool2006/szabo.best.vwh.net/idea.html. Cited 31 July 2019
4. S. Nakamoto, Bitcoin: A Peer-to-Peer Electronic Cash System (2008), https://bitcoin.org/bitcoin.pdf. Cited 31 July 2019
5. P. Dai, N. Mahi, J. Earls, A. Norta, Smart-contract Value-transfer Protocols on a Distributed Mobile Application Platform (2017), https://qtum.org/user/pages/01.home/Qtum%20whitepaper_en%20v0.7.pdf. Cited 31 July 2019
6. G. Wood, Ethereum: A Secure Decentralised Generalised Transaction Ledger. Ethereum Project (2014), https://gavwood.com/paper.pdf. Cited 31 July 2019
7. A. Hertig, How Ethereum Works (2019), https://www.coindesk.com/information/how-ethereum-works. Cited 31 July 2019
8. Payment Application Data Security Standard: Frequently Asked Questions (2008), PCI Security Standards Council. "https://www.pcisecuritystandards.org/minisite/en/docs/PA-DSS_v3.pdf. Cited 31 July 2019
9. Payment Card Industry (PCI) Payment Application Data Security Standard-Requirements and Security Assessment Procedures version 3.0 (2013), PCI Security Standards Council. https://www.pcisecuritystandards.org/minisite/en/docs/PA-DSS_v3.pdf. Cited 31 July 2019
10. M. Di Ferrante, R. Mercer, Towards Blockchain Transaction Privacy (2017), https://www.ieee-security.org/TC/EuroSP2017/posters/poster6.pdf. Cited 31 July 2019
11. M. Conti, S. Kumar, C. Lal, S. Ruj, A survey on security and privacy issues of bitcoin. IEEE Comm. Surveys Tutorials. **20**, 3416–3452 (2018)
12. P. Koshy, D. Koshy, P. McDaniel, An analysis of anonymity in bitcoin using P2P network traffic, in *Financial Cryptography and Data Security (FC 2014)*, ed. by N. Christin, R. Safavi-Naini (Springer, Heidelberg, 2014), pp. 469–485
13. Y. Sompolinsky, A. Zohar, Secure high-rate transaction processing in bitcoin, in *Financial Cryptography and Data Security (FC 2015)*, ed. by R. Böhme, T. Okamoto (Springer, Heidelberg, 2015), pp. 507–527
14. S. Ma, Y. Deng, D. He, J. Zhang, X. Xie, An efficient NIZK scheme for privacy-preserving transactions over account-model blockchain, in: Cryptology ePrint Archive, Technical Report 2017/1239. The International Association for Cryptologic Research (2017). https://eprint.iacr.org/2017/1239. Cited 31 July 2019

15. M. Andrychowicz, S. Dziembowski, D. Malinowski, L. Mazurek, Secure multiparty computations on bitcoin, in *Proceedings of 2014 IEEE Symposium on Security and Privacy* (IEEE, New York, 2014), pp. 443–458
16. F. Zhang, E. Cecchetti, K. Croman, A. Juels, E. Shi, Town Crier: an authenticated data feed for smart contracts, in *Proceedings 2016 ACM SIGSAC Conference on Computer Networks and Communications* (ACM, New York, 2016), pp. 270–282
17. M. Gray, C. Hajduk, Anatomy of a Smart Contract. Microsoft Corporation (2017), https://github.com/Azure/azure-blockchain-projects/blob/master/bletchley/AnatomyofASmartContract.md. Cited 31 July 2019
18. M. Gray, C. Hajduk, Anatomy of a Smart Contract 2. Microsoft Corporation (2017), https://azure.microsoft.com/en-us/blog/scanatomy-2. Cited 31 July 2019
19. M. Gray, C. Hajduk, Cryptlets Deep Dive. Microsoft Corporation (2017), https://github.com/Azure/azure-blockchain-projects/blob/master/bletchley/CryptletsDeepDive.md. Cited 31 July 2019
20. A. Kosba, A. Miller, E. Shi, Z. Wen, C. Papamanthou, Hawk: the blockchain model of cryptography and privacy-preserving smart contracts, in *Proceedings of 2016 IEEE Symposium on Security and Privacy* (IEEE, New York, 2016), pp. 839–858
21. M. Bartoletti, L. Pompianu, An empirical analysis of smart contracts: platforms, applications, and design patterns, in *Financial Cryptography and Data Security (FC 2017)*, ed. by M. Brenner, K. Rohloff, J. Bonneau, A. Miller, P.Y.A. Ryan, V. Teague, A. Bracciali, M. Sala, F. Pintore, M. Jakobsson (Springer, Heidelberg, 2017), pp. 494–509
22. K. Delmolino, M. Arnett, A. Kosba, A. Miller, E. Shi, M. Bartoletti, L. Pompianu, Step by step towards creating a safe smart contract: lessons and insights from a cryptocurrency lab, in *Financial Cryptography and Data Security (FC 2016)* ed. by J. Clark, S. Meiklejohn, P.Y.A. Ryan, D. Wallach, M. Brenner, K. Rohloff (Springer, Heidelberg, 2016), pp. 79–94
23. L. Luu, D. Chu, H. Olickel, P. Saxena, A. Hobor, Making smart contracts smarter, in *Proceedings of 2016 ACM SIGSAC Conference on Computer Networks and Communications* (ACM, New York, 2016), pp. 254–269
24. V. Buterin, Thinking About Smart Contract Security. Ethereum Project (2016), https://blog.ethereum.org/2016/06/19/thinking-smart-contract-security. Cited 31 July 2019
25. N. Atzei, M. Bartoletti, T. Cimoli, A survey of attacks on Ethereum smart contracts (SoK), in *Principles of Security and Trust (POST 2017)*, ed. by M. Maffei, M. Ryan (Springer, Heidelberg, 2017), pp. 164–186
26. G. Bello, A.J. Perez, Adapted PA-DSS Standards (2019), https://tinyurl.com/yabykwf8. Cited 31 July 2019

Blockchain-Based Certification for Education, Employment, and Skill with Incentive Mechanism

Liyuan Liu, Meng Han, Yiyun Zhou, Reza M. Parizi (ID) **, and Mohammed Korayem**

Abstract Nowadays, more and more companies become employee centric enterprises and have a data-driven culture. Employees, as a unique capital value, is linked to the company's profitability. Hiring the appropriate employee and decreasing hiring liability workplace violence are two main tasks in the employment process. Most companies are outsourcing background screening to third parties to ensure the efficiency and professional compare with the traditional in-house check. However, background screening still is a pain point in human resource industry, especially for employment, education and skill verification. Sometimes, background screening is prolonged and inaccurate. For overseas recruitment, background screening will be more troublesome due to the information asymmetry. Therefore, we propose a novel E^2C-Chain, which is a two-stage blockchain to improve education, employment, and skill verification system. The first stage aims to create new blocks when a trust organization verifies the education and employment information of the candidate. In the second stage, we comprehensively address the challenge of how to encourage the participants in the blockchain platform. We employ a Vickrey-Clarke-Groves (VCG) incentive mechanism to find the Nash Equilibrium and ensure social cost minimization. We also present the theoretical proofs and extensive simulations to demonstrate beneficial properties and efficiency of our proposed system.

L. Liu · M. Han (✉) · Y. Zhou
Data-driven Intelligence Research (DIR) Laboratory, Kennesaw State University, Marietta, GA, USA
e-mail: mhan9@kennesaw.edu

R. M. Parizi
College of Computing and Software Engineering, Kennesaw State University, Marietta, GA, USA

M. Korayem
CareerBuilder, LLC, Peachtree Corners, GA, USA

© Springer Nature Switzerland AG 2020
K.-K. R. Choo et al. (eds.), *Blockchain Cybersecurity, Trust and Privacy*, Advances in Information Security 79, https://doi.org/10.1007/978-3-030-38181-3_14

1 Introduction

Corporations face a vital hurdle in recruitment when they need to verify applicants' credentials, such as employment history, education, and skills. They keep spending much money on the employees' background screening and outsourcing to third parties. Background screening industry developed speedily. CareerBuilder reported 72% companies background check everyone they hired [1]. Regarding the ResearchAndMarket's report, the employment screening services market is supposed to increase from $3.74 billion to $5.46 billion by 2025 [2]. Compare with the traditional in-house checks, third-parties' inspection improve recruitment quality, such as enhancing the efficiency and saving the in-house resources, etc. Even though the third party employment screening benefits to employment process, there still exist fraud and opacity in employee credentials. According to the survey of HireRight, 88% employers misrepresentation their credentials on the resume [3]. The duplicity resume will result in altered recruitment. With the report from CareerBuilder [1], there is 75% of employers affirmed that they had recruited inappropriate employees, the average cost of one unseemly hiring is around $17,000. The mistake of hiring is a cost not only the monetary loss of employers but also lost the time and human resource to re-hire and re-training a new candidate, and neutralizing the employees' morale [4].

According to CareerBuilder's 2016 annual report [1], education, employment, criminal and credit score are top credentials which employers most acknowledged in background screening. Figure 1 displays the proportion of top credentials regarding CareerBuilder's statistical information. Since the development of smart government and credit bureaus, there are several credentials unique databases that employers could retrieve secure information from that. For example, the criminal and identity information could collect from government and identity databases; credit records could get from credit bureaus' databases; clinical and insurance databases are storing drug usage reports. These databases systems have more reliable management that could ensure information authenticity. However, unlike other database systems, there do not exist universally and secure databases that store employment information. Therefore, how to guarantee the authenticity of education and employment information is the most significant challenge to employers. Moreover, the third-party background screening is time-consuming, as a background screening company BARADA introduced [5], the background screening for one employee is between 2 to 5 business days. Commonly, the waiting period of background screening has another potential risk that results in the talents get another opportunity, and employers lost great talents. Also, employers are hard to verify the skills that employees lists on their resume until employee pass the test that employers required.

Blockchain, as a distributed, digitized, secure, open record of all cryptographic data exchange technology start to change the world in many fields [6]. Since use blockchain, participates can verify the transactions without a central certifying authorization. It has implied for many industries which rely on the record, store and track transactions secure, accurate, and unmodifiable. It can change many filed such

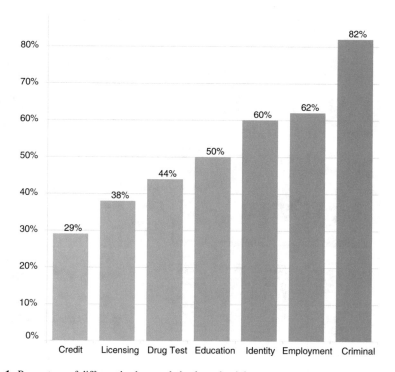

Fig. 1 Percentage of different background check credentials

as supply chain [7], healthcare [8], Internet of Things [9, 10], agriculture [11] et al. In this study, we consider that business recruitment has similar ones. The truthful education, employment, and skill records of candidates need secure, accurate and unmodifiable either. However, it is common that there exists information asymmetry between employee and employer. It will not only affect a financial problem but also cost time, social trust, and other enterprise problems. Therefore, this motivated us to propose blockchain-based education employment and skill certification framework: E^2C-Chain. Also, helping enterprises improve their management of human capital.

The basic idea of E^2C-Chain is incorporating blockchain technology with professional accomplishment, expert skills to education and employment history on the distributed ledger. The information is stored in each block and will unmodifiable, trackable, and secure. It will also solve the overseas employment problems which make information globally.

However, we confront several challenges when we initial establish E^2C-Chain.

- To our best knowledge, the blockchain-based education employment and skill verification is still an open question.
- How to encourage the participants to verify others' skill is another question. The cost of each participant for completing a skill verify is private. It is challenging to encourage all verifiers to describe their real costs.

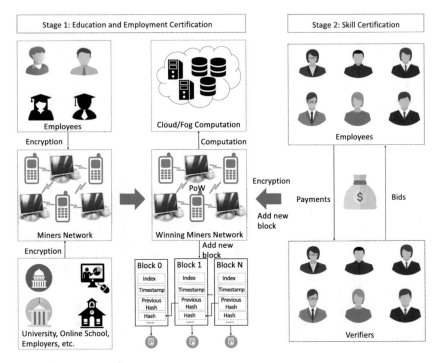

Fig. 2 Architecture of E^{2}C-Chain

- It is hard to choose the optimal set of participants that minimize the cost of requesters. The incentive mechanism needs to be placed in the peer-to-peer verify process.

Hence, we propose a two-stage incentive blockchain system to address the challenges above. In the first stage, when the trust organizations, such as universities, enterprises claim proof of employees' records, a new transaction is then created. It helps to store candidates' education and employment history permanently. The second stage mainly focuses on generating skill certifications for employees. When an employee requests a skill, it is enabled to send the verify request to potential participants that verify the proposed expert skills. To encourage the participants, we employ the Vickrey-Clarke-Groves (VCG) incentive mechanism to find the Nash equilibrium. We also prove that the proposed mechanism is individually rational and truthfulness and computation efficiency. The framework of the E^{2}C-Chain is demonstrated in Fig. 2.

Our contributions are concluded below:

- E^{2}C-Chain provides a trusted source of employees' information that is unmodifiable and permanently. It offers more immutable, fair, trust, and direct pathways between employers and employees.

– We implement Vickrey-Clarke-Groves (VCG) game to find the Nash Equilibrium. This incentive mechanism encourages verifiers to bid their reward price and reach the social cost minimization.
– E^2C-Chain is a secure and incentive chain that protects all nodes' private information. With zero-knowledge proof (ZK-SNARK), the task can be completed without disclosing any information beyond the validity of the statement itself.

The rest of this paper is organized as follows. Section 2 introduces the related works of different technologies. The architecture and overview of the E^2C-Chain are presented in Sect. 3. Section 4 formulates the incentive mechanism and provides theoretical investigation. Section 5 displays experimental results of the two-stage E^2C-Chain. Lastly, Sect. 6 concludes the study.

2   Related Work

The previous block hash, transaction data, and timestamps are three principal components in each blockchain. It is an append-only transaction ledger that enables to store and write new records. We will discuss the related works from three aspects.

Firstly, we studied the literature related application of blockchain in different domains, especially for human resource industry. Recently, there are many researchers focus on blockchain applications. There are several different domains, such as Internet of Things (IoT) [12], cyber-physical systems [13], education [6], supply chain management [14], and crowdsourcing and crowdsensing [15], etc. It is evident that the characteristics of blockchain, such as non-modifiable, anonymity, security, can revolute employment market fairer, more efficient, and universal. However, there is not abundant research focus on human research industry.

Regarding recent research, most education, employment, and skill certification based blockchain studies are in the beginning step. This problem is an open question from now. The highlights researches are concluded in the Table 1 below. Turkanovic et al. [16] proposed a framework called "EduCTX" which is a novel blockchain-based higher education credit platform. They also performed the implementation of the model using the Ark Blockchain Platform. Grather et al. [17] also presented a blockchain-based education platform to issue the education certificates for students. They defined their system overview in their paper, and illustrated the

Table 1 Literature of education and employment based blockchain

Literature	Application	Implementation	Incentive mechanism
Turkanovic et al. [16]	Education	Yes	No
Grather et al. [17]	Education	Yes	No
Chan et al. [18]	Education Employment	Yes	Mentioned
Pinna et al. [19]	Employment	Yes	No
Rooksby et al. [20]	Education	Yes	No

implementation details includes certification authorities management and smart contract. Chen [18] introduced his blockchain based system and named "Echo." He illustrated that using Echo, the employment information such as skill, and career can be verified. Pinna et al. [19] proposed a system using blockchain to protect temporary employment' right. In their system, the employees will get fair and legal payout regarding their work performance. And this system also can help employers automatically manage the contracts through smart contract. However, most of them are not illustrate how to encourage peer-to-peer verification in their system.

Secondly, we start to study how incentive mechanisms help to improve blockchain systems. Game theory algorithms are the critical and fundamental theories of incentive mechanisms. Vickrey-Clarke-Groves (VCG) and Stackelberg game are two main algorithms used to solve the tradeoffs in the wireless network environments. Vickrey-Clarke-Groves (VCG) mechanism is a mechanism that is truthful and enables to assist in accomplishing a social welfare maximization solution. Stackelberg game is a strategy that finds the nash equilibrium that serves best each part in a game. Several studies employ VCG or Stackelberge game in a blockchain environment. Most of them are focus on the computation resource allocation between miners and edge service providers. Jiao et al. [21] deployed an auction game between edge computing service provider and the miner who need the computation resources. With their auction mechanism, it can optimize the social welfare; at the same time, it can guarantee the individual rational, truthfulness, and computation efficiency of authors proposed method. Gu et al. [22] implemented a VCG auction mechanism to solve the storage transactions problem. They performed their model using the Ethereum platform, and the experimental results showed their method could construct a safe, efficient, and economic resource trading. Xiong et al. [23] employed Stackelberg game to manage the computation resource of blockchains proof-of-work puzzle in the edge computing environment.

To our best knowledge, there are a few incentive mechanisms that use game theory algorithms to reward the verifiers in blockchain peer-to-peer verification process at the moment. In this study, we implement VCG as the fundamental of the incentive mechanism. VCG is frequently used in edge computing, wireless networks, crowdsourcing, and crowdsensing domains etc. Li et al. [24] formulate the offloading games for the mobile edge computing environment. With the optimal incentive scheme, when the users' experience, the process of decision making will reach the equilibrium that social welfare will be maximization incorporate with VCG. Li et al. [25] employed VCG in their research in the mobile crowdsensing field. They proposed the algorithms theoretically to help the platform more efficient and beneficial to seek the participates. Zhou et al. [26] proposed a new framework in the crowdsensing area. They used VCG to reward the participators, implemented the edge computing to reduce the high computation traffic and burden, suggested incorporate with deep learning algorithms, such as Convolutional Neural Networks (CNN) to filter the fake and unrelative information which selfish participates offered. With the case study, their framework can reach high robustness.

Since most blockchains are stored sensitive, valuable records, how to make a secure blockchain system will be one crucial research area. We thirdly review the related publications of the blockchain privacy-preserving mechanisms. There are many researchers focus on designing privacy-preserving algorithms to protect the transaction data in blockchain. Kosba et al. [27] introduced a novel method called "Hawk," it is a smart contract system that decentralized, the transactions data will not be stored in the appearance on the blockchain, it will create a private smart contract and use RSA to make sure the data is cryptography and security. Lu et al. [28] presented a novel privacy-preserving network named "CreditCoin" in the IoT environment. With their blockchain-based incentive mechanism, the announcement network will be efficient anonymous the vehicular's announcement protocol. Yue et al. [29] developed a novel APP named Healthcare Data Gateway that enables to store, control and share the patient data since the patients' data are sensitive, they provided a new method to protect the data private. Recently, the zero-knowledge proof is modern cryptography in blockchain. For example, Lu et al. [30] proposed a private and anonymous decentralized crowdsourcing system named ZebraLancer. This system is atop an open blockchain that can prevent data breach.

From the related works, we find our proposed E^2C-Chain has the significant contributions that not only address the problem of how to complete the education, employment and skill verification in blockchain but also implement incentive mechanism to improve the peer-to-peer verification system.

3 E^2C-Chain Overview

There are two stages in E^2C-Chain. As Fig. 2 shows, education and employment verification are performed in the first stage. The system requires employees to enter their education and employment history first. Also, an economic system will reward several E^2C-coins to employees regarding their completion of information. In order to quantify the verification quality, the system enables to produce a sufficient weight that represents users' verification weights. Higher weights affect higher evaluation quality. Some trust organizations, such as universities, online schools, employers issue proofs of employees about their employment and education information can also receive the E^2C-coins. To guarantee the trustful of organizations, trust organizations have to make an official confirmation when they sign up. When an employee requests an employment or education verification, trust organizations also send a history certification. Then a new transaction is created. The transaction will generate a hash with the SHA-256 algorithm, and PoW consensus is employed and determine the winning miners. The creator of the new block will be the first miner that solved the hash function. In the verification process, ZK-SNARK is applied to preserve sensitive data. The trust document will be stored to the new block without revealing that information, and without any interaction between the prover and verifier. The first stage transaction verification algorithm is shown in Algorithm 1. The new block ID is generated to follow the steps below. After the education and employment certification stored in the blockchain, it will be unmodifiable, permanently and trustful.

Algorithm 1 First Stage Transaction Verification

Input: Transactions
Output: New Certification Block ID
  1: Verify Transaction: $R_{Employment}$, $R_{Education}$
  2: Verify PK_p
  3: **if** PK_P is match **then**
  4:     **Reject Transaction**
  5: **else**
  6:     Transaction Verified
  7:     New cBlock ID $\leftarrow f(ID_u, ID_b)$
  8: **end if**

In the second stage, users input their professional skills to the system, and the system specifies some E^2C-coins regarding their profile completeness. After users determine the skills are demanded to be verified, users also declare the price of each skill that they willing to pay to the verifiers. To protect the privacy of users, ZK-SNARK will be fulfilled to stage two as well. The critical point of stage two is the incentive mechanism. We employ VCG to encourage the verifiers that complete the verification process. In this stage, every skill s has its price p decide by the requester. Based on the VCG algorithm, a set of winners will be selected, and the payment will be chosen. Each verifier has a sufficient weight represents their verification quality. When the sum of all winners' weight reaches a qualifying score, the skill verification process is completed, and the record can be stored to a new block. After each success verification, the weight of verifiers will be increase regarding their past performance. PoW is used in this stage to determine the winning miners as well.

In E^2C-Chain, six elements are included: Nodes which represent all users. Transaction is a certification request that broadcast to the network and collect into the blocks; it could be either education, employment, or skill verification. The third essential element is Blocks, which are storing records permanently, such as each employment, education, and skill verification information. Chain is a list of verifying certification blocks in a particular order. Miners are the fifth critical component; miners are the particular nodes which solve the SHA-256 hashed puzzles, and help to affirm a new block and add to blockchain. Last but not least, consensus is a set of mechanisms and systems to make sure blockchain works. In this study, Proof of Work (PoW) is employed to determine the winners of miners.

ZK-SNARK is a technique to protect sensitive data in this study. ZK-SNARK is a non-interactive zero-knowledge proof. With ZK-SNARK, the duplicated interaction is not required between requester and verifier; it enables us to perform soundproof. Each user has a public key Pu_k, and a private key denotes to Pr_k. The Pu_k as a user's encrypted information and no other party knows the user's identifications. The user could send a concatenation of the encrypted information Ω. The concatenation can be denoted as $CPr_k(\Omega)$ and is sent to the miners. The miners confirm it if the user's input information is authentic by decrypting $CPr_k(\Omega)$ with the user's public key. However, the users' are anonymous, and the miners cannot know any identity information of users [31]. Figure 3 shows the process of ZK-SNARK. The verifiers

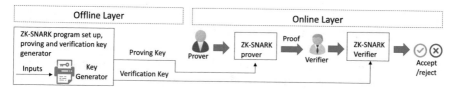

Fig. 3 ZK-SNARK process

Table 2 Notations and description

Notations	Description
ξ	Employee who request skill verification
V_s, v_i	Set of each skill verifiers and verifier
S, s_i	Set of skills and skill
D_s	Description for skill s_i
ω_i	Effective weight for verifier v_i
β	The score allow create block of skills
U_i	Utility of verifier v_i
W, W_s	Set of winners and winners of skill s_i
N_V, N_w	Number of verifiers and winners of s_i
b_i, b_{-i}	Bid of verifier v_i Bids if v_i is not attend
ζ_i	Cost of verifier v_i
ρ_i	Payment of verifier v_i for s_i
B_s	Budget of employee for each skill s_i
γ_s	The price verifier claimed to verify s_i

and the provers can easily verify and complete the verification process, protect the completeness of computation, and keep the sensitive employment and education records secure.

4 VCG Incentive Mechanism

As introduced in the previous sections, we employed VCG as the incentive mechanism in the skill verification process. It aims to attract participants to take part in verifying proposed skills of requesters. In this study, we prove that our proposed incentive mechanism is truthfully, rationally, and computation efficiency. Firstly, we illustrate the frequently used notations as Table 2 shown.

We consider employee ξ has a set of S=$\{s_1, s_2, s_3, \ldots, s_i\}$ proposed skills by employees, each proposed skill need to be verified by a set of verifiers V=$\{v_1, v_2, v_3, \ldots, v_i\}$ while, the total number of verifiers is N_V. For each skill s_i, there exist a description of s_i such as "Programming C++", "Data Analytics" defined as $s_i=\{D_s\}$. Employees first determine the skills that need to be verified, then E^2C system will send the verification request for each potential verifier. Any communication detection algorithms or machine learning algorithms can decide the potential verifiers. Each verifier has its effective weight denotes to ω_i. This weight represents the verification quality in this process. As same as the method to detect the potential verifiers, the effective weight also could be determined by some algorithms regarding each verifiers' age, education level, job title, relationship, etc. For example, a deep neural network enables to predict a weighted score that when the users input their information. When we sum all the verifiers' effective weights, and it reaches one qualifying score, it means the verification is sufficient and qualified to be written in the E^2C-Chain. We use β to present if the skill verification is qualified to store in a new block.

$$\sum_{v_i \in W_s} \omega_i \geq \beta \tag{1}$$

Budget is another element that necessitates to be considered for requesters. When the verifiers received the tasks, the verifiers who willing to participate will provide the bid price, $\forall\{v_i\} \in V_s$, the bid of v_i denotes as b_i. Based on the theory of VCG algorithm, a set of winners $W_s=\{W_1, W_2, W_3, \ldots, W_j\}$ will be selected to complete the verification process, the number of winners j defined as N_w. The total payment cannot exceed the budget B of requesters designed for each skill verification task; it can be defined as Eq. 2.

$$\sum_{v_i \in W_s} \rho_i \leq B_s, \tag{2}$$

The utility of verifier will be maximized in the auction process. When the verifiers are selected as the winners, their utility will be the difference between ρ_i and ζ_i, the utility can be defined as:

$$U_i = \begin{cases} \rho_i - \zeta_i, & \text{if } v_i \in W_s \text{ for } s_i. \\ 0, & \text{otherwise.} \end{cases} \tag{3}$$

4.1 Desirable Properties

There are three desirable properties need to be considered when we design the incentive mechanism.

- Truthfulness: It is truthful that in an auction mechanism every verifier ξ reports the true cost ζ_{true}. The verifiers' utility U_i will not be increased when they report the cost is different from his true value, denotes as ζ_{false}. When a verifier provides an inappropriate cost ζ_{false}, he or she may lose the chance to be selected as a winner and the utility will be 0 as Eq. 3 shown.

- Individual Rationality: Each verifier will get a non-negative utility when he bid the true cost ζ_{true}, $U_i \geq 0$, $\forall i \in U$. In order to receive more utility, the verifiers have to bid their price rationality.
- Computational Efficiency: The incentive mechanism will be computationally efficient if the outcome can be computed in polynomial time.

According to the previous research [32–34], we get some definitions as following:

Definition 1 (Monotonicity) The verifier winner selection process is monotone. The winner selected with bid price γ_s^* and S^* will still win γ_s' and S' with any $\gamma_s^* \geq \gamma_s'$, $S^* \leq S'$.

Definition 2 (Critical payment) There has a critical payment ρ_{ci} for the winning verifier v_i that claim his bid price γ_s individually. v_i will win if $\gamma_s' \leq \rho_{ci}$, otherwise he will lose.

Theorem 1 *An auction mechanism will be truthful if and only if it satisfies monotonicity and existing a critical payment.*

4.2 Optimal Social Cost Solution

In our second stage, to encourage more and more verifiers to participate in the verification is crucial. In the meantime, it is essential that minimizing the social cost when the requester rewards the winning verifier. The object of VCG algorithm is minimizing the social cost that is suitably employed in this study. Our objective function that minimizes the sum of social cost for each skill s_i can be described as the following:

$$\min \sum_{v_i \in W_s} \zeta_i \tag{4}$$

$$s.t. W_s \subseteq V_s$$

It had been proven that VCG mechanisms are truthfulness and individual rationality in [35]. According to the VCG algorithm, the each winner's payment ρ_i equal the difference between the total cost for the other when verifier i is not participating and the total cost for the others when verifier i joins. The payment equation can be defined as Eq. 5 displayed:

$$\rho_i = \sum_{v_j \neq v_i} \zeta_j(W_{-i}^*) - \sum_{v_j \neq v_i} \zeta_j(W_i^*) \tag{5}$$

Algorithms 2 and 3 show how to select the winning verifiers and how to determine the payment in the second stage. We first discuss the algorithm of the winners' selection process. When the requester sends the notification of verification requests, each verifier v_i bids their cost ζ_i. The system first sorts the set of ζ_i ascendingly, then selects the winners' set that presents the minimum social cost. When the sum of the cost for winners exceeds requesters' budget B_s, another selection round will be performed.

Algorithm 2 Set of Winning Verifiers Selection

Input: Verifier Set V_s, Cost ζ_i for verifiers, Budget B_s
Output: A set of winning verifiers

1: Initialization:
2: k=$argsort_{i \in V_s}(\zeta_i)$
3: W=$\emptyset$, C=0, j=0
4: **while** j $\leq$ k **do**
5:    **if** $C \leq B_s$ **then**
6:       Append v_{j+1} to W
7:       C=C+ζ_j
8:       j=j+1
9:    **end if**
10: **end while**
11: **return** $W = [W_1, W_2, W_3, \ldots, W_{j+1}]$

Algorithm 3 shows the determination of verification price for each skill verification task. The price determination is following the VCG-based mechanism. As same as Algorithm 2, we sort all the costs for winners ascendingly, then determine the price for each winning verifiers following Eq. 5. It will return a set of payment for each verifier of skill verification task s_i.

Algorithm 3 Price Determination

Input: Winning Verifiers Set W, Cost ζ_i for verifiers, Verifier Set V_s
Output: A set of price P for winning verifiers

1: m=$argsort_{v_i \in W}(\zeta_i)$
2: P=$\emptyset$, j=0
3: **while** j $\leq$ m **do**
4:    $\rho_i = \sum_{v_j \neq v_i} \zeta_j(W_{-i}^*) - \sum_{v_j \neq v_i} \zeta_j(W_i^*)$
5:    Append ρ_i to P
6:    j=j+1
7: **end while**
8: **return** $P = [\rho_1, \rho_2, \rho_3, \ldots, \rho_n]$

4.3 Proof of Designed Properties

In this section, we show the theoretical proofs of each designed property. Our proposed E^2C-Chain is truthfulness, individual rationality, and computation efficiency. Firstly, we proof the truthfulness of our incentive mechanism as Theorem 2 described.

Theorem 2 *Our proposed skill verification system is truthful.*

Proof Regarding Theorem 1, our proposed mechanism will be truthful if and only if it satisfies monotonicity and existing a critical payment.

- **Monotonic** Algorithm 2 is monotonic. Let v_i denotes as one winner of the winning verifiers set when verifying the skill s_i; the cost is ζ_i. When the v_i bidding as ζ_i^*, and $\zeta_i^* \leq \zeta_i$, regarding Algorithm 2 line 2–11, when sort all the verifier v_i with their ζ_i, v_i will be selected in advance with bidding price ζ_i^*. v_i will always win if his or her bidding with $\zeta_i^* \leq \zeta_i$ with skill task s_i. Therefore, the winner selection process is monotonic.
- **critical payment** There existing a critical payment ρ_{ci} for the winning verifier v_i that claim his bid price γ_s individually. Suppose the critical payment ρ_{ci} for each verifier v_i and skill task s_i is equal to the critical cost ζ_{ci}. If the verifier nu_i bidding with a cost $\zeta_i^* > \zeta_{ci}$, regarding to Algorithm 3 line1 and line4, the payment $\zeta_i* > \zeta_j$ since all the cost will be sorted in the beginning. Therefore, in the sorted list, the index of verifier v_i is behind v_j. The verifier v_i will not be the winner.

Our proposed mechanism will be truthful if and only if it satisfies monotonicity and existing a critical payment. We have proven for any s_i, the winner nu_i will always win if he or she bid with $\zeta_i^* \leq \zeta_i$. Also, we proven that there exist a critical payment ρ_{ci} for each verifier v_i in Definition 2. Therefore, Theorem 2 can be proven.

We then proof the system is individual rational as Theorem 3 shown.

Theorem 3 *Our proposed skill verification system is individual rational.*

Proof For each verifier v_i, there existing a critical cost ζ_{ci} which equal their payment $\rho_i = \sum_{v_j \neq v_i} \zeta_j(W_{-i}^*) - \sum_{v_j \neq v_i} \zeta_j(W_i^*)$. A verifier's utility will be nonnegative when v_i is selected as a winner, there must have $\zeta_i \leq \zeta_{ci}$. Otherwise, the utility of verifier will be 0. Theorem 3 can be proven because the individual rationality is guaranteed.

Theorem 4 *Our proposed skill verification system is computation efficiency.*

Proof The time complexity of Algorithms 2 and 3 are O(n) which indicates the implementation time complexity of our proposed skill verification mechanism is adequate.

5 Experiments Results

5.1 Incentive Mechanism

In order to evaluate the performance of the second stage incentive auction mechanism, we simulate random numbers of some variables and test it. The limited qualify score fixed as $\beta \in \{50, 60, 70\}$, The number of verifiers fixed as $N_V \in \{40, 60, 80, 100\}$. The cost of each verifier ζ_i is distributed over [1,50] uniformly, and the effective weight ω_i is randomly chosen from [1,5]. The verifiers' asking price γ_i is set from [1,30]. We first compare the social cost of different verifier numbers by β, as Fig. 4 shown.

From this figure, we observed that the social cost would decrease with the increasing number of verifiers, higher β value, higher social cost. Figure 5 shows the relationship between the number of winners and the β score by different numbers of the verifier. It shows when β value gets higher, and there does not have enough verifiers, all the verifiers can be the winner, but the skill certification cannot be issued since the sum of winners' effective weight would not reach the qualifying score β.

We also test the utilities of winning verifiers using our proposed VCG-based skill verification model. We randomly choose two winning verifiers defined as "Random Verifier 1" and "Random Verifier 2". The utility of random verifier 1 shows as Fig. 6, the true cost of random verifier 1 is $\zeta_{rv_1}=5$. If the verifier asks truthful price, which is 5, he will get the optimal utility 5. However, if he overbids greater than 10, he will not be selected, and his utility is 0. The true cost of random verifier 2 is $\zeta_{rv_2}=2$. If the verifier asks price truthfully for 2, he will reach the optimal utility is 7. If he overbids a value greater than 8, then he will not be selected, and his utility will

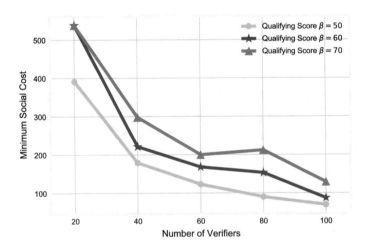

Fig. 4 The social cost of different number of verifiers

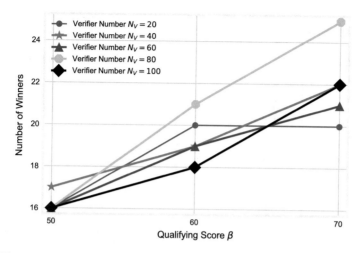

Fig. 5 The winners number of different qualifying score β

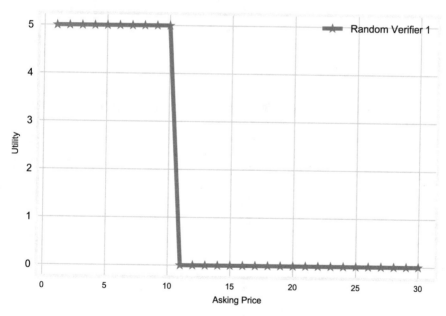

Fig. 6 Utility of random verifier 1 with different asking price

drop to 0 (Fig. 7). We also test the random verifier 3 and 4 as Figs. 8 and 9 shown. Compare with Figs. 6 and 7, with the different sets of qualifying scores, and the system is still truth. The verifiers need to bid the truthful cost that ensures they got the optimal utility (Figs. 10 and 11).

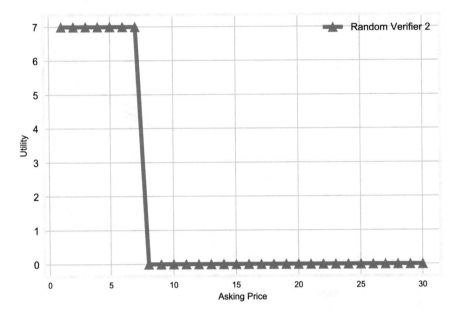

Fig. 7 Utility of random verifier 2 with different asking price

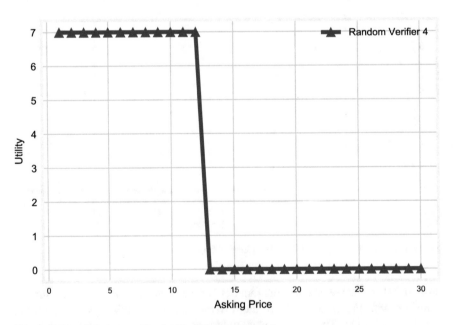

Fig. 8 Utility of random verifier 3 with different asking price

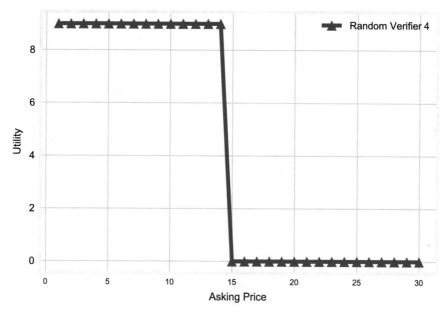

Fig. 9 Utility of random verifier 4 with different asking price

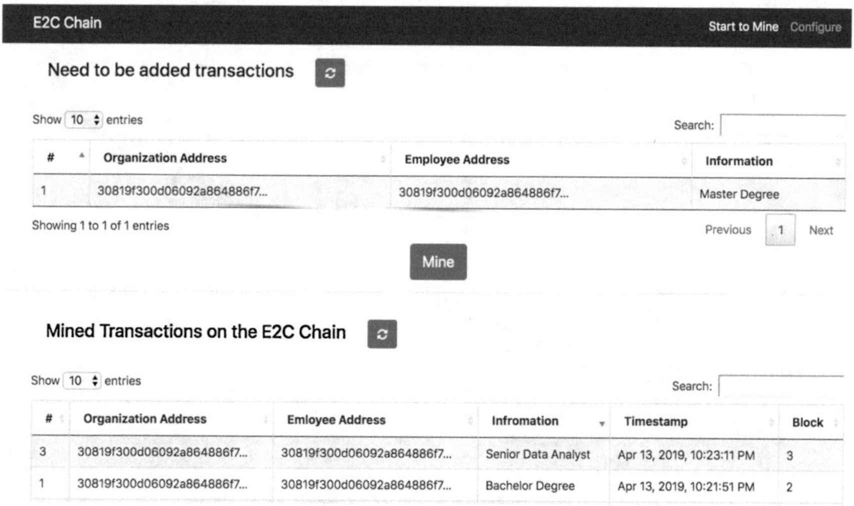

Fig. 10 E^2C-Chain API screen

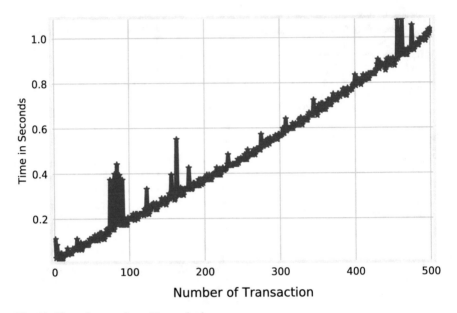

Fig. 11 Time of transaction with easy hash

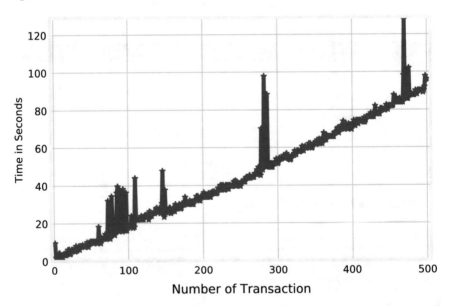

Fig. 12 Time of transaction with hard hash

We also increase the difficulty of SHA256, the time of one transaction increase significantly as Fig. 12 shown. Figure 13 shows the times of transaction encryption with 500 transactions.

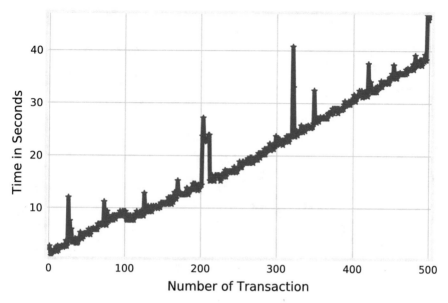

Fig. 13 Time of transaction encryption

5.2   *Implementation and Evaluation of E$_2$C-Chain*

We initial implement the proof of concept our first stage verification E^2C-Chain. We simulate pairwise transactions with a local implementation of blockchain. The simulations are running on a MacOS of 1.6GHz Intel Core i5. We first initialized the wallets and then generated transactions. The transactions are included organization, employee, and information. We also use PoW in our blockchain. The difficulty of the SHA256 set as "2" which is easy. The miners allow to solve the function and earn the reward. We also create Flask API to maintain blockchain nodes. Figure 10 shows the API of E^2C-Chain with several example transactions.

Because of the peer-to-peer architecture for our proposed E^2C-Chain, DoS attacks apt to less compared with traditional solutions. In the permission system, if a node has inadequate behavior, he will be forbidden to access the network. This process also can handle Sybil attacks. Furthermore, data encryption will also protect sensitive individual information. We also show the simulate time assumption from 1 to 500 transactions in Fig. 11.

We test different hash function with 500 transactions, and the running time is shown in Fig. 14. We compare SHA-256, SHA-384, and SHA-512 in this case. With the results of the experiment, SHA-512 costs the least time, and SHA-384 takes longer compare with others. The more details of implementation and evaluation will be discussed in future work.

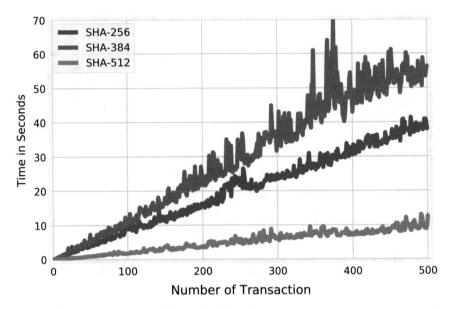

Fig. 14 Time of transaction with different hash function

6 Conclusion

In this study, we first proposed a two-stage incentive blockchain to help improve the human resource industry. With E^2C-Chain, the employees' employment, education and skill history data can be stored in the blockchain unmodifiable and permanently. It offers more immutable, fair, trust, and direct pathway between employers and employees, especially for overseas recruitment. We employed Vickrey-Clarke-Groves (VCG) algorithm as the theoretical background to encourage verifiers to participate in the skill verification process. We found a Nash equilibrium that helps to select the set of winning verifiers and determine the price for each verifier. With the incentive auction mechanism, it can reach the social cost minimization. E^2C-Chain assists employers in targeting the best talents immediately and precisely, and support employees to move forward to their advanced career life.

References

1. B. Goldberg, 75% of employers have hired the wrong person, here's how to prevent that (2016), https://resources.careerbuilder.com/news-research/prevent-hiring-the-wrong-person
2. BusinessWire: $5.46 billion employment screening service market to 2025 - global analysis & forecasts by services & application - https://www.researchandmarkets.com. https://www.businesswire.com/news/home/20180202005232/en/5.46-Billion-Employment-Screening-Service-Market-2025

3. HireRight, Hireright survey finds 88 percent of employers have found a misrepresentation on a resume (2016), https://www.hireright.com/news/press-release

4. L. Liu, M. Han, Y. Wang, Y. Zhou, Understanding data breach: a visualization aspect, in *International Conference on Wireless Algorithms, Systems, and Applications* (Springer, Berlin, 2018), pp. 883–892

5. BaradaAssociates: How long do pre-employment background checks take? (May 2019), https://baradainc.com/how-long-do-pre-employment-background-checks-take/

6. M. Han, Z. Li, J.S. He, D. Wu, Y. Xie, A. Baba, A novel blockchain-based education records verification solution, in *Proceedings of the 19th Annual SIG Conference on Information Technology Education, International World Wide Web Conferences Steering Committee*, pp. 178–183 (2018)

7. E. Hofmann, U.M. Strewe, N. Bosia, *Supply Chain Finance and Blockchain Technology: The Case of Reverse Securitisation* (Springer, Berlin, 2017)

8. M. Mettler, Blockchain technology in healthcare: The revolution starts here, in *2016 IEEE 18th International Conference on e-Health Networking, Applications and Services (Healthcom)* (IEEE, New York, 2016), pp. 1–3

9. A. Dorri, S.S. Kanhere, R. Jurdak, Blockchain in internet of things: challenges and solutions. arXiv preprint. arXiv:1608.05187 (2016)

10. Y. Zhou, M. Han, L. Liu, Y. Wang, Y. Liang, L. Tian, Improving iot services in smart-home using blockchain smart contract. in *2018 IEEE International Conference on Internet of Things (iThings)* (IEEE, New York, 2018), pp. 81–87

11. Y.P. Lin, J. Petway, J. Anthony, H. Mukhtar, S.W. Liao, C.F. Chou, Y.F. Ho, Blockchain: the evolutionary next step for ICT e-agriculture. Environments **4**(3), 50 (2017)

12. S. Zhu, W. Li, H. Li, L. Tian, G. Luo, Z. Cai, Coin hopping attack in blockchain-based IoT. IEEE Internet Things J. **6**(3), 4614–4626 (2018)

13. G. Liang, S.R. Weller, F. Luo, J. Zhao, Z.Y. Dong, Distributed blockchain-based data protection framework for modern power systems against cyber attacks. IEEE Trans. Smart Grid **10**(3), 3162–3173 (2018)

14. N. Kshetri, 1 blockchain's roles in meeting key supply chain management objectives. Int. J. Inform. Manag. **39**, 80–89 (2018)

15. M. Li, J. Weng, A. Yang, W. Lu, Y. Zhang, L. Hou, J.N. Liu, Y. Xiang, R. Deng, CrowdBC: A blockchain-based decentralized framework for crowdsourcing. IEEE Trans. Parallel Distrib. Syst. **30**(6), 1251–1266 (2018)

16 M. Turkanović, M. Hölbl, K. Košič, M. Heričko, A. Kamišalić, Eductx: A blockchain-based higher education credit platform. IEEE Access **6**, 5112–5127 (2018)

17. W. Gräther, S. Kolvenbach, R. Ruland, J. Schütte, C. Torres, F. Wendland, Blockchain for education: lifelong learning passport, in *Proceedings of 1st ERCIM Blockchain Workshop 2018, European Society for Socially Embedded Technologies (EUSSET)* (2018)

18. S. Chan, Blockchain based professional networking and recruiting platform (2017). https://icos.icobox.io/uploads/whitepaper/2017/11/59f9568215146.pdf

19. A. Pinna, S. Ibba, A blockchain-based decentralized system for proper handling of temporary employment contracts, in *Science and Information Conference* (Springer, Cham, 2018), pp. 1231–1243

20. J. Rooksby, K. Dimitrov, Trustless education? a blockchain system for university grades, in *New Value Transactions: Understanding and Designing for Distributed Autonomous Organisations, Workshop at DIS* (2017)

21. Y. Jiao, P. Wang, D. Niyato, Z. Xiong, Social welfare maximization auction in edge computing resource allocation for mobile blockchain, in *2018 IEEE international conference on communications (ICC)* (IEEE, New York, 2018), pp. 1–6

22. Y. Gu, D. Hou, X. Wu, A cloud storage resource transaction mechanism based on smart contract, in *Proceedings of the 8th International Conference on Communication and Network Security* (ACM, New York, 2018), pp. 134–138

23. Z. Xiong, Y. Zhang, D. Niyato, P. Wang, Z. Han, When mobile blockchain meets edge computing. IEEE Commun. Mag. **56**(8), 33–39 (2018)

24. L. Li, T.Q. Quek, J. Ren, H.H. Yang, Z. Chen, Y. Zhang, An incentive-aware job offloading control framework for mobile edge computing. arXiv preprint. arXiv:1812.05743 (2018)
25. J. Li, Z. Cai, J. Wang, M. Han, Y. Li, Truthful incentive mechanisms for geographical position conflicting mobile crowdsensing systems. IEEE Trans. Comput. Social Syst. **5**(2), 324–334 (2018)
26. Z. Zhou, H. Liao, B. Gu, K.M.S. Huq, S. Mumtaz, J. Rodriguez, Robust mobile crowd sensing: when deep learning meets edge computing. IEEE Netw. **32**(4), 54–60 (2018)
27. A. Kosba, A. Miller, E. Shi, Z. Wen, C. Papamanthou, Hawk: the blockchain model of cryptography and privacy-preserving smart contracts, in *2016 IEEE Symposium on Security and Privacy (SP)* (IEEE, New York, 2016), pp. 839–858
28. L. Li, J. Liu, L. Cheng, S. Qiu, W. Wang, X. Zhang, Z. Zhang, Creditcoin: A privacy-preserving blockchain-based incentive announcement network for communications of smart vehicles. IEEE Trans. Intell. Transp. Syst. **19**(7), 2204–2220 (2018)
29. X. Yue, H. Wang, D. Jin, M. Li, W. Jiang, Healthcare data gateways: found healthcare intelligence on blockchain with novel privacy risk control. J. Med. Syst. **40**(10), 218 (2016)
30. Y. Lu, Q. Tang, G. Wang, Zebralancer: Private and anonymous crowdsourcing system atop open blockchain, in *2018 IEEE 38th International Conference on Distributed Computing Systems (ICDCS)* (IEEE, New York, 2018), pp. 853–865
31. Z. Guan, G. Si, X. Zhang, L. Wu, N. Guizani, X. Du, Y. Ma, Privacy-preserving and efficient aggregation based on blockchain for power grid communications in smart communities. IEEE Commun. Mag. **56**(7), 82–88 (2018)
32. J. Wang, J. Tang, D. Yang, E. Wang, G. Xue, Quality-aware and fine-grained incentive mechanisms for mobile crowdsensing, in *2016 IEEE 36th International Conference on Distributed Computing Systems (ICDCS)* (IEEE, New York, 2016), pp. 354–363
33. J. Xu, Z. Rao, L. Xu, D. Yang, T. Li, Mobile crowd sensing via online communities: incentive mechanisms for multiple cooperative tasks, in *2017 IEEE 14th International Conference on Mobile Ad Hoc and Sensor Systems (MASS)* (IEEE, New York, 2017), pp. 171–179
34. Z. Duan, M. Yan, Z. Cai, X. Wang, M. Han, Y. Li, Truthful incentive mechanisms for social cost minimization in mobile crowdsourcing systems. Sensors **16**(4), 481 (2016)
35. N. Nisan, T. Roughgarden, E. Tardos, V.V. Vazirani, *Algorithmic Game Theory* (Cambridge University Press, Cambridge, 2007)

Printed in the United States
By Bookmasters